BREAKDOWN OF WILL

In this challenging and provocative book, the researcher who originally proposed hyperbolic discounting theory presents important new findings that confirm its validity and describes implications that undermine our most basic assumptions about how self-control works. Hyperbolic discounting theory has provoked much recent controversy in psychology, economics, and the philosophy of mind. It begins with a startling experimental finding: People devalue a given future event at different rates, depending on how far away it is. This phenomenon means that our preferences are inherently unstable and entails our present selves being pitted against what we can expect our future selves to want. Although the notion of temporary preferences upsets conventional utility theory, it offers radical solutions to problems that have defeated utility theory: Why do people knowingly participate in addictions, compulsions, and bad habits? What is the nature of will? What makes a will weak or strong? Do we in fact need a concept of will at all?

The author argues that our responses to the threat of our own inconsistency determine the basic fabric of human culture. He suggests that individuals are more like populations of bargaining agents than like the hierarchical command structures envisaged by cognitive psychologists. The forces that create and constrain these populations help us understand much that is puzzling in human action and interaction: from addictions and other self-defeating behaviors to the experience of willfulness, from pathological overcontrol and self-deception to subtler forms of behavior such as altruism, sadism, gambling, and the "social construction" of belief.

This book uniquely integrates approaches from experimental psychology, philosophy of mind, microeconomics, and decision science to present one of the most profound and expert accounts of human irrationality available. It will be of great interest to philosophers concerned with the mind and action theory. By questioning some of the basic assumptions held by social scientists about rational choice, it should be an important resource for professionals and students in psychology, economics, and political science.

George Ainslie began doing research on intertemporal conflict while still in training at Harvard Medical School, the Harvard Laboratories of Experimental Psychology, and the National Institutes of Health. The results have been published in journals ranging from *The Journal of the Experimental Analysis of Behavior* and *Behavioral and Brain Sciences* to *Law and Philosophy* and the *American Economic Review*, as well as many book chapters and a book, *Picoeconomics*. He now does his work at the Veterans Affairs Medical Center, Coatesville, Pennsylvania, and maintains a website at picoeconomics.com.

BREAKDOWN OF WILL

GEORGE AINSLIE

Veterans Affairs Medical Center, Coatesville, Pennsylvania

CAMBRIDGE
UNIVERSITY PRESS

PUBLISHED BY THE PRESS SYNDICATE OF THE UNIVERSITY OF CAMBRIDGE
The Pitt Building, Trumpington Street, Cambridge, United Kingdom

CAMBRIDGE UNIVERSITY PRESS
The Edinburgh Building, Cambridge CB2 2RU, UK
40 West 20th Street, New York, NY 10011-4211, USA
10 Stamford Road, Oakleigh, VIC 3166, Australia
Ruiz de Alarcón 13, 28014 Madrid, Spain
Dock House, The Waterfront, Cape Town 8001, South Africa

http://www.cambridge.org

© George Ainslie 2001

First published 2001

Printed in the United States of America

Typeface Meridien 10/13 pt.   *System* QuarkXPress 4.01 [AG]

A catalog record for this book is available from the British Library.

Library of Congress Cataloging in Publication Data
Ainslie, George, 1944–
Breakdown of will / George Ainslie.
p.   cm.
Includes bibliographical references and index.
ISBN 0-521-59300-X (hb) – ISBN 0-521-59694-7 (pb)
1. Will.   2. Choice (Psychology)   3. Self-defeating behavior.   I. Title.
BF611.A295   2001
153.18 – dc21   00-058604

ISBN 0 521 59300 X hardback
ISBN 0 521 59694 7 paperback

To the late Richard Herrnstein and his students,
who have kept the study of motivation alive.

CONTENTS

Contents

PREFACE

I wrote *Breakdown of Will* in response to Cambridge editor Terry Moore's suggestion that I summarize *Picoeconomics*. This book is simpler and, I think, clearer. I have also added a great deal, both of research and theory, that I have discovered since *Picoeconomics* was published in 1992.

I've assumed no familiarity with hyperbolic discounting or intertemporal bargaining, so readers of *Picoeconomics* will find some repetition. However, if you've read the earlier book, you shouldn't assume that this book will therefore be a rehash of ideas you've seen before. In everything I've written I've thought it best to build from the ground up, rather than referring the new reader to works that may be hard to get; drafts of parts of this work have appeared not only in *Picoeconomics* but also in articles in Jon Elster's and Ole-Jorgen Skog's *Getting Hooked* and Elster's *Addiction: Entries and Exits, The Journal of Law and Philosophy*, and a precis in *Behavioral and Brain Sciences*.[1] However, *Breakdown of Will* pulls these works together and goes beyond them.

You may be surprised by the conversational style I use. I've adopted this style partly for readability – as a discipline against too many subordinate clauses – but also from a belief that the supposed benefit of an impersonal voice ("the language of scholars") is false. The fact that someone uses formal language doesn't mean she's objective, and formal language makes it harder to guess at her actual thought processes. The procession of dispassionate sentences becomes a kind of priestly cant, a curtain drawn around the Wizard of Oz, potentially just as misleading as the emotionality that might be provoked by conversation.

Specialists in the fields I've drawn from may have a more substantial objection: that I've mixed the results of controlled experiments with less "hard" sources, like clinical observations, thought experiments, historical writings, and even personal experiences. But I'm not pretending to prove once and for all any of the possible implications of hyperbolic discounting. This discounting itself rests on so many parametric experimental findings that I can call it firmly established, but there are many ways it could affect how our motives interact. I have only developed some models that I find parsimonious, and have cast about for diverse sources of information to test this parsimony. Once researchers have seen the possibilities for modeling minds as the populations of diverging interests that are shaped by this discounting, I hope that more systematic pattern matching will gradually approach a unique fit.

Many people helped me write this book. Especially helpful were Jon Elster and the diverse group of creative investigators he gathered for his seminars on irrationality. United by nothing more than the topic, we obeyed his summons to the far reaches of two continents over a period of almost 20 years. Like Nathan Detroit's floating crap game in *Guys and Dolls,* we moved to wherever he could enlist support for this eccentric endeavor: to Paris, Collioure, Oslo, Chicago, and New York. Sometimes there was a single meeting; sometimes we were a task force that worked on a book; *The Multiple Self, Choice Over Time, Getting Hooked,* and *Addiction: Entries and Exits* were all products of these colloquia, not to mention large parts of the books and articles written individually by the members, the most productive of whom was Jon himself. He has been the guiding spirit of the modern study of irrationality.

The roots of this book go back even before Jon's project, to the late Richard Herrnstein's behavioral laboratory at Harvard. Had I thought to dedicate *Picoeconomics,* it would certainly have been to him; I make that belated gesture now. A second-year medical student with a vague idea about crossing discount curves, I was lucky enough to find his lab in 1967, the very year he and Shin-Ho Chung published the first study of his matching law as applied to delay. When I pointed out that the matching formula implied a hyperbolic discount curve (I'd been using the power function by my teacher at Yale, Frank Logan), he set me up in his laboratory with snap lead racks and an advisor (Howard Rachlin, who has also been a helpful critic over the years); then he waited patiently for the six years it took to show that pigeons have the expectable intertemporal conflict. During that time and afterward he was always open to discussing new ideas, and usually knew someone who had been doing something along the same line. It was as an invited speaker in one of his classes, some years later, that I first tried out the prisoner's dilemma model of bargaining among successive selves. I published work with him on temporary preference, discussed at length the theories in his and my papers of the early nineties, and worked with him in the Russell Sage Foundation phase of Jon Elster's project. He was the closest thing I ever had to a mentor.

I owe thanks to many people at the Veterans Affairs Medical Center, Coatesville, Pennsylvania, for help on the articles that led to this book. John Monterosso was especially helpful in conducting both human and animal experiments, finding relevant articles in several literatures, and reading drafts and debating my ideas; he recently did most of the work of starting a behavioral rat laboratory from scratch, including most of the design. Andrew Henry obtained many articles for me. Pamela Toppi Mullen, Barbara Gault, and Kathy Meeker helped in the research and in critiquing ideas. Lynn Debiak drew crisp figures, and Wanda Sandoski often spent a frantic day helping me meet a deadline. For the book itself I thank John Monterosso, my wife Elizabeth, and two anonymous referees for valuable criticism; such clarity as I've been able to achieve comes from Elizabeth's painstaking reading of every line. Finally, thanks to Terry Moore for his unwavering support of the project.

PART I

BREAKDOWNS OF WILL: THE PUZZLE OF *AKRASIA*

CHAPTER 1

INTRODUCTION

There have been plenty of books and articles that describe how irrational we are – in consuming drugs and alcohol and cigarettes, in gambling, in forming destructive relationships, in failing to carry out our own plans, even in boring ourselves and procrastinating. The paradoxes of how people knowingly choose things they'll regret don't need rehashing. Examples of self-defeating behaviors abound. Theories about how this could be are almost as plentiful, with every discipline that studies the problem represented by several. However, the proliferation of theories in psychology, philosophy, economics, and the other behavioral sciences is best understood as a sign that no one has gotten to the heart of the matter.

These theories almost never mention failures of will.[1] This is just not a concept that behavioral scientists used much in the twentieth century. Some writers have even proposed that there's no such thing as a "will," that the word refers only to someone's disposition to choose. Still, the word crops up a lot in everyday speech, especially as part of "willpower," something that people still buy books to increase.

It's widely perceived that some factor transforms motivation from a simple reflection of the incentives we face to a process that is somehow *ours*, that perhaps even becomes *us* – some factor that lies at the very core of choice-making. We often refer to it as our will, the faculty by which we impose some overriding value of ours on the array of pressures and temptations that seem extrinsic. People usually ascribe control of temptation to the power of will and the unpredictability of this control to the freedom of will. Unfortunately, there has been no way to talk about such a faculty in the language of science, that is, in a way that relates it to simpler or better-understood elements. Without addressing

3

this factor, science paints a stilted picture of human experience in general. However, quantitative motivational research has produced a distinctly new finding that promises to account for the phenomenon of will – with elements that are already familiar to behavioral science. That, in a sentence, is the topic of this book.

1.1 A BRIEF HISTORY OF SELF-DEFEATING BEHAVIOR

A lot has been said about the will since the classical Greeks wrote about why people don't – or shouldn't – follow their spontaneous inclinations. Plato quoted Socrates describing what can go wrong when people weigh their future options:

> Do not the same magnitudes appear larger to your sight when near, and smaller when at a distance? . . . Is not [the power of appearance] that deceiving art which makes us wander up and down and take the things at one time of which we repent at another? . . . Men err in their choice of pleasures and pains, that is, in their choice of good and evil, from defect of . . . that particular knowledge that is called measuring.

Aristotle gave this disorder a name, *akrasia*, "weakness of will."[2] Thus a human faculty, not called will until later, was defined by the situation in which it failed.

Normally, a person was said to follow "reason," to weigh her options in proportion to their real importance; but sometimes an option seemed to loom too large, a process called "passion." Passion was the enemy of reason. As this dichotomy evolved, it began to define a functional anatomy of the self. Reason was the major part of your real identity; passion was something that *came over you* – the term was often contrasted with "action," something you *do*.[3]

The self used reason to defend itself from passions and, if successful, developed a "disposition" to behave temperately. Reason and a temperate disposition were the good guys; passion and *akrasia* were the bad guys, perhaps the *other* guys. The Roman physician Galen said that their relationship was that of a man to an animal: "Irascible" passions could be tamed, but "concupiscible" passions (appetites, like sex and gluttony) were too wild and could be controlled only by starving them.[4]

The Judeo-Christian theological view of "weakness of the flesh" developed in parallel with the Greek rationalist one. A noteworthy difference was that the theological view made reason somewhat external to the self, and passion more internal. Reason was the word of God, and a function called will was, to a large extent, supplied by God's grace. Passion was sin, a relentless part of man's identity since Adam's fall; but passion was sometimes augmented by external possession in the form of demons. The self swayed between reason and passion, hoping, in its reflective moments at least, that God would win:

> I do not even acknowledge my own actions as mine, for what I do is not what I want to do, but what I detest. But if what I do is against my will, it means that I agree with the law and hold it to be admirable. But as things are, it is no longer I who perform the action, but sin that lodges in me . . . the good which I want to do, I fail to do; but what I do is the wrong which is against my will; and if what I do is against my will, clearly it is no longer I who am the agent, but sin that has its lodging in me. I discover this principle, then: that when I want to do the right, only the wrong is within my reach. In my inmost self I delight in the law of God, but perceive that there is in my bodily members a different law, fighting against the law that my reason approves and making me a prisoner under the law that is in my members, the law of sin.[5]

The assertion that the individual will had somewhat more power than this, and thus might not depend on the grace of God, was rejected as one of the great heresies, Pelagianism.[6]

Other philosophies and religions have all included major analyses of the passions. They also discuss how to avoid them. Buddhism, for instance, concerns itself with emancipation from "the bond of worldly passions" and describes five strategies of purification, essentially: having clear ideas, avoiding sensual desires by mind control, restricting objects to their natural uses, "endurance," and watching out for temptations in advance.[7] However, the ways that non-Western religions enumerate causes of and solutions to self-defeating behaviors seem a jumble from any operational viewpoint of trying to maximize a good.

Despite all the attention paid, not many really new ideas about self-control have appeared over the years, even in the great cultural exchanges that brought the whole world into communication. One significant advance was Francis Bacon's realization that reason didn't have its own force, but had to get its way by playing one passion against another: It had to

> set affection against affection and to master one by another: even as we use to hunt beast with beast. . . . For as in the government of states it is

sometimes necessary to bridle one faction with another, so it is in the government within.[8]

The implication was that passion and reason might be just different patterns in the same system. Furthermore, they might be connected not by cognition but by some internal economic process, in which reason had to find the wherewithal to motivate its plans.

Another new idea was the Victorian discovery that the will could be analyzed into specific properties that might respond to strengthening exercises. We'll look at these in detail later (Section 5.1.4).

Even as some nineteenth-century authors were dissecting the will, others began to get suspicious of it. Observers had long known that the will could get bogged down in minutiae, a problem that medieval scholastics called a "scrupulous conscience."[9] In early Victorian times Soren Kierkegaard warned of a more general but insidious affliction that seemed to come from the very success of willpower in controlling passion – a loss of what the existential school of philosophy, Kierkegaard's heirs, came to call "authenticity." The existentialists said that authenticity comes from a responsiveness to the immediacy of experience, a responsiveness that is lost when people govern themselves according to preconceived "cognitive maps."[10]

At the turn of the twentieth century, Freud described a division of motivational processes into those that serve long-range goals (the "reality principle") and those that serve short-range ones (the "pleasure principle"). But the long-term processes are always distorted by an alien influence, "introjected" from parents, making them rigid. Freud rarely used the word "will," and used it trivially when he did; but his farsighted processes and the "superego" that made them rigid would have been recognizable to his audience as components of will and willpower.[11]

Interest in the will grew steadily until about the time of World War I. After that the concept of will suddenly became highly unfashionable, even distasteful – as if people blamed it for their countries' steadfastness in commanding millions of soldiers to face murderous fire and perhaps for the fortitude that led the soldiers to obey.[12] Whatever the reason, the twentieth century saw our concepts of impulsiveness and self-control become diffuse. We continued to analyze reason in the form of utility theory, which defined that perfect rationalist, Economic Man. Passion and *akrasia*, however, are another story entirely, as are any devices that might be needed to overcome them. Explanations of them are ad hoc and higgledy-piggledy.

Willpower had become a popular Victorian virtue without any examination of where it came from. When it became tainted there was no agreed-upon way to analyze what was wrong, or what alternatives there might be, or even precisely what function it was supposed to perform.

1.2. HOW TO STUDY SELF-DEFEATING BEHAVIOR

Something is obviously wrong or at least incomplete about the way we've understood *akrasia* and self-control. I believe that new findings make it possible to say a lot about the will and the reasons why it succeeds and fails where it does; but first, we have to look at what's already been said. Behavioral scientists still study weakness and strength of will, although usually without those specific concepts in their minds – sometimes without even the concept of motivation. But these scientists don't talk to most of their colleagues. Like so many fields where people are probing a mystery, decision science has split into schools whose members agree within their groups on certain assumptions and ways of doing research. Reading other schools' writings means forgoing the shorthand you've become adept at in your own school, not to mention the confidence that what you write yourself will have a willing audience. Mostly, we don't bother.

But these schools have separately discovered many different tools to work on the will problem. Before we start work, we need to look at the available methods. Here's an informal list of the schools that have studied will-related decisions:

Behaviorism is the school that has designed most of the systematic experiments on utility theory. The behaviorists have made especially good use of animal models. Lower animals are different from people, of course, but their subcortical brain structures are similar, including the systems that govern motivation, and this similarity is reflected in a similar response to most (but not all) schedules of reward. For instance, animals can become addicted to all the substances that affect people. Based on their ability to judge how rich different sources of reward are, animals often seem to be more rational than people.[13]

The neurologist Paul MacLean once observed that the human cortex rides on lower brain functions like a man riding a horse. Although we

7

can't use animals to study some higher functions – wit, irony, or self-consciousness, for instance – we can use them to study the horse we all ride. And when a mental process can be demonstrated in animals – like a conflict between motives at successive times – it spares us speculation about subtle causes like quirks of culture.

However, the careful experiments that the behaviorists do have been overshadowed by their righteousness about method. To the average educated person, a behaviorist is somebody who believes that the mind doesn't exist, and that people's behavior can be accounted for entirely by the observable stimuli that impinge on them. Even the academic community tired of this brand of logical positivism and stripped the behavioral school of most of its glory. As a source of carefully controlled data, however, it remains unsurpassed, and its data are the starting place of this book.

Cognitive psychology, often as applied to social psychology, is currently the most widespread approach to both research and theory dealing with irrational behavior. It generally has high standards of experimental proof and has described many examples of maladaptive behavior. However, its theorists seem to have gone out of their way to avoid dealing with the process of motivation, seeing it as at most some kind of internal communication that a higher judge – the irreducible person – can and often should disregard. Thus its theories of irrationality have been restricted to finding errors of perception or logic.

Economics is the field that deals with rational decision-making in the real world. In modern times it has embraced the assumptions of utility theory, as characterized by Paul Samuelson: "The view that consumers maximize utility is not merely a law of economics, it is a law of logic itself." Gary Becker showed that economic concepts could handle even nonmonetary incentives like drug highs and the risk of jail.[14]

However, economists have made some unrealistic assumptions about decisions: that they're all deliberate, that they're based only on external goods (as opposed to rewards that you might generate in your own head), and that they're naturally stable in the absence of new information. Since this stability should make decisions consistent, economic theories have attributed irrationality only to inadequate information or steep discounting of the future, explanations that are both inadequate, as we'll see.

Philosophy of mind looks at model-making itself, and has pioneered thought experiments whereby every reader can test a particular theory.[15]

8

However, it has stayed within the conventional assumptions of a unitary self – unitary in the sense of not housing contradictory or unconscious elements. If anything should allow exploration of a more molecular model of the self, it should be thought experiments; but the seeming paradoxes that some have demonstrated have not led analysis beyond standard utility theory. They remain paradoxical.

Psychoanalysis was the first major attempt to confront self-contradictory behaviors with utility analysis. As an explorer of scientifically virgin territory, Freud sketched out several different models – one based on motivation ("libido"), one based on consciousness, one based on organization ("id," "ego," "superego"), and so on. But he didn't work out how the various models got along with each other. Without the discipline of either controlled observation or conceptual parsimony, psychoanalysis grew overinclusive, until it resembled the polytheisms from which it drew some of its observations.

Oversold in the middle third of the twentieth century, psychoanalysis has lately been the target of vigorous attacks aimed at its standards of observation and proof. The essayist Frederick Crews concluded that

> the designer of psychoanalysis was at bottom a visionary but endlessly calculating artist, engaged in casting himself as the hero of a multivolume fictional opus that is part epic, part detective story, and part satire on human self-interestedness and animality.[16]

It hasn't been fashionable to ask whether even a fictional opus that once had such immense popularity among intelligent people may offer insights worth keeping.

Actually, Freud brought together a lot of previous work that describes disunity of the self, and this has gone into limbo with him.[17] Worse, people who have found his answers wrong or incomplete have stopped asking his questions, and these questions have to be in the forefront of any attempt to explain impulsiveness and impulse control: Is all behavior motivated? How can someone obey internally contradictory motives? How can you hide information from yourself? How can self-control sometimes make you worse off? On many questions I'll start with Freud's ideas – because, in my view, after modern criticism tackled the ball carrier, no one ever picked up the ball.

Bargaining research, a new discipline, has used elementary games to see how small groups of competing agents can reach stable relationships. It is especially suggestive when it shows how such a group can reach stable decisions that are not in all or any member's best interest. However, until now, bargaining research has not seemed applicable to conflict within the individual because of the supposed unity of the person. Given a rationale for disunity, we'll find it useful.

Chaos theory, an even newer theory of analysis, has been applied to other subjects – the weather, for instance – to explore how outcomes may depend on a recursive feedback system. It has also shown how such a system may lead to similar patterns at different levels of magnification and even to the growth of the different levels themselves. So far chaos theory has lacked any important motivational example. However, the fundamental unpredictability of the human will, which has defied attempts to explain it by antecedent causes, makes it look like some of the natural phenomena where the chaos approach has proven useful. As we find recursive processes in the will, chaos theory will become relevant.

Sociobiology has studied competition among populations of reward-seeking organisms, so it has developed concepts that might be useful for populations of behaviors – the range of behaviors that an organism tries out – as well. Behaviorists have proposed that reinforcement acts on behaviors the way natural selective factors act on organisms.[18] This suggests some way that sociobiological theory might apply to conflicting motives.[19]

Neurophysiology has produced increasingly precise findings on brain mechanisms, including those that create motivation. It's possible to see, for instance, exactly where and by what neurotransmitters cocaine rewards the behaviors that obtain it;[20] but pinpointing the transmitters doesn't explain how a conflict between alternative rewards gets resolved or why it fails to get resolved in some cases. It may be, for instance, that some alcoholics have inherited settings in their reward mechanisms that make alcohol more rewarding for them than for most people; but this doesn't tell us why many alcoholics are conflicted about their drinking – why they often decide not to drink despite the intensity of this reward and, having decided this, why they sometimes fail to carry out their own decision. Neurobiology will be useful here mainly as a check on reality, as a body of findings with which any motivational theory must at least be consistent.

Theology shouldn't be disregarded. It has studied a part of our decision-making experience that seems to lie outside the will and has been least influenced by the lure of utility theory. Despite its own theory that its insights come mystically, by faith, revelation, or some such nonempirical route, theology actually demands that its tenets ring true to experience. Sin, for instance, seems synonymous with the self-defeating behaviors that the more scientific disciplines have talked about; the debates that have occurred over the power of the individual will to overcome sin have appealed to what is, in effect, clinical experience. But what this inspirational approach has gained in sensitivity it has lost in testability, and it becomes arbitrary when it tries to nail down its insights in a systematic way. Like psychoanalysis, it will be a source more of questions than of answers. But the questions are important ones.

Finally, any explanation of *akrasia* has to be at least compatible with *subjective experience* and might well find evidence there. Some behavioral scientists sniff at experiential evidence as "folk psychology" and warn of the days when psychologists tried to gather data using trained introspectors. While common sense is suggestive at best and, as theory, almost always inconsistent and ad hoc, it is by far the largest body of human observations. Useful samples of common experience appear in the writings of the preexperimental (Victorian) psychologists and of later clinicians who have interviewed patients, as well as in those works of fiction that have rung true with generations of readers. Jon Elster has been especially insightful in sorting the pieces of our written heritage by their motivational implications.[21]

1.2.1 My Approach to the Problem

So how should we assemble a working tool kit from all of these methods? I'll suggest one way, obviously not the only one possible. But as far as I can tell, it's the only proposal so far that reconciles the familiar paradoxes of motivation with basic research.

I warn the reader in advance that this approach is *reductionistic*. That is, I assume that every change in thinking, feeling, wanting, planning, and so on, has a physical basis in the nerve cells of the brain, which in turn depend on chemical changes within the cells, and so on. I'm not saying that thinking and feeling are best studied by studying the chemistry of cells – only that all explanations of behavior should at least be consistent with what's known in the physical and biological sciences.

Nonreductionistic (and antireductionistic) theories have been created for a reason, of course. In the past, reductionistic theories ignored causes that were hard to observe or to imagine – that is, too hidden or complex

11

or internally fed back – like cognitions, or intuitions, or will. "Scientific" explanations therefore made people seem like robots.[22]

By the same token, my proposals are *deterministic*. Aside from some irrelevant arguments about whether the movements of subatomic particles are strictly determined (see Section 8.3.2), the physical sciences assume that all things that happen are shaped completely by prior causes, which have causes in turn. I do, too. I don't mean that these causes can be found. Some are probably too hidden or complex or internally fed back ever to be useful for practical prediction; but again, explanations of behavior should never depend on some uncaused or otherwise imponderable factor.

Students of human behavior often rebel against reductionism and determinism in favor of holistic, humanistic approaches so that science can still examine feelings, not to mention the many other private subtleties that can be introspected but not tested. However, I'll argue that these subtleties – among them self-deception, self-control and its loss, self-esteem and its loss, and freedom of will itself – are completely consistent with a reductionistic theory of choice.

So please don't be put off by my warning. The humanist reader will find protection, even ammunition, in the model of choice I'm going to propose.

1.3 SUMMARY

The human bent for defeating our own plans has puzzled writers since antiquity. From Plato's idea that the better part of the self – reason – could be overwhelmed by passion, there evolved the concept of a faculty, will, that lent reason the kind of force that could confront passion and defeat it. The construct of the will and its power became unfashionable in twentieth-century science, but the puzzle of self-defeating behavior – what Aristotle called *akrasia* – and its sometime control has not been solved. With the help of new experimental findings and conceptual tools from several different disciplines, it will be possible to form a hypothesis about the nature of will that does not violate the conventions of science as we know it.

CHAPTER 2

THE DICHOTOMY AT THE ROOT
OF DECISION SCIENCE

Do We Make Choices By Desires or By Judgments?

Our ideas about deciding divide into two kinds, each of which goes back to ancient times. Theorists from classical Greece to the present have focused on two conspicuous experiences in choice-making, wanting and judging, and have built models around each of them. Models based on wanting say that people weigh the feeling of satisfaction that follows different alternatives and selectively repeat those behaviors that lead to the most satisfaction. Models based on judging take a hierarchy of wants as given and focus on how a person uses logic – or some other cognitive faculty – to relate options to this hierarchy. The weighers, who include the British empiricist philosophers like David Hume, the psychoanalysts, and behaviorists like B. F. Skinner, developed satisfaction-based models that are called "hedonistic" or "economic" or "utilitarian." On the other side, the German idealists, Jean Piaget, and modern cognitive psychologists like Roy Baumeister and Julius Kuhl have centered their explanations on judgments; this approach is called "cognitive" or "rationalistic."

Skinner said that not only choice but also deliberation depend on differential reinforcement:

> The individual manipulates relevant variables in making a decision because the behavior of doing so has certain reinforcing consequences.

His explanation of addictions is simple: "The effects induced by [addictive] drugs reinforce the behavior of consuming them."[1] By contrast, cognitivist writers attribute addiction and other "misregulations" to various kinds of interpretive errors, as we're about to see.

13

These two orientations to choice-making don't contradict each other's facts, but they imply incompatible assumptions about the fundamental process of choice. There are times when everyone is conscious of weighing her satisfactions and times when everyone figures out what to do by logic; but when the weighings and the deductions dictate contradictory choices, what decides the winner? I *want* to have a love affair, but I *judge* it to be imprudent, or unethical, or sinful. How do I decide? No theory about how the wants and the judgments compete for dominance has taken us beyond Plato's contest between passion and reason.

The starting place that people haven't been able to agree upon is whether the root process – the bottom line – is a matter of hedonism or of cognition. Does the fundamental determinant maximize some quantity like utility or reward, or does it somehow step outside of hedonic attraction and make overriding judgments?

People's ability to resist temptation at least sometimes, even while feeling its pull, has made the cognitive process seem intuitively more likely. After sufficient learning, reason seems to triumph over passion. Most cognitive writers see the weighing of satisfactions as a subordinate activity, one of several possible ways to make a decision and probably not one of the best. This opinion won out among the ancients and has remained dominant among philosophers of mind. They have recently been joined by many psychologists, including a number of clinicians concerned about self-defeating behaviors and even self-induced illnesses.[2]

Cognitivism attributes self-defeating behavior to mental error – for instance, to illusions that have led to faulty puzzle-solving; where it alludes to motivation at all, the cognitive school assumes that the person is free to choose her motives and thus isn't ultimately moved by them. One philosopher asks, "Should I give less weight to some of my desires because they are not my present desires?" – implying that the "giving" of weight is not itself determined by weights.[3] In a summary of "self-regulation" – a cognitive word for willpower – psychologists Roy Baumeister and Todd Heatherton give motivation a tangential role in the form of its cognate, emotion:

> Misregulation occurs because [people] operate on the basis of false assumptions about themselves and about the world, because they try to control things that cannot be directly controlled, or because they give priority to emotions while neglecting more important and fundamental problems.[4]

14

Misjudgment, not temptation, is said to be the problem, except in cases where the misjudgment leads you to "give priority" to your feelings; by allowing for that, these authors let the concept of temptation in, but through a back door. Psychologist Janet Polivy uses the word "motivation" itself, but for her, "motivations are signals," and determination of their relative strengths determines only which ones are "most likely" to prevail. Psychologists Jack Brehm and Beverly Brummett go so far as to say that "emotions have the character of motivational states"; but these are only hortatory: They just "have the function of urging an adaptive response to an actual or potential outcome of greater than average importance." In such views, we can always choose what influences to listen to. To oversimplify a bit, but not much, cognitive theories say that emotion/motivation just provides one more challenge for reasons to meet. If we succumb to temptation, the problem lies with our reasoning. Our overwrought brains are prone to logical errors, so that we overgeneralize or generalize from the wrong things.[5] Cognitive psychology revives Socrates' dictum that nobody knowingly does wrong.

The cognitive picture of choice is certainly recognizable in everyday experience. The trouble is, it doesn't get us beyond the observational level of explanation. Pronouncing motivation to be just one of many factors that appeal to reason ends the analysis of choice. There's no way to nail down the relationship of motive and judgment if the judge is a homunculus inside the mind who's sometimes swayed by motives and sometimes not.

By contrast, utility theory follows the discipline that your options have to compete for your favor on the basis of some elementary motivational quality – call it "reward" – a common dimension along which all options that can be substituted for each other have to compete. Reward is supposed to operate on your choices the way natural selection operates on species: It keeps the successful candidates and drops the others. Utilitarian writers in fields from economics to abnormal psychology depict people as simply trying to maximize their satisfactions. To them, this is reason's role; it's just straight thinking. Its enemy isn't passion per se, or the misuse of logic, but the simple miscalculation of your main chance. So utility theorists have narrowed the scope of cognitive failure to a single dimension, estimation of reward.

According to utility theory, rationality isn't found only in human beings, but occurs naturally in lower animals; even titmice and crabs have been described as fine-tuning their behavior to conditions so as to miss almost no rewards.[6] The hypothetical person who achieves as much acumen as these animals is Economic Man.

An artificial concept at his creation, Economic Man[7] is now looked upon as normal. Paul Samuelson pioneered the transformation of economics into the study of his behavior. Samuelson's fictional hero has crept into the thinking of all utility-oriented writers, so that their concept of irrationality has become synonymous with a failure to maximize expected income.[8]

Utility theory has been a great success at predicting preference, at least among alternatives that are roughly simultaneous – so much so that the whole gamut of choice analysts, from sociobiologists through behavioral psychologists to economists and sociologists, accept utility as the elementary basis of choice. It doesn't always describe how people choose, but at least it pinpoints the costs of departing from this basis. Utility theory has been used to demonstrate the excessive cost of behaviors like sticking to an investment just because it has already been made, or borrowing money at a higher rate of interest to avoid tapping savings that earn a lower rate.[9]

However, utility theory has had trouble explaining why people go on doing these things, sometimes while saying, "I know it's irrational, but . . ." Why do people often fail to choose their best deal from among familiar alternatives, even though rats in a maze succeed? The failure of investors to maximize their prospects in light of good information is a puzzle in the very center of economics, and it's just the tip of an iceberg.

Choices that violate the norm of utility maximization can be seen everywhere. The prosperity of modern civilization contrasts more and more sharply with people's choice of seemingly irrational, perverse behaviors, behaviors that make many individuals unhappier than the poorest hunter/gatherer.[10] As our technical skills overcome hunger, cold, disease, and even tedium, the willingness of individuals to defeat their own purposes stands in ever sharper contrast. In most cases these behaviors aren't naive mistakes, but the product of robust motives that persist despite an awareness of the behaviors' costs.

The substance addictions are the most conspicuous example of this puzzle. Observers often blame the biological properties of the substance, even though experienced addicts knowingly readdict themselves after they're sober. Addictions without physiological substances, like gambling and credit card abuse, have the same characteristics as drug addictions when carried to the same extent: a rush of feeling that preoccupies the addict, the relentless narrowing of alternative opportunities through alienation of family, friends, and employers, and even the adaptation of brain chemicals involved in pleasure, so that deprivation of the activity leads to symptoms of withdrawal – nausea, sweating, and other physical side effects.[11] These nonsubstance addictions form a conceptual link to a large class of ordinary "bad habits," habits that people say they want to be rid of even while indulging in them: promiscuity, episodic rage, chronic procrastination, a bent for destructive relationships – all the patterns that the classical Greeks would have called *akratic*. Unlike substance abuse, these behaviors can't be blamed on the distortion of "natural" motivation by a molecule.

Ironically, the straightforward simplicity of utility theory seems to have put it out of business as an explanation for irrational behavior. If choice is just a matter of estimating maximal reward, the role of motivation in bad choices will be trivial, since any failure of maximization can only come from an error in the estimating process.[12] Utility theory has been at great pains to find a way around this conclusion.

2.1 IS ADDICTION EITHER A MISTAKE OR A SIMPLE PREFERENCE?

A popular solution is the suggestion that addiction occurs only in two special cases – when a person doesn't know its consequences or when she doesn't care. In the first case, you're supposed to have committed yourself to the poorer, earlier alternative before you knew its cost – so that the hangover or damage to relationships is a surprise. Certainly this could be a factor in how people first get addicted to something. Despite the fact that most smokers, for instance, know the dangers of smoking before they start, it may be that they can't picture how strong their craving will become once they're addicted. It's believable that alcoholics and drug addicts can't imagine how their other options will narrow after they've had their habit for a while. Thus there probably is a "primrose path" that leads many people to addiction.[13]

However, the popular impression that addictions trap people by the threat of withdrawal has proven not to be true. It's not the case that once you start, you can't stop. In reality addicts stop many times, even withdrawing deliberately to cheapen their habits. Furthermore, the primrose path theory doesn't explain why sober addicts have a great tendency to be readdicted or why active addicts try to stop by committing themselves in advance – for instance, by taking disulfiram, a drug that makes alcohol sickening. Once an addict has become familiar with her options, conventional utility theory requires that any craving strong enough to lead to a relapse has to be strong enough to command a consistent preference for the addiction. People might be deceived into taking up an addictive habit but not into restarting a familiar addiction once they've escaped.

For similar reasons, we can rule out the theory that addicts just don't care much about the future – that they devalue delayed events. Their devaluation may well be greater than usual,[14] but the "rational addict" whom economists Gary Becker and Kevin Murphy picture wouldn't ever try to kick her habit and certainly wouldn't try to restrict her own future range of choice by taking disulfiram. The rational addict who thinks that the high is worth the consequences when the opportunity is at hand should think so at a distance as well, and should always keep her options open in case new information makes another choice seem better.[15]

Straightforward value estimators have no reason to use strongarm tactics on themselves. If your struggle with temptation can be bypassed simply by gaining insight into your best prospects, volition as a mechanism becomes superfluous. Your calculation of your main chance flows smoothly into action, and will disappears. Will may even be a superstitious concept, the philosophical equivalent of cherubim or seraphim, a theoretical decoration without any explanatory function. In the 1940s Gilbert Ryle insisted that this was the case.[16] He asked whether "willing" added anything to the simple state of being motivated to perform an action; answering his question in the negative, he dismissed the will as a "ghost in the machine." If you estimate that you'll be better off without chocolates and this is enough reason to stop eating them, does an organ called the will have to be any part of the process?

2.2 DOES ADDICTION COME FROM PROCESSES THAT VIOLATE THE USUAL LAWS OF MOTIVATION?

Facing the somewhat counterintuitive conclusion that the will doesn't exist,[17] utility theorists have looked outside of the evaluation process for a way to explain why self-control takes effort at best and sometimes fails miserably. Two areas of research have sometimes looked promising: classical conditioning and brain physiology.

18

2.2.1 Classical Conditioning: Does Addiction Come from a Different Kind of Reinforcement?

Perhaps some factor that bypasses utility kicks in – something that reinforces a behavior without actually rewarding it. There's an experimental model of how you can apparently elicit a behavior without motivating it: "classical" conditioning.[18] When a stimulus picked at random is regularly followed by the emotionally meaningful events that can trigger apparent reflexes – food that produces salivation, pain that produces a racing heart, and so on – the random stimulus starts to produce behavior very similar to the reflex, without anything seeming to reward or punish this behavior. At first glance, conditioned behaviors seem to be *pushed* by prior events – the "conditioned stimuli" – rather than *pulled* by an expectation of subsequent ones.

Some writers suggested that impulsive behaviors like drinking might be conditioned, so that they could come over the person whether or not she wanted them. Even Freud, usually a utility theorist, sometimes used the concept of a "repetition compulsion" that was independent of reward or punishment; the few times he called on it, he'd been at a loss to explain a particular behavior on the basis of motivation.[19] However, it's now well known that the kinds of movements that are usually voluntary can't come under the control of conditioning. An alcoholic can't be made to bend her elbow by the conditioned stimulus of a bar.

A more robust idea involves a special class of inborn responses that can't be emitted deliberately or shaped by reward or punishment but have to be triggered reflexively – pushed instead of pulled. These responses are said to need genetically determined triggers – "unconditioned stimuli," – but conditioned stimuli that have been paired with them also become triggers. The supposedly unmotivatable responses are secretions and smooth muscle contractions – the domain of the autonomic nervous system – and, mostly by implication, emotions and hungers. If these latter two can be conditioned, the argument goes, then maybe conditioned stimuli can impose motives on a person that she otherwise doesn't want, and those conditioned motives can overwhelm her normal (or rational) ones. "Two-factor theory" states that cravings are what get conditioned in an addict; they occur when she encounters a stimulus that's been associated with them in the past. Even though you don't drink because a conditioned muscle reflex makes you, you may drink because the sight of a bottle elicits a conditioned craving great enough to overcome your other motives. Factor one is the conditioning that pushes the craving on you; factor two is the drinking that is pulled by the hope of satisfying the craving.[20]

This scenario has intuitive appeal. Many people have had the experience in a restaurant of resolving not to order dessert, only to have their resolve broken by the appearance of the dessert cart. Couldn't it be the conditioned appetite aroused by the sight and smell of the desserts that causes the motivation to change? But however familiar this experience is, conditioned craving can't be the ultimate explanation for self-defeating behavior for two reasons: Conditioning probably isn't independent of reward; and even if it is, conditioned motives should come to be anticipated and weighed like any other kind. The reader not interested in why ordinary reward is probably what reinforces conditioning can skip to Section 2.2.1.2.

2.2.1.1 There Seems to Be Only One Kind of Reinforcement. Some overlap was always recognized between motivatable and unmotivatable responses; for a long time some conditioned patterns were reported in the "voluntary" (skeletal) muscles, like those that govern eyeblinks, for instance, and voluntary urination has long been known to be controlled by "involuntary" (smooth) muscle. Furthermore, potential unconditioned stimuli (food, shock, etc.) were observed to be identical with motivating stimuli; that is, all stimuli that can induce conditioning have some motivational value as well.[21] Nevertheless, the theoretical dichotomy wasn't seriously challenged until subtler experiments were done in the 1970s.

These experiments showed the following:

- Many responses previously thought to be unmotivatable can be shaped by incentives if these are delivered soon enough after the response; thus involuntary responses in humans can be made voluntary by delivery of the right biofeedback. It has even been reported that deprived narcotic addicts stop developing physiological symptoms of withdrawal when these are punished by shock.[22]
- Conditioned responses have to vie with one another for expression: Old addicts who see reminders of their drug use, for instance, sometimes reexperience the drug high but sometimes the drug craving; the possible responses must compete, just as rewarded responses must.[23]
- Conditioned stimuli compete with and can even be overridden by

contrary incentives; the crucial test is whether the behavior can be changed or suppressed by the apt targeting of differential reward, and this has sometimes proven possible. For instance, monkeys conditioned to raise their heart rates at a warning cue for unavoidable shock can learn to slow their heart rates instead if slowing prevents additional shock from occurring.[24]

- Given the overlap of conditioning and goal-directed learning, some common means of deciding which governs behavior has to exist:

  > The two procedures cannot require different "laws of learning" because, even if different laws existed, no basis would exist at the moment of selection with which the organism could "decide" which set of laws to invoke.[25]

- Perhaps most importantly, close examination shows that conditioned responses are not just copies of unconditioned responses emitted to a new stimulus, like Windows icons dragged to a new part of the screen, but are different responses that must have been taught afresh – and taught by reward, unless yet another kind of reinforcement is invoked.[26]

Computer modeling of the common behavioral experiments has shown that a single process can explain selection of both classical (pushed) and goal-directed (pulled) responses, thus putting detail in a theory that had often been proposed.[27] Without necessarily accepting the actual equivalence of the reinforcement that governs conditioning and the reinforcement that governs choice, many researchers have concluded that only *information* can be linked by simple pairing – that all *responses* depend on adequate motivation.[28] This is to say that seemingly conditioned (pushed) responses in nature are actually shaped by some reward factor (pulled). Perhaps salivation makes food taste better; an arousal response may make pain less painful; and so on.[29]

The problem for the theory that conditioning is a separate selective force acting on behavior isn't its nonexistence, either in the laboratory or in ordinary appetites. On the contrary, conditioning is a familiar phenomenon. The problem is that conditioning per se connects only information – one stimulus to another, like a bell and the taste of food – and does not transfer responses, even autonomic or, presumably, emotional responses. Responses like salivation certainly arise to conditioned stimuli, and these responses often closely resemble the responses elicited by unconditioned stimuli, but the evidence I've just outlined suggests that they occur only insofar as they're motivated.

The distinction that probably made two different kinds of response selection seem necessary was that conditioning could induce both pleasurable and aversive experiences, while reward-based choice was thought to seek only pleasure.[30] Conventional theory could explain the reexperience of the drug high as rewarding, for instance, but how could someone be motivated to participate in the dysphoric craving? Given the inadequacy of conditioning as an explanation, this problem might seem to have no solution. Actually, the research I'll be describing supplies one, but this will require more background (see Sections 4.3.1 and 10.1). I'll leave that for the moment and make the second, simpler argument about conditioning as a cause of impulsiveness.

2.2.1.2 Conditioned Motives Are Still Weighed. Whether or not conditioning is a separate kind of response-selecting principle, there's nothing about being conditioned that should make an appetite different from other appetites. We don't pick our other appetites, either. Once we've become familiar with how our appetites respond to dessert carts, there's no reason that we shouldn't weigh our prospects as we do ordinarily. If the desserts stimulate appetite and the appetite increases their prospective rewardingness, this experience should also become familiar and get evaluated in comparison with alternative experiences. According to conventional utility theory, if the experience of appetite-followed-by-food is worth more than the experience of abstention-followed-by-whatever-benefits-accrue at the time the food is at hand, then it should also be worth more when anticipated from a distance. An addict should have no more motive to avoid a conditioned craving than to avoid any other future wish. Whatever conditioning is, it's just a part of the ordinary mechanism of motivation.[31]

2.2.2 Does Impulsiveness Come from Brain Chemistry?

Many scientists hope that understanding the physical basis of reward will provide an answer to that question. We certainly know more about it than we did a generation ago. At first the problem seemed impenetrable. In the 1950s researchers despaired of finding a common characteristic of things that could reward. Behavioral psychologist David Premack finally said that rewards reliably share only the common trait of being rewarding – the psychological equivalent of the economists' abdicating slogan "there's no accounting for tastes."[32]

Even as Premack was saying that, however, neurophysiologists were using brain electrodes to find how and where reward happened in the brain. They located several places in the midbrain – a part that hasn't changed much from lower vertebrates to man – where electrical or chemical stimulation produced intense pleasure. They could tell because (1) an animal with an electrode in one of these places would ignore both hunger and increasing exhaustion in order to work for repeated stimulation, sometimes to the point of collapse,[33] and (2) some human patients who had electrodes implanted for pain control described this pleasure.[34] It still wasn't possible to say what this meant for ordinary rewards that occur naturally, although brain stimulation at the sites that were sensitive to electrical reward often generated appetites like hunger, thirst, and sexual appetite as well.

In recent years, brain reward research has become more exact. Neurophysiologists have found that most or all recreational substances, from alcohol and marijuana to cocaine and heroin, are mediated by stimulating release of the neurotransmitter dopamine in one small part of the midbrain, the nucleus accumbens.[35] The site that animals will stimulate electrically to the point of exhaustion is the same site that crack abusers will stimulate chemically to the point of exhaustion. Many complex motivational effects have been described after stimulating and/or recording from the neighborhood of this nucleus, including the following:

- The stimulation of many sites produces both appetite in a satiated animal and reward in a hungry one, suggesting that these processes may not be simple opposites.[36]
- Sensory events that attract attention but aren't otherwise rewarding or punishing elicit activity from these sites, thus suggesting that direction of attention may be intimately related to reward.[37]
- A few sites that respond to reward also respond to pain and threat, suggesting that in some way the nervous system may find a common meaning in these seeming opposites (see Section 4.1.4).[38]
- Sites that respond to reward when it's unexpected come to respond to information that predicts the reward, and cease responding to the reward itself once it is thoroughly expected – suggesting

23

that one step in the reward process is produced only by surprising events.[39]

Another line of research has shown that impulsiveness itself – a preference for smaller, earlier over larger, later rewards or an inability to wait for delayed rewards – can be manipulated by changing activity in other neurons, which use serotonin as a transmitter.[40]

This is exciting research. It suggests mechanisms that might give some people a high inborn susceptibility to drug reward, and it shows how taking a drug over time can reduce the brain's sensitivity to other kinds of reward. It also underscores the likelihood that choice is fundamentally based on some kind of hedonic evaluation, as I'll now describe. However, it doesn't repair the flaw in conventional utility theory: It doesn't suggest why people fail to maximize reward as they themselves see it, that is, why people should perceive a need for self-control.

2.2.3 There Must Be a Single Dimension of Choice

Cognitively oriented writers have said that reward is only one reason, sometimes a perverse reason,[41] for judging an outcome to be good, and that we hold the determination of what rewards us in our own hands. When we "give importance" to something, our reason seems to be setting up what passions will move us. But when reward is manipulated directly in the brain, it validates Aristotle's comment: It may do no good for a person to have a rational belief; "appetite leads him on, since it is capable of moving each of the [bodily] parts."[42]

The ability of neurophysiological reward to override all other considerations leads us toward a utility-based relationship of cognition and motivation: As utility theorists have said, reason has to serve reward, albeit only in the long run. Freud put it succinctly, speaking of passion as the "pleasure principle" and reason as the "reality principle":

> Actually the substitution of the reality principle for the pleasure principle implies no deposing of the pleasure principle, but only a safeguarding of it. A momentary pleasure, uncertain in its results, is given up, but only in order to gain along the new path an assured pleasure at a later time.[43]

This is to say that reason depends on reward in the sense that reward gives reason its purpose. But at the same time, short-range pleasure seems to be the enemy of long-range pleasure, which must be "safeguarded" by something like reason.

As I've described (Section 1.1), Francis Bacon was the first to point out that reason could have force only if it had some connection to motivation. His point was amplified by the philosopher Spinoza. Discussing how cognitions might control passions ("affects"), Spinoza said, "No affect can be restrained by the true knowledge of good and evil insofar as it [the knowledge] is true, but only insofar as it is considered as an affect." And "An affect cannot be restrained nor moved unless by a stronger opposing affect."[44] That is, reason has to acquire the same kind of power, the same movingness, that passions have, if it is sometimes to overcome them. Reason and passion must bid for control of the person's behavior using the same kind of currency. This seemingly elementary point has been surprisingly controversial and keeps having to be rediscovered; witness a Russian article of not so long ago:

> When 2 [value] centers are formed simultaneously, 1 drive is extinguished only by a stronger drive, e.g., the wish for pleasure (sexual drive) is superseded by the striving for self-esteem. This eliminates the dualistic view that emotions associated with concepts are distinguished from those associated with drives, and intellectual and instinctual actions are separated.[45]

Neurophysiologists Peter Shizgall and Kent Conover have gone beyond mere rediscovery by finding evidence for an "evaluative circuitry" in the brain that creates just such a currency for comparing diverse objects of desire. As they point out:

> For orderly choice to be possible, the utility of all competing resources must be represented on a single, common dimension.

But if passion and reason both affect the allocation of common resources, then reward looks like the needed common dimension.[46]

Thus it's possible to define a role for reason within an entirely motivation-driven decision-making process. However, this still doesn't solve the puzzle of addiction. So what if our cognitions are shaped to maximize reward? Whether utility theorists call the thing to be maximized reward, or reinforcement, or utility, or even money, they have no way of identifying a bad kind. Utility theory says that reward is sought, and more is better than less. Period. It allows delayed reward to be devalued, of course; but this in itself doesn't suggest why we seek at one time the same reward we reject at another. There is still no reason to have a will or for that will to require effort.

2.3 SUMMARY

The puzzle of self-defeating behavior has provoked two kinds of explanation, neither of which has been adequate. Cognitive theories have stayed close to introspective experiences of the will and its failure but have shrunk from systematic causal hypotheses, perhaps because they make a person seem too mechanical. Utility-based theories have accounted well for many properties of choice, but seem to predict neither self-defeating behavior nor any faculty to prevent it. Hypotheses to reconcile self-defeating behavior with maximization of utility have cited naiveté, short time horizons, conditioned cravings, and the physiological nature of reward, but all of these explanations have failed on experimental or logical grounds.

CHAPTER 3

THE WARP IN HOW WE
EVALUATE THE FUTURE

If the headache would only precede the intoxication, alcoholism would
be a virture.

Samuel Butler

Lore abounds not only about how people mistrust their own future
preferences, but how they sometimes engage in strategic planning
to outsmart the future selves that will have these preferences. Here is
Ulysses facing the Sirens or Coleridge moving in with his doctor to be
protected from his opium habit. We know that the stakes in this intertemporal game sometimes reach tragic proportions. Yet we can't reconcile this game with utility theory's basic meat-and-potatoes notion
that people try to maximize their prospects. The irony of smart people
doing stupid things – or having to outsmart themselves in order not to –
appears in literature again and again, but without an explanation.

This quandary may have been one reason for the popularity of cognitive explanations, which at least stay close to intuition. The problem
hasn't undermined utility theorists, but it has cramped their style. They
go from success to success in areas like finance and sociobiology, where
tough competition selects strongly for individuals who function like
calculating machines. However, their attempts to explain self-defeating
choice on a rational basis have been unconvincing; the most notable
has been the effort by economists Gary Becker and Kevin Murphy to
show how a person who sharply devalues the future might maximize
her prospective pleasure by addictive behavior. Their proposal is basically that devaluation of the future leads to addictive behaviors, which
further increase this devaluation. They suggest no rationale for fearing
future choices, much less for trying to restrain them.[1] Utility theorists

27

have mostly stayed away from the subject. Some writers have thrown up their hands altogether by concluding that there are options that, although substitutable for one another, can't be weighed against each other.[2] While science stands by, mystified, people keep wrecking their own lives.

3.1 THE HYPERBOLIC CURVE THAT DISCOUNTS FUTURE EVENTS

Another solution to the self-harm puzzle has always been logically possible, but utility theorists and cognitivists alike keep ruling it out, perhaps because its implications would require the rethinking of basic assumptions about rationality: People indeed maximize their prospective rewards, but they discount their prospects using a different formula from the one that's obviously rational. It will take a little arithmetic to illustrate this possibility clearly.

Few utility theorists question the assumption that people discount future utility the way banks do: by subtracting a constant proportion of the utility there would be at any given delay for every additional unit of delay. If a new car delivered today would be worth $10,000 to me and my discount "rate" is 20% a year, then the prospect of guaranteed delivery today of the same car would have been worth $8,000 to me a year ago, $6,400 two years ago, and so on (disregarding inflation, which merely subtracts another fixed percentage per unit of time).

Utility theory operates the same way for reward itself, although it has to use a fanciful unit of measure like the "utile." If drinking a bottle of whisky is worth 100 utiles to me right now and my discount rate for drinking is 20% per day, the prospect of today's drinking would have been worth 80 utiles to me yesterday, 64 utiles the day before, and so on. Furthermore, if the drinking has a cost of 120 utiles that has to be paid the day after in the form of a hangover, reproaches from my family, and so on, and I discount these at the same rate, the net utility of drinking today will be $100 - (120 \times 80\%$, or 96), or 4 utiles. So I should decide to drink. If I foresaw this episode from a day away, the net value would have been $(100 \times 80\%) - (120 \times 80\% \times 80\%)$, viz., $80-76.8$, or 3.2 utiles. At that point I would still have decided to drink.

The arithmetic is simple. You just multiply each discounted value on any day by 80% for each anticipated day of further delay and find the difference: 3.2 utiles for one day in advance, 2.56 utiles for two days in advance, and so on. The discounting method can be summarized for delays of any length by the formula

$$\text{Value} = \text{"Objective" value} \times (1 - \text{Discount rate})^{\text{Delay}}$$

This discount function is called "exponential" because it calculates value by an exponential, or power, function of the discount rate.[3]

With exponential discounting, the difference in the utility of drinking in our example gradually gets smaller, but the important thing is that it never goes negative or even gets to zero. If I'd choose to drink when the opportunity was right at hand, I'd also choose to drink when it was a week or a year away. If I'd choose not to drink from the vantage point of some delay – if, say, my discount rate were just 10% – then I'd still choose not to drink when the opportunity was immediately at hand, as well as at all other distances. (The net value of drinking would be −8 utiles at no delay, −7.2 utiles one day in advance, −6.48 at two days, and so on.)

This arithmetic seems to describe the consistency many people show toward large purchases – bankers, at least, and others who decide "rationally"; but it misses the mark for drinkers, or at least for people whose drinking is serious enough to involve hangovers and reproaches from their families. People who are strongly drawn to drinking – or taking drugs, or gambling, or kleptomania, or any other thrills of the kind that people later regret – typically experience swings of preference between indulging their habit and giving it up. And the swings are often influenced by how close an opportunity for indulgence is. People trying to control a bad habit tend to keep a distance between themselves and opportunity – avoid the streets where their favorite bars are located and similar strategies.[4]

Faced with this instability of choice – economists have taken to calling it "dynamic inconsistency," but it amounts just to a temporary preference for the poorer alternative – writers have come up with various fudge factors to make it fit the principle that people strictly maximize their exponentially discounted prospects for reward (see the introduction to this chapter). The most obvious suggestion is that people discount different kinds of reward at different rates. If I discount drinking by 40% per day but discount not having a hangover the day after (worth 120 utiles) by 20%, then the net utility of an immediate drinking bout would be $100 - (120 \times 80\%)$, or 4 utiles; but its net utility a day in advance would be $(100 \times 60\%) - (120 \times 80\% \times 80\%)$, 60 − 76.8

or −16.8 utiles. I would drink if the chance were at hand but not if it were delayed.

The trouble with this solution is that many cases of temporary preference involve the same kind of reward on both sides of the choice; a difference in discount rate for different kinds of reward can't be a factor. The punishment for gambling to win money is to lose money. Likewise, people in experiments do things like choosing a shorter period of relief from noxious noise over a longer but later period of relief from the same noise if and only if the shorter, earlier period is imminent. It makes no sense to hypothesize that the earlier relief is discounted at 40% but the later relief of the same kind is discounted at 20%.[5]

Long ago philosophers noted that avarice was a bad habit partly because it was self-defeating – that impatience for riches usually made people poorer in the long run.[6] If the basic reward-weighing mechanism is the same among all the higher animals – the same assumption that lets us study addictive drugs in rats, for instance – we can see this self-defeating phenomenon clearly in quantitative experiments. For instance, pigeons will choose a shorter, earlier access to grain over a later, larger one when the shorter one is immediate and not when it's delayed; and some of them will actually peck a colored key in advance to prevent themselves from later getting offered a differently colored key that produces the smaller reward – showing that in some way the pigeons themselves are responding to their own tendency to choose the smaller, earlier reward as a problem.[7]

In light of such findings, it's not enough to say that the kinds of things that reward impulses are discounted more steeply than the kinds of things that reward rational choices. Exponential discounting can't account for temporary preferences in knowing subjects. On the other hand, any kind of nonexponential discounting should lead to maladaptive behavior.

The main theoretical rival to the exponential curve is *hyperbolic* – more bowed than an exponential curve; when goods at both very short and very long delays would be valued the same as with exponential discounting, goods in between would be valued less[8] (Figure 1). If people devalue future goods proportionately to their delay, their discount curve will be hyperbolic.

The greater bowing means that if a hyperbolic discounter engaged in trade with someone who used an exponential curve, she'd soon be relieved of her money. Ms. Exponential could buy Ms. Hyperbolic's win-

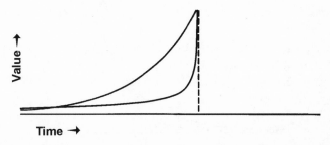

Figure 1. An exponential discount curve and a hyperbolic (more bowed) curve from the same reward. As time passes (rightward along the horizontal axis), the motivational impact – the *value* – of her goals gets closer to its undiscounted size, which is depicted by the vertical line.

ter coat cheaply every spring, for instance, because the distance to the next winter would depress Ms. H's valuation of it more than Ms. E's. Ms. E could then sell the coat back to Ms. H every fall when the approach of winter sent Ms. H's valuation of it into a high spike. Because of this mathematical pattern, only an exponential discount curve will protect a person against exploitation by somebody else who uses an exponential curve.[9] Thus exponential curves seem not only rational, in the sense that they're consistent, but also adaptive. At first glance, it looks as if natural selection should have weeded out any organism that didn't discount the future exponentially.

Nevertheless, there's more and more evidence that people's natural discount curve is not only nonexponential, but specifically hyperbolic. The simplest sign is that such curves cross if they're from alternative rewards available at different times.

The experiment used to test whether a subject's discount curves cross is simple: You offer subjects a choice between a small reward at delay D versus a larger reward of the same kind that will be available at that delay plus a constant lag, L. A subject gets the small reward at delay D from the moment she chooses or the larger reward at delay D + L. If she discounts the choices according to conventional theory, her curves will stay proportional to each other (Figure 2A). If she chooses the larger reward when D is long but switches to the smaller reward as D gets shorter, she's showing the temporary preference effect that implies a discount curve more bowed than an exponential one (Figure 2B).

This research strategy has one potential problem: If people really discount the future with highly bowed curves that cross, then when D is

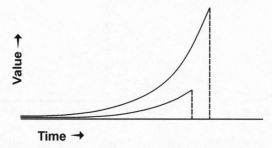

Figure 2A. Conventional (exponential) discount curves from two rewards of different sizes, available at different times. In the experimental design described in the text, the delay *D* is the distance between when the subject chooses and when the earlier and later rewards will be available, and the lag *L* is the distance between when the earlier and later rewards will be available, shown by the vertical lines. At every point at which the subject might evaluate them, their values stay proportional to their objective sizes.

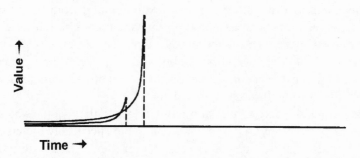

Figure 2B. Hyperbolic discount curves from two rewards of different sizes available at different times. The smaller reward is temporarily preferred for a period before it is available, as shown by the portion of its curve that projects above that from the later, larger reward.

long they'll be motivated not only to choose the later, larger reward but somehow to forestall the change of choice that occurs as D gets shorter. Like the pigeons that learned to peck the colored key to forestall the tempting, other-colored key, subjects might have learned ways to make up for this tendency. Otherwise, they'll have been at risk of exploitation by other people who have learned these ways – as in the overcoat example. An experiment like this might not uncover their natural, spontaneous preferences, but only those that they had been educated to express. This kind of learned compensation might be a serious obstacle to observation.

The best way around this obstacle should be to use the kind of reward that the subject experiences ("consumes") on delivery and also the kinds that don't lend themselves to mental arithmetic. When experimenters have used this kind of reward, people have shown a persistent tendency to reverse their preferences as D changes, evidence that their basic discount curves cross and are thus more hyperbolic than exponential: People exposed to noxious noise and given a choice between shorter, earlier periods of relief and longer, more delayed periods choose the shorter periods when D is small and the longer periods when D is long. College students show the same pattern when choosing between periods of access to video games. Retarded adolescents show it in choosing between amounts of food. Certainly at the gut level, people's discount curves cross.[10]

Furthermore, it turns out that whatever method people may have learned in order to compensate for hyperbolic discounting, it doesn't spoil temporary preference experiments. Even money, the archetypical token reward – "token" in the sense that it has its effect only by letting subjects buy other rewards later, and invites the counting and comparing of alternatives – turns out sometimes to be chosen differently, depending on D. If I ask a roomful of people to imagine that they've won a contest and can choose between a certified check for $100 that they can cash immediately and a postdated certified check for $200 that they can't cash for three years, more than half of the people usually say they would rather have the $100 now. If I then ask what about $100 in six years versus $200 in nine years, virtually everyone picks the $200. But this is the same choice seen at six years' greater distance.

This is an experiment you can perform for yourself. I recommend it as a way of getting direct experience with this unexpected warp in people's outlook. You might want to confront the people you ask with the fact that they've changed their preference on the basis of their vantage point, and ask how they explain it. Answers involving inflation or uncertainty about getting the later amount obviously make no sense, since the lag between the alternatives is the same in both examples. Some subjects have suggested that the promise of immediate money has a sensory (sensuous?) quality that money at any delay doesn't have, and other subjects say that the three-year lag doesn't seem as long when postponed; neither of these explanations is inconsistent with the notion of a high spike of value at short delays. The one explanation that might preserve exponential discounting is that a student expects to graduate within the next three years, and thus thinks she needs the money significantly more right now than she will at three, six, or nine years. However, getting the temporary preference effect doesn't depend on having young and perhaps temporarily poor subjects or, for that matter, on making the smaller value of D zero. Various groups of subjects have shown the change of preference over a range of D values. Some excellent recent work has made it possible to describe the exact shape of subjects' discount curve in similar amount-versus-delay experiments.[11] It's clearly hyperbolic for all age groups, although older subjects discount the future less steeply than younger ones, introverts less steeply than extroverts, and ordinary adults less steeply than heroin addicts or even smokers.[12]

Subjects working for actual cash don't always show the temporary preference effect. The factors that determine whether they'll show it or not have just begun to be explored, but the early findings are revealing: For instance, when subjects had to choose between amounts of money such that choice A produced a conspicuously larger reward than choice B, but choice A led to poorer subsequent payoffs for both choices, the outcome depended on an important detail of the design: Where choice of a larger amount reduced the *amounts* to choose between on subsequent turns, most subjects soon discovered the strategy of picking the smaller amount in the current choice so as to have better choices later. However, where choosing the larger amount led to greater *delay* before subsequent choices, thus reducing total income in trials of fixed duration, subjects tended to keep picking the larger amounts and getting smaller subsequent returns. They were lured into what the experimenters called "melioration," taking what by itself seems the best choice without considering the bigger picture. Amounts are well defined and obvious, lending themselves to conscious scrutiny; delays are vague unless you specifically count the seconds. As we might expect, when the experimenters pointed out to their subjects the greater delay that came from choosing the larger reward, these subjects, too, started choosing the smaller one.[13]

Hyperbolic discounting is even more evident in lower animals, which shows that it isn't some quirk of human culture. In scores of experiments, animals have always chosen rewards in inverse proportion to their delays – and, similarly, punishments in direct proportion. Animals also do what crossing discount curves predict: In amount-versus-delay experiments they choose the smaller, earlier reward when D is short and the larger, later reward when D is long. It was the consistency of animal findings that led Herrnstein nearly forty years ago to propose a universal law of choice, which he called the "matching law": that rewards tend to be chosen in direct proportion to their size and frequency of occurrence and in inverse proportion to their delay.[14] Many researchers have since offered variations to fine-tune the matching law to describe individual differences in impatience, but the best seems to be one of the simplest:[15]

$$\text{Value} = \text{Amount} / (\text{Constant}_1 + (\text{Constant}_2 \times \text{Delay}))$$

In practice the constants seem to stay close to 1.0, which simplifies the equation still further. When I discuss the likely consequences of hyperbolic discounting, I'll be using this formula.

3.2 IMPLICATIONS OF HYPERBOLIC DISCOUNTING

Does this apparent universality of hyperbolic discounting mean that utility theorists through the ages have been wrong – that philosophers and bankers and welfare economists should have been calculating the worth of goods using the deeply bowed curves of Figure 2B? This can't be true either. We saw in the overcoat example that exponential discounting is better than hyperbolic discounting, in the sense that exponential discounters win out in competition with hyperbolic discounters.

The conventional answer would almost certainly be that since only exponential curves produce consistent preferences, they're the ones that are objectively rational, and that people should learn to correct their spontaneous valuations to fit them. After all, science has long known that the intensity of many other subjective experiences is described by hyperbolic curves[16] and that people can learn to correct such impressions. It soon becomes second nature to a child that the telephone pole down the street is as tall as the one nearby, even though it forms a smaller image on her retina. Even where spontaneous impressions are misleading, you learn to trust instruments for measuring objective size – light by your camera's light meter, distance to travel by an odometer or map, and so on – without feeling that you're wrestling with some inner resistance. You develop "object constancy." Can't people learn to value reward in proportion to its objective amount, just as we learn to gauge objective brightness and distance?

That's what conventional utility theory calls for; but despite data from your clocks and calendars, such an adjustment seems to occur irregularly, sometimes not at all. It usually takes some kind of effort (willpower again) to evaluate a smaller present satisfaction as less desirable than a greater one in the future. This is where the analogy of delay to other sensory impressions like length breaks down: You may move through time toward a goal just as you move through space toward a building, and the matching law formula describing your spontaneous valuation of a goal is indeed close to the formula for the retinal height of the building.[17] But the building doesn't seem to get larger as it gets closer, whereas the goal often seems to get more valuable. Insofar as you fail to make the correction in value that corresponds to your correction of retinal height, poorer goals that are close can loom larger than better distant goals. Although people develop some faculty for utility constancy, it takes effort and remains tenuous.

These observations provide additional help with the question we discussed earlier: Which is more basic, cognitive or motivational evaluation? If cognitive judgments ultimately control choice, it should make no difference whether you're estimating the size of a building or a reward; either way, an evaluation with full knowledge should parallel the objective size of the objects in question, and any choices that depend on this evaluation should follow without further effort. If hedonistic effects are primary, however, the two cases will differ: A larger image on the retina doesn't of itself pull a person one way or another and thus doesn't resist cognitive transformation. But if reward is the fundamental selective force of choice, then however you perceive or categorize it, you're still acted upon by its direct influence. You should often prefer lesser alternatives during the period when they're imminent; and this is just what the foregoing research describes. Thus experience suggests that there's a raw process of reward that constitutes the active determinant of value. While it can be perceived abstractly, it doesn't occur differently because of this abstraction.

In the following comparison of lines, the second one continues to look longer, even after we've measured them and found that they are the same length:

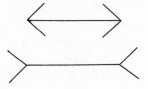

In the same way, knowing that, all things considered, eating another dessert or putting off going to the dentist will make me less happy in the long run doesn't of itself reduce my urge to do these things. Still, any sensible person would argue that we learn not to do them – most of the time, anyway. Doesn't this mean that we've learned to change our discount curves?

Yes and no. If we infer someone's curve from her expressed preferences, then as she gets older and wiser, we'll see her apparent curve get shallower and less bowed; often we'll see her act exactly as if she discounted future goods exponentially at the rate of inflation plus 3% or so a year. But as we've seen, there will be situations where she'll be both more impatient and more inconsistent than that. These are signs of the persistence of another curve – one that is both steeper and has a tendency to cause reversals of preference. The banker-like curve seems to represent an added accomplishment, not a fundamental change.

This is what we should expect. If a person could learn to change the discount curve she was born with, there would always be a strong incentive to do so as much as possible: If some distant prospect – a Christmas present, say – was worth only 3 utiles to you now, but by some trick you could make it worth 5 utiles, you could make yourself 2 utiles richer just by doing this trick. If you could act directly on your discount curves, you could coin reward for yourself, so to speak. We'd expect everyone to exploit this trick all the time, as much as they could. If it was the kind of trick you had to keep doing, it would be like candy or a tranquilizer, something you did *instead* of getting impatient. If it was the kind of trick you could do once and for all, then your impulsive urges to drink or smoke or spend should just disappear. The point is that we study people – and animals, for that matter – after whatever curve-flattening they're capable of should have already happened. The hyperbola we detect is what has survived this learning. The trick of behaving as if your curve were exponential has to be an effortful, sometime thing, not a modification your basic curve.

Of course, nature doesn't always put things together in the simplest way. The widespread appearance of hyperbolic discounting may not mean that it's a universal form, the underlying pattern from which all other valuation patterns are derived. The appearance of hyperbolic discounting in some situations and exponential discounting in others may turn out to have an explanation now hidden from us. But theories should always start in the simplest way. Let's assume that the ubiquitous hyperbola is the basic discount curve – that our basic instinct is to evaluate future events by dividing their amount by their delay – and see where its implications lead us.

3.2.1 How Utility Theory Can Predict Inconsistency

The most basic implication is that you'll tend to prefer smaller, earlier rewards to larger, later ones temporarily, during the time that they're imminent. Then the obvious task is to find out what kind of effort could sometimes make your expressed preferences look exponential. Hyperbolic discounting is a shock for utility theory. Suddenly the pavement moves beneath our feet, and we have to take the simple concept of maximizing expected reward not as a description of basic human nature but just as a norm that we try to implement. Only if a person is lucky or skillful can she achieve such consistency in the face of this screwball valuation system.

The good news is that hyperbolic discounting, and its consequent temporary preferences, will let utility theory move beyond its stalemate with cognitivism. Let's return to the problems that the two approaches have had in explaining *akrasia*. In cognitive models the person ultimately stands outside of her emotions – emotions being the closest cognitivist equivalent of motivation – and says, "This experience is misleading. I'll select my behavior instead on the basis of accurate calculations of its value." The trouble is that there's a lot of leeway in the calculation process, as cognitive research itself has shown; when someone has a choice among different ways of calculating value, how does she choose the one she'll use? To be sure, everyone has had the experience of mistrusting an emotion or even disowning it. We inhibit an emotion sometimes or "nurse" one. To some extent we can indeed mold the influence that in turn molds us. But when I stand outside of my emotions, what am I standing on? In other words, what determines my choice of cognitions?

The argument between the cognitive and utilitarian schools has been about whether choice is fundamentally determined by some kind of internal marketplace, or else by a planned economy, in effect an internal bureaucracy of principles and logic. The conventional view of a person's self-command structure is definitely bureaucratic, on the model of a corporation or an army, where superior agents simply pass commands down to inferior ones. However, closer examination of corporations and armies has shown that despite the establishment of hierarchical command structures, they remain marketplaces where officers must motivate rather than simply ordering behaviors.[18] Sheer instructions aren't enough to control someone's behavior, as bureaucrats have discovered again and again; any system that tries to govern behavior by regulations develops an underground economy of motives – of favors and obstructions, and hiding places from supervisory procedures – that ultimately determines what gets done.[19]

Utility theory says that the experience of reward is the fundamental selective factor for behaviors, so that you can't stand outside of that experience and choose dispassionately among rewards. You might as well say, "The thermometer tells me not to feel cold, so I won't." The utilitarians' problem has been that they've assumed a person's evaluation of rewards (or emotions) to be exponentially discounted, and hence consistent over time; as a result, utility theory hasn't been able to account for self-defeating choices, or for the various kinds of uniquely human effort that we call forth to avoid them. If we simply maximize our prospective reward, what use do we have for self-control? What role is there for a will, either strong or free?

My argument is that exchanging hyperbolic discounting for the exponential kind in the reward-maximizing process supplies utility theory with its missing element. Utility theory can now explain the seductiveness of self-defeating choices; and the assumption that a person has to strictly maximize her expected, discounted reward explains why she doesn't automatically learn to be objective, the way she does with sizes and distances. Reward has its effect directly, and intellectual adjustment takes place only tangentially. With hyperbolic instead of exponential discounting, utility theory now says that people will naturally go for smaller, earlier over larger, later rewards. We're unable *not* to choose the reward that looms largest when discounted to the moment of choice. *Akrasia* is just maximizing expected reward, discounted in highly bowed curves.

3.2.2 The Self as a Population

Hyperbolic discounting shifts the main problem for utility theory. We're no longer at a loss to explain shortsighted choices. Now we have to account for how people learn the adaptive controls that let them behave like bankers. How does an internal marketplace that disproportionately values immediate rewards grow into what can be mistaken for either the reasoning self of the cognitivists or the long-range reward maximizer of conventional utilitarians?

We can no longer regard people as having unitary preferences. Rather, people may have a variety of contradictory preferences that become dominant at different points because of their timing. The orderly internal marketplace pictured by conventional utility theory[20] becomes a complicated free-for-all, where to prevail an option not only has to promise more than its competitors, but also act strategically to keep the competitors from turning the tables later on. The behaviors that are shaped by the competing rewards must deal not only with obstacles to getting their reward if chosen, but also with the danger of being unchosen in favor of imminent alternatives.

How does a marketplace of hyperbolically discounted choices ever come to look like a single individual? If I discount future reward hyperbolically, and make whatever choices maximize my discounted prospective reward at the moment I make them, then my choices won't consistently follow the same set of goals over time, the way they would if I were ruled either by reason or by exponentially discounted passion. If I'm a susceptible person[21] and I'm close to a bottle of whisky or a box of chocolates, or perhaps a provocation to rage or panic, I'll value these options differently than when I'm far away from them. Often I'll choose in the opposite direction when I'm close and when I'm distant, which means I'll regularly do things at one time and undo them at another. Obviously if what I do in a particular situation regularly gets undone later, I'll learn to stop doing it in the first place – but not out of agreement with the later self that undoes it, only out of realism. I'll keep trying to find ways to get what I want from this particular vantage point, things that won't get undone, and take precautions against a future self that will try to undo them. In this way I'll be like a group of people rather than a single individual; often these people will be as different as Jekyll and Hyde.

An agent who discounts reward hyperbolically is not the straightforward value estimator that an exponential discounter is supposed to be. Rather, it is a succession of estimators whose conclusions differ; as time elapses, these estimators shift their relationship with one another between cooperation on a common goal and competition for mutually exclusive goals. Ulysses planning for the Sirens must treat Ulysses hearing them as a separate person, to be influenced if possible and forestalled if not.

To take an everyday example: You may hate to go to bed at a prudent hour, even though you hate even worse getting up in the morning without enough sleep. Your mind this morning curses your mind of last night and tries to forestall your expected mind of tonight, but runs up against the effect of hyperbolic discount curves: Your mind holds a population of reward-seeking processes that have grown to survive in contradiction to each other, and that endure despite each other.[22] You keep on staying up late when the chance is at hand and the morning is far away – unless you can do something to bring the incentives to sleep, which are larger in the long run, to bear on your evening self.

What can you do? If a person is a population of processes that have grown in the same mind through the selective action of reward, what factors, if any, impose unity on this population? For single moments we can model unity easily. The process by which diverse needs interact to produce a single decision doesn't have to be different from the process that motivates a social group to reach agreement.

Separate individuals can have widely diverse interests that conflict with the interests of others, because they have separate organs for reward that can act differently at the same time. One person can be tearful while her neighbor is rapturously happy, or seek out parties while her neighbor avoids them, without there being any necessary confrontation between these opposite choices. What coordinates diverse interests in separate people is limitation of resources. If there's only one room to sit in, the sad person and the happy one will have to see each other, and each will have to deal with the other's effect on her own mood. If they're roommates, they'll have to decide whether or not to use the room for a party that evening. It seems reasonable to suppose that analogous constraints impose at least some unity on the competing processes within the individual person, but that this unity is incomplete insofar as contradictory goals can coexist.

There may or may not be separate neural centers for different kinds of reward. As we've discussed, there's evidence that the reward process is at least concentrated in specific location(s) rather than diffused throughout the brain.[23] The question doesn't matter much when you have only one set of limbs – or, more to the point, a finite channel of attention that has to direct those limbs. There may be a lot of people or part-people in your mind, but they're all constrained to coordinate what they do by the fact of being permanent roommates. If a given behavior can be influenced by more than one center, these centers must compete for the exercise of this influence, and whatever process governs this competition will act in effect like a single comprehensive reward center.[24] Insofar as one behavior can be replaced by another, it has to compete with the other for expression, and this competition operates as a single reward clearinghouse for all substitutable behaviors – all behaviors among which a person can choose. This is the constraint that unifies a person's behavior at any given moment.

Integration over time is more difficult. Any explanation has to account for our observations not only of unity but also of varying degrees of disunity, ranging from preference reversals in "normal" people to Jeckylls and Hydes. The key factor is doubtless the highly concave shape of the discount curves in Figure 2B, which limits what the market of choice can do to unify a person's purposes over time. Ulysses' wish to sail home and his wish to hear the Sirens will be integrated only for individual moments; this piecemeal integration will make different options dominant, depending on when the choice occurs. There will be a regular conflict between the mental operations that win out when the lure of the Sirens' song is dominant and those that win out when the prospect of finishing the journey is dominant.

You could call the mental operations selected for by a particular kind of reward the person's "interest" in that reward. Interests within the person should be very similar to interests within a social group, those factions that are rewarded by ("have an interest in") the goal that names them (e.g., "the petroleum interest," "the arts interest"). Since a person's purposes should be coherent except where conflicting rewards dominate at successive times, it makes sense to name an interest only in cases of conflict. I wouldn't be said to have separate chocolate and vanilla ice cream interests, even though they're often alternatives, because at the time when I prefer chocolate I don't increase my prospective reward by forestalling a possible switch to vanilla. But I may have an ice cream interest and a diet interest, such that each increases the prospective reward in its own time range by reducing the likelihood of the other's dominance. Put another way, I don't increase my prospective reward in either the long or short range by defending my choice of chocolate against the possibility that I may change to vanilla; but I increase my prospective long-range reward by defending my diet against ice cream, and I increase my prospective short-range reward by finding evasions of my diet for the sake of ice cream. Whichever faction promises the greatest discounted reward at a given moment gets to decide my move at that moment; the sequence of moves over time determines which faction ultimately gets its way.

Where alternative rewards are available at different times, each will build its own interest, and one interest will be able to forestall the other only if it can leave some enduring commitment that will prevent the other reward from becoming dominant: If my diet interest can arrange for me not to get too close to ice cream, the discounted prospect of ice cream may never rise above the discounted prospect of the rewards for dieting, and the diet interest will effectively have won. However, whenever the value of ice cream spikes above that of dieting, the ice cream interest may undo the effect of many days of restraint. The ultimate determinant of a person's choice is not her simple preference, any more than the determinant of whether a closely contested piece of legislation becomes law is simple voting strength in the legislature; in both processes, strategy is all.

This process – power bargaining made necessary by finite means of expression – may be all that unifies a person. Philosophers and psychologists are used to speaking about an organ of unification called the "self" that can variously "be" autonomous, divided, individuated, fragile, well-bounded, and so on,[25] but this organ doesn't have to exist as such. The factor that impels toward unity the various behavioral tendencies that grow from a person's rewards may be the realization that they are, in effect, locked up in a room together.

If this room is divided, so that only some of the person's learned processes ever have access to particular resources for expression, she starts to behave like two people. This actually happened when neurosurgeons developed an operation for epilepsy that cut the main connection between the cerebral hemispheres, the corpus callosum. The right half of the brain controlled the left hand and the left half, the right hand; if the two halves were fed information separately, they sometimes fought over a decision to the extent that one hand restrained the other by the wrist. Conversely, when convention or necessity makes two people act in concert over long periods – for example, in some identical twinships and some marriages – the site of the marketplace seems to shift somewhat from the individual to the pair.[26] But where in the pair? Here the choice-maker is clearly not an organ but a process, something in the empathic engagement between the two twins; and if that is true for the pair, why not for the individual or the neurosurgeon's half-individual? The constraint of limited resources for expression may be all that impels a person toward selfhood; and the success of her currently dominant interests in bargaining with interests that will be dominant in the future may be what determines the kind of unity her self will have.[27]

Are ordinary people really populations of interests rather than something more solid? It's disturbing to think of yourself as so fluid, so potentially unstable, held together only by the shifting influence of available rewards. It's like being told that atoms are mostly empty and wondering how they can bear weight. Yet the bargaining of interests in a society can produce highly stable institutions; perhaps that's also true of the internal interests created by a person's rewards. Shortly we'll look at the patterns of choice that hyperbolic discounters would be likely to follow, and see if these patterns look like familiar properties of personality.

Of the basic discounting phenomenon there can no longer be much doubt. Remarkably, hyperbolic discounting seems to occur over all observable time ranges. Subjects choosing between hypothetical amounts of money at delays of years show it as much as those choosing between differences in food, or comfort, or direct brain stimulation, over periods of seconds. Economist Charles Harvey has pointed out that the most long-range planning that ever occurs – choices to preserve the environment or leave money to grandchildren – follows a hyperbolic discount pattern rather than the exponential one that the planners themselves sometimes claim to be using. He points out that exponential discounting of goals decades away at even moderate rates would make them relatively worthless in a competitive economy; it's only the comparatively high tails of hyperbolic curves that could make us concern ourselves with the distant future at all. Accordingly, respondents to a random household survey on the hypothetical value of saving lives 25, 50, and 100 years from the present demonstrated that "if [exponential] discount rates are computed under the assumption that they vary with time, the mean annual discount rate is 7% today and 0% in 100 years."[28] That is, the more delayed an option is, the less discounted it is, just the pattern that hyperbolic discounting predicts.

Economists David Laibson and Christopher Harris have recently modeled people's lifetime saving/spending patterns with hyperbolic curves, and have found that they predict many observed behaviors that exponential curves don't. For instance, hyperbolic curves make a preference for illiquid savings rational – such savings serve as commitments – and thus can explain why people borrow on credit cards at 18% to avoid dipping into savings that are earning far less (see Section 6.2).[29]

3.3 THE ADAPTIVENESS OF HYPERBOLIC DISCOUNTING

If our basic discount curve has been hyperbolic, then the biggest job of civilization must have been to change people's spontaneous choice into something that produces fewer internal conflicts and reversals of preference. Before assuming that this has been the case, we should ask an obvious question: How could such a curve, with such potential to put an individual at a competitive disadvantage, survive the process of natural selection?

Sociobiologists, who used to believe that animals maximize their expected intake of resources over time, have now also done experiments demonstrating the hyperbolic shape of the basic discount curve.[30] However, despite their interest in evolution, these authors haven't tried to reconcile this finding with survival of the fittest. I'll suggest two ways that highly bowed discount curves could have survived natural selection. They could have preserved genes at the expense of the individual, or they could have been a harmless by-product until too recently to have affected evolution. Arguments about evolutionary fitness can aim only for plausibility, not proof. Take your pick.

1. The evolution of species occurs through the survival of genes, not of individuals. There are many familiar cases where an individual organism must sacrifice itself to maximize survival of its genes. Maybe hyperbolic discounting is a way to get an animal to do that: The anger that makes an animal fight to defend its young probably isn't much different from the anger that recruiting sergeants exploit in wartime, and neither is in the individual's own long-range interest. If cool reason prevailed, the animal would survive more often and the gene-bearing offspring less often. Similarly, bearing young is probably never in an animal's selfish interest. Of course, it may be that many human mothers in previous centuries accepted the roughly 15% risk of eventual death in childbirth out of altruism, or from cultural pressures that made the alternatives worse, but impulsive romances must have made a big contribution too. Even in modern times,

> [C]ourtship leads to romantic love, a temporary suspension of reason, in which the couple is conveyed by the most compelling of short-term rewards, into marriage, a commitment with a lifetime horizon.[31]

The mechanism by which individuals come to reduce their rational utility for the sake of a larger group has been controversial even since

Erasmus first praised the seeming folly of having children or going into politics.[32] Hyperbolic discounting is one candidate.

2. It's also possible that hyperbolic discounting has been carried along as a hitherto harmless by-product of vertebrates' basic perceptual tooling. As I described earlier, all higher animals get sensory impressions in proportion to the *change* in level of stimulation, rather perceiving its absolute level. The same perceptual processes that make you sense a change in light or temperature proportionately to its previous intensity may prepare you to evaluate delays the same way.[33] This wouldn't have been a great problem for animals that couldn't change the environments in which they evolved. Where survival has demanded foresighted behavior – sleep at a certain time, or hoarding of food or mating in a certain season – instinctual mechanisms have evolved to convert such long-range interests into short-range rewards. The animal experiences an immediate appetite to sleep or hoard or mate, and there's no intertemporal conflict unless a devious experimenter creates one.

By contrast, people have learned to manipulate both their environment and their instinctual appetites. We learn to divorce sleep from darkness, to cultivate appetites for hoarding what we don't need, to mate without reproducing, indeed to obtain many of the rewards of mating vicariously, through fiction or fantasy, and in general to cultivate motives that overwhelm the incentives of nature. We've also changed our environments radically from the ones in which we evolved. We've increasingly taken our long-range plans into our own hands, and are threatened to the same extent by the operation of our hyperbolic discount functions. As we overcome the historical limitations imposed by poverty and primitive technology, the scope of the decisions governed directly by these discount functions becomes broader. Evolution hasn't had time to respond to these, if indeed it has mechanisms available. It's unlikely that modern humans will ever grow wheels instead of feet, for instance, adaptive as that might be.[34]

Thus there's good reason to believe – and nothing to keep us from believing – that the human race evolved with a very regular but deeply bowed discount curve for evaluating the future. That hypothesis can explain a lot about why people defeat their own plans so relentlessly. However, it raises more questions than it answers. How do people become consistent choice makers? How do painful options interact with pleasurable ones? Why do we often choose according to logical categories? How do "higher" mental functions fit in?

The answers will come by deducing how a bent for temporary preference can be expected to create a marketplace of choice within the individual, the behavior of which depends on strategy rather than the simple value comparisons depicted by exponential curves. For that reason, I've suggested that this approach represents the most microscopic application of economic thinking – micromicroeconomics, perhaps, or picoeconomics.[35]

3.4 SUMMARY

There is extensive evidence that both people and lower animals spontaneously value future events in inverse proportion to their expected delays. The resulting hyperbolic discount curve is seen over all time ranges, from seconds to decades. Because a hyperbolic curve is more bowed than the exponential curve that most utility theories go by, it describes a preference pattern that these theories would call irrational: It predicts temporary preferences for the poorer but earlier of two alternative goals during the time right before the poorer goal becomes available. Regular temporary preferences, in turn, predict that a population of conflicting interests will grow and survive within the individual, sometimes leading to choices that are self-defeating in the long run. A self that is a marketplace for such interests differs radically from the conventional image, and needs exploring in detail.

CHAPTER 4

THE WARP CAN CREATE INVOLUNTARY BEHAVIORS

Pains, Hungers, Emotions

If people temporarily prefer shortsighted alternatives on a regular basis, how do they talk about the experience? It's not something that's supposed to be happening. It not only makes us ineffective in following our own long-term plans, it puts us at risk of exploitation by people who find out what our temporary preferences are. Therefore we might be expected to try to keep it from happening, and when we can't, to conceal it, perhaps even from ourselves. How we try to prevent it is the main subject of this book, and I'll get to it in the next chapter. First we should examine how temporary preference actually feels, since this discussion may otherwise seem rather removed from real life. It will turn out that many diverse experiences that have been thought to require special mechanisms can be explained instead by hyperbolic discounting.

4.1 ZONES OF DURATION OF TEMPORARY PREFERENCES

First of all, a temporary preference probably produces different experiences, depending on how long it lasts. Very short ones might not be noticed as preferences, while very long ones might seem wholehearted and not temporary at all.

4.1.1 Addictions

If we start roughly in the middle – not seconds or years but hours or days – we can see the clearest examples, which lead to the common clinical tragedies as well as personal frustrations. These are the "bad habits" that we're aware of wanting to avoid but that we find ourselves willfully giving in to: pigging out on food, throwing our smoking resolution overboard, taking a stupid risk, getting mad at the wrong person, or perhaps just putting off for another day something we should have done a long time ago. Isolated examples of this kind are called "impulses." When we do one of these things repeatedly, it has the feel of an addiction, whether or not it gets us into enough trouble to be officially diagnosed. We look forward with worry to the possibility that it will happen again, but once it's happened, we pursue the bad behavior with energy; afterward, we feel regret or guilt and wonder how to stop it from happening again.

Sometimes it feels as if all human life is like that: "We have left undone those things which we ought to have done; and we have done those things we ought not to have done, and there is no health in us."[1] Yet we cling to the idea that we're basically consistent planners who are just subject to odd aberrations, "weaknesses of the flesh."

As I mentioned earlier, people sometimes think of addiction as caused by a specific chemical property of a drug or alcohol, but even specific physical symptoms like withdrawal can be caused by gambling and other activities that don't involve a substance. We do know that differences of inborn neurophysiology cause different tendencies to become behaviorally dependent, both in people and in lower animals.[2] But these findings suggest only that some individuals are equipped to get more pleasure than others from a particular substance. Different capacities for pleasure don't explain why individuals can't weigh the costs and benefits of taking the substance and decide just how much is worth the cost. The mere fact that we can observe the brain mechanism that makes a particular event rewarding doesn't mean that this kind of reward behaves differently than other rewards.

In any case, addictions to substances are just the most obvious examples of robust, alternating preferences for conflicting goals. More numerous are the activities that are temporarily preferred but that are clearly not "hardwired" to reward. The lure of gambling has been a mystery, but there's no denying its addictive potential.[3] Some people get equally hooked on overspending money, kleptomania, dangerous sex, and other kinds of thrill. The defining feature of "addiction," as I'm using the term, is that the imminent prospect of such activities is strongly rewarding, but they're avoided if foreseen from a distance and regretted afterward. When the person's preference in either direction lasts long enough to be a decisive preference – when she consciously strives to avoid the activity, then changes direction and just as deliberately indulges in it – I'll speak of this activity as "temporarily preferred in the addiction range of duration," regardless of whether there are measurable physiological changes like tolerance or withdrawal.[4]

Even among addictions, some reversals of preference last longer than others. The person who's failing to stop smoking may still stub out her cigarette seconds after she's lit up, while an alcoholic bender can last a week or two. The common feature of the temporary preferences in the addiction range is the full reversal of intentional behavior.[5]

4.1.2 Compulsions

Some temporary preferences are longer than the addictions and may seem closer to what the person "really" wants; there may never be a time when she works wholeheartedly to avoid them. Sometimes they turn out to have been temporary after many years, and sometimes they can be identified only by signs of ambivalence. Regret may still occur, for instance, and the person may even expect the regret while indulging in the behavior, but this behavior has a more deliberate, consistent quality than an addiction. In fact, the bad behavior may amount to becoming a control freak of one kind or another – going overboard on dieting until it is called "anorexia nervosa," cultivating the self-defeating love of detail that is called "obsessive-compulsive personality," or becoming stoical about feelings until she can no longer recognize them, a condition that clinicians have called "alexithymia."[6]

As with the addictions, some of these long-range but ambivalent preferences may never be recognized as psychiatric conditions. They're apt to be called "character flaws." The person may be a miser or a workaholic, or have a need to control the people around her. Usually the people I'm talking about here have some sense that they're getting less satisfaction than other people – that they'll regret their commitments to these strange projects, which seem like disciplines gone haywire. And yet, even while noticing this, they feel trapped in their behaviors and are apt to revert to them after attempts at reform. They systematically cultivate a habit like miserliness or self-starvation even while they feel imprisoned by it, admitting more or less overtly that it's not their richest option in the long run. There's a kind of security in these activities that the person can't give up, and often a seductive logic that they're maximizing her well-being: her wealth, or safety, or self-control itself. She might be said to have "sold out" to them, and in previous writings

I've used the word "sellouts" for long-range preferences that are not in your longest-range interest. However, since most or all of these preferences have a controlled, systematic quality, the more familiar word "compulsions" is apt.[7]

The reader might wonder why temporary preference should be the main quality I'm picking to characterize compulsions and addictions. The miser who never doubts the wisdom of maximizing money and the heavy drinker who's unaware of any major downside to drinking are incurring losses just like the people who struggle hard against these traits. We might only guess that these people *would* regret the behaviors if they had more foresight. Does the temporary or ambivalent quality of a preference define it that much?

Again, yes and no. From the social welfare point of view, choices that tempt the person in the short run and betray her in the long run should be regarded as traps, whether or not the person ever discovers her loss. But neither utility theory nor cognitive theory has any trouble explaining why a person keeps doing harmful things when she doesn't know any better. Cigarette smoking was just as harmful before the harm was proven and publicized, but the behavior of smoking wasn't puzzling at all. The cases that need explaining are those where people keep doing this kind of thing while knowing they'll regret it and even while trying to stop. It's only temporary preference that confounds conventional theory. Addictions and compulsions in this sense describe internal self-control problems, and that's why they're puzzling.

4.1.3 Itches

Going in the other direction on the spectrum of durations, there are unwanted behaviors that are preferred so briefly that they never feel deliberate. That is, they require your participation but lack clear periods of conscious preference. A conspicuous example is the psychogenic itch, which will abate if you don't scratch it but which you nevertheless have a strong urge to scratch. Personal mannerisms like nail-biting, or linking sentences with "um," or hair-pulling, or "nervous" coughing are also voluntary behaviors in the sense that you can stop doing them when you think about them; however, your motives to do them would be described as urges rather than appetites.[8] Pathological examples include the "tics" of Tourette's syndrome, which are actually brief, embarrassing verbal outbursts, and attentional patterns like persistent self-consciousness, obsessional doubts, and hypochondriacal worries. Clinicians have even reported an urge for certain epileptic patients to self-induce seizures and for schizophrenic patients to voluntarily trigger their own hallucinations.[9] The feature that distinguishes these patterns from the addictions is that a person will seek something that keeps her from obeying the urge – an engaging task or a restraining device or medicine – even in the midst of giving in to it. She never "wants" the behavior, and could reduce or eliminate the urge by consistently not giving in to it; but nevertheless she tends to give in repeatedly. Since these patterns all have the temporal properties of a psychogenic itch, I'll call them "itches."

To say that itches are rewarding may stretch the intuitive meaning of the word; but if we use "reward" in its most basic sense – whatever makes the choice it follows more likely to be made again – we'd have to say that the maintenance of this kind of urge is rewarding. In fact, this seemingly irrational pattern can be produced in an animal using only conventional rewards and periods of nonreward.

In a behavioral experiment, pigeons had to emit more and more pecks to get a single delivery of grain. When more than a certain number of pecks was required, the subjects didn't stop pecking, but they did choose an option that removed the opportunity to peck. Just as with the human behaviors just listed, a bird would peck regularly, but at the same time would work to avoid the stimulus that elicited this pecking. If a process of temptation and temptation avoidance weren't involved, it would have been simpler for the subjects just not to peck when it became no longer worthwhile. Similarly, monkeys will sometimes work so that cocaine won't be available for a time, even though they work to get it when it is.[10]

Imagine that you like to walk for recreation, and every day you face a choice of two possible routes, one of two miles and the other of three miles. Along the two-mile walk, someone has always left a nickel lying slightly out of your path every 50 yards or so; on the three-mile walk, there are no coins. With turning aside and bending down 60 times to pick up the nickels, the two-mile walk takes about an hour, so that you make about $3 per hour for your pains. The three-mile walk also takes an hour. Unless they were in dire need of money, most people would probably prefer the walk without the nickels – or would come to prefer it after some experience. Of course you could just resolve not to pick up the nickels, but this would take extra effort. The aversiveness of this walk would doubtless come from the nickels' breaking into attention just often enough to disrupt any ongoing reverie. If the nickels occurred every five yards at the beginning or end of the walk, they would be less objectionable.

Itches, like the urge to pick up the nickels, compete against other urges in the marketplace of choice, and their sometime success is evidence that the basic selective process – reward – has occurred. Figure 3A depicts a pattern of rewards that satiate quickly but also regenerate quickly; choosing these rewards interferes with a low but steady level of ("baseline") reward from other sources, which always starts to regenerate at about the time when a brief spike of reward again becomes available. As this time approaches, the aggregate value of the baseline reward fails to climb as rapidly as the value of a spike (Figure 3B). The urge represented by the spike may recur several times a minute, and thus can have considerable nuisance value despite the transitory nature of relief from each individual urge. However strongly the person is motivated to respond to an individual urge in the way that perpetuates its recurrence, most of the time she'll welcome the chance to be rid of the whole cycle of urge and relief.

The difference between addictions and itches is the length of time that they're preferred. The intensely rewarding phase of addictions lasts for periods ranging from minutes to hours or even days, and the hangover phase before that kind of reward is again available is proportionately long. If the time between spikes in Figure 3A is weeks instead of seconds the figure is a good representation of a binge pattern. The gratification of an itch lasts for seconds, but is available again in seconds. The person bites a fingernail and is then free of the urge, but only momentarily.

There's no sharp line between the duration of preference that characterizes itches and that which characterizes addictions. The satiated smoker who repeatedly lights and then extinguishes a cigarette represents a borderline case on a continuum of preference durations from the addiction range to the itch range. So do retardates who nurse their stereotyped self-stimulation symptoms.

The example of itches is important, because it shows how something experienced as aversive can be built entirely out of a sequence of reward and nonreward. As periods of temporary preference get shorter, they seem to lose the subjective quality of being your "own," of being what the psychoanalysts call "ego-syntonic." And yet your participation in choosing them is clear: You don't *have* to scratch, or worry your canker sore, or bite your nails; it isn't physically painful not to, and if you never

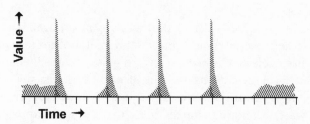

Figure 3A. Aversion as a cycle of brief, intense reward (rightward hatching) that interrupts an ongoing baseline reward (leftward hatching) for a relatively longer time. If the time units are hours or days, this describes an addiction; if they're a few seconds, it describes an itch; it they're small fractions of a second, it could describe a pain.

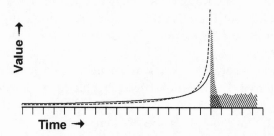

Figure 3B. Hyperbolic discount curves drawn from a single spike in an aversion sequence, such as that in figure 3A. (Each curve is the sum of the curves from each moment of reward; see figure 6 and its accompanying footnote.) The spike has less area than the baseline reward to which it is an alternative; but because it's taller it will be preferred just before it's available.

do it you'll soon lose the urge. But these activities may nevertheless be robust. Given this example, it may be profitable to explore what could be happening if there were temporary preferences that were briefer still.

4.1.4 Pains

At the shortest end of this continuum there may be a cycle so rapid that positive and negative elements blend together in consciousness: If the brief spike of the reward for scratching an itch occurred even more briefly, and was always followed by a brief trough of nonreward, this combination might reward an ultra-short-latency response like attention but deter longer-latency responses like moving a muscle. In that case, the spikes in Figure 3A would be separated by fractions of a second that were small enough to produce flicker fusion – the experiential overlap that, in a different modality, makes the frames of a movie seem continuous.

Imagine that instead of the walk with nickels, you just have the chance of reading an engaging story but with a distraction: A nearby tape recorder plays an unrelated but even more engaging story in 5-minute episodes every 30 minutes. At these intervals, switching back and forth probably wouldn't be very annoying. But if the times gradually became shorter – for instance, 1 minute of tape recording for every 6 minutes of reading, or 5 seconds for every 30 – it would get so that the disruption of the story you were reading would make the otherwise enjoyable tape recording a nuisance. The recording would take on the properties of an itch. If the distraction were shorter still, say a varied and highly stimulating pattern of words or sounds that you heard for 1 second in every 6, or even 0.1 second in every 0.6, the distraction would get more irritating and your sense of directing your attention voluntarily would get less. The brief distractions might totally dominate the intervals between them, so that you no longer seemed to have two sequential experiences, reading and distraction, but rather the single experience of reading *with* distraction, or maybe being unable to read at all.

You might choose to get the 5- and 30-minute pattern, even from the perspective of distance, depending on what other options were available. As the cycle got shorter, the costs of shifting your attention would make it undesirable at a distance, but in the period when the tape was imminent you'd still choose to have it turn on; in a still more rapid cycle, you'd actively leave it in the middle of a cycle, but not, perhaps, while the shorter, more interesting tape was actually playing. As the intervals got very short, there would be a set of values for which you'd work to get rid of the pattern at any time in the cycle. Your attention would still be drawn to the sounds, although you might learn to deflect it with effort. However, in terms of your physical behavior, you'd no longer have any tendency to *move* toward the sounds; in fact, you'd wholeheartedly want to move away from them. You'd then be having an experience constructed entirely from alluring elements, which attracted attention but repelled motor behavior.

It's hard to know what importance this possibility has in real life. If the two components blend in consciousness, they can't be identified by introspection, and no one has studied very short rewards alternating with nonreward in the laboratory. However, this model suggests how to solve another problem where conventional utility theory has glossed over a major inconsistency: the problem of pain.

Casual introspection has usually led people to the conclusion that pain is the opposite of pleasure or satisfaction, and many philosophers and psychologists have based their views of motivation on this polarity. However, as soon as the early behaviorists began to study the components of behavior precisely, they realized that the two were not exact opposites. Pleasure led to memories of the behaviors that preceded it and a tendency to repeat those behaviors; pain led to a tendency not to repeat the behaviors it followed, but it didn't erase the memories. If anything, painful memories were more vivid than pleasurable ones and had a greater tendency to recur. They led to strong emotions that might even grow and get worse in the absence of new pains.[11]

If you believe in an independent cognitive apparatus that stands outside of motivation and doesn't apportion attention on the basis of reward, you can still think of pleasure and pain as exact opposites in spite of this asymmetry; but you're then left with the question of how memories compete for a person's attention. If someone remembers painful things only because it's rational – as a way to avoid injuries, for instance, or because she judges that she ought to – why does she rehearse painful memories that she believes are useless or even harmful? Why create dread before the next visit to the dentist by rehearsing the pain of the previous one? And why should memories of pain sometimes get worse over time?

In fact, this doesn't seem to be why someone remembers pain. We remember pain because it's vivid – the memory of it has the same ability to draw our attention that joy or enthusiasm does, except that we experience this draw as an unwanted urge rather than a welcome chance for satisfaction. There seems to be a marketplace for our attention just as there is for motor behaviors, and painful memories seem to compete much as itches do, or cravings for a cigarette.

This line of questioning brings us to ask why people have to pay attention to pain itself. We may think of it as a reflex, as something we can't help doing; but on close examination this isn't true for moderate pains, and there are ways people learn to react without aversion even to severe pains like those of childbirth, dental work, and surgery. Doctors have long noticed that pain seems to be a matter of subjective response. People who are injured in the heat of sports competition, or in battle, often don't notice their injury until the action stops. They can report when and where the injury happened, but it doesn't have an emotional meaning until later. Part of this is the natural anesthesia of the endorphins that the body generates during excitement; but these are often still present when the action stops and your attention goes to your injury. At that point you have an urge to "surrender" to the pain, that is, to open yourself to an intense, aversive emotional reaction. It's hard to resist this urge, even though it may make you faint or put you into circulatory shock – but people sometimes learn to do it. For instance, after the battle for Okinawa in World War II, doctors observed that American soldiers often went into shock after fairly minor wounds, while the local peasants, presumably more used to dealing with pain, waited calmly for major wounds to be treated.[12]

In situations where pain is predictable and unavoidable, people have often developed attention-patterning techniques to fend off the urge for this emotional reaction. "Natural" childbirth, for instance, depends on being well practiced in repetitive behaviors to perform during the long, stimulus-deprived period of labor – behaviors that have no effect except to provide a preoccupying task as an alternative to the urge to get involved in your pain. Similarly, dentists have learned that patients report less pain from drilling if there are auditory stimuli like music or conversation that they can pay attention to; this is the puzzling "audio-analgesia" effect. For people who have a special talent for focusing their attention – "good hypnotic subjects" – it's even possible to learn to have major surgery with only hypnotic suggestion as anesthesia. These patients feel exactly where and when the cuts are occurring, but they "handle" the feelings with nonpainful interpretations (e.g., the sensation of being warmed by the sun on a beach) that can compete successfully with the obvious interpretation of being carved up.[13]

The reader might be able to observe this competition personally. The next time you have a moderately painful procedure done, like a tooth filled, have it done it without local anesthesia and notice the contest between your ongoing thoughts and the jarring, disorganizing experience of pain, an urge that gets more demanding the longer there's a continuous run of its stimulus (e.g., drilling). The importance of this observation is that pain has to bid for domination in the marketplace of choice, just as opportunities for pleasure do. Although its defining feature is that people don't want it, it shares a lot of characteristics with the itches and even the addictions – choices that are generally unwanted but that present people with a problem because they're temporarily preferred.

I'm suggesting that pain may be a rapidly cycling itch, just as an itch is a rapidly cycling addiction. I submit that this hypothesis is the first complete solution to the problem of pain, the puzzle of how an event can attract attention while deterring physical behavior. Whether or not this turns out to be the specific mechanism of pain, it has to be true that pain is a combination of reward for some initial enabling response that "opens the floodgates" and some consequent obligatory nonreward. To the extent that there's an urge to open the gates, the person will participate in pain in the same way that she participates in itches, although perhaps so quickly and automatically that it doesn't often feel like a choice. People usually have to be taught to make it a choice by a pain-management program, and even then the urge to open the gates remains strong.

Some other experiences seem to have the same motivational profile as pain. Panic episodes and traumatic flashbacks, for instance, are unwanted but hard to resist; they feel totally involuntary but are marginally controllable through learned attention patterns. The same is true of the urges of obsessive-compulsive disorder, which often border on the pain range, and of the kind of grief that doesn't resolve but takes on a life of its own.[14] A trivial example that the reader might experiment on without dentistry is shivering. Stand outdoors without a coat on a cold day and notice the urge to shiver. You can suppress shivering with focused effort, but as soon as your attention strays, you're apt to shiver without thinking; and once you've begun shivering, it's hard to stop. Shivering isn't very aversive and presents no clinical problem, but teaching techniques to avoid other aversion responses – I'll refer to the whole category as "pains" – is a big part of behavior therapy.[15]

4.1.5 Distinguishing Rewards From Pleasures

The hypothesis that reward is a necessary component of pain and other aversive experiences seems absurd at first. It sounds as if I'm saying that pain is basically pleasurable or that people are really masochists. I'm not. There are certainly cases where pain increases sensual pleasure, and there have been experiments where animals have been fooled into doing more of a behavior the more it brought on pain;[16] but these cases are a tiny part of how pain manifests itself, and they're not what I'm talking about.

Rather, I'm describing how hyperbolic discounting causes a split between *reward* and *pleasure*. In conventional utility theory they're the same thing: Reward per se is pleasurable, and if it commits you to a later unreward or to a different process called pain, you should be able to decide simply whether it's worth the cost. Conventionally, the definition of reward – "any experience that tends to cause repetition of the behaviors it follows" – is not significantly different from the definition of pleasure, which might be "any experience that you perceive as desirable." With hyperbolic discounting, by contrast, brief rewards can seduce you even after you know that they commit you to a greater subsequent absence of reward. Very short-term rewards like the itches and pains I've just discussed can create urges that are virtually irresistible but that are never experienced as desirable. Short-term rewards, the hypothesis predicts, produce very different experiences from longer-term rewards.

It's not useful to ask whether pain "feels like" reward; that question refers intuitively to reward as a synonym of pleasure. The influence of reward has to be inferred from the experience that pain feels irresistible – or, better, very difficult to resist, a difficulty that measures the amount of reward that has to be bid against it, and hence its own rewardingness. There is little direct evidence on how aversive stimuli reward attention; however, among the cells in the nucleus accumbens that respond to rewarding stimuli, there are some that respond to both rewarding and aversive stimuli – which at least suggests that they may have part of their mechanism in common.[17]

In discussing pains, I'm talking not only about rewards that aren't pleasurable, but also about behaviors that aren't voluntary. Why isn't this doubletalk? That impression comes from the same habits of thought that make temporary preference seem so paradoxical. People try to be well-informed managers of their wishes, who scrutinize all decisions for consistency and give a go-ahead only on reflection. A reward is therefore thought of as something you choose consistently over time, and a "deliberate" choice has to be something that maximizes reward in that sense, or else it's called irrational. However, the process of scrutiny requires conscious notice and takes time; given how quickly attention, for instance, can respond to short-range rewards, only some of the processes that are selected for their consequences can feel voluntary.

The other consequence-based processes are still different from true reflexes like knee jerks, which are driven by the stimuli that precede them (pushed), but these other processes don't generate pleasure. Some are just "second nature." We each have many small, unremarkable behaviors that are unreportable even if we try – mannerisms, postures, breathing patterns, and the facial expressions that we learn about only when someone says that we look angry or anxious. However, if we identify and try to change these movement patterns, we notice that they aren't arbitrary, that they've been keeping us more comfortable than their alternatives do. Research has shown that even while we're asleep, our behavior can be shaped by differential comfort.[18] Thus our behaviors can grow to obtain reward without the well-scrutinized process we call "volition." The choices that respond to reward are a broader category than what are usually called voluntary or deliberate choices or even conscious choices.

These examples aren't startling. No one would object to saying that reward-dependent behaviors are those that would feel deliberate if we took notice of them. However, the reward-dependent category must be even broader than that. While it may seem odd to speak of the sensation of pain as even partially rewarding, remember that I'm using "reward" to name any factor that increases the future occurrence of the process it follows. To the extent that we can choose what we pay attention to, phenomena like itches and pains will have to have their rewards just like the sensations that are experienced as pleasures. Otherwise, they'd have no vividness, and we'd have to force ourselves to pay attention to any ones we thought were necessary by an effort of self-control.

I'm saying that if a painful sensation attracts attention, it must necessarily have some rewarding property; and even if obligatory periods of little or no reward follow or are mixed with this sensation, the experience as a whole will still tend to be labeled with the attention-drawing part, because only things that draw attention make good labels. A toothache is aversive ultimately because it interferes with ongoing pleasure – You can't eat, play, or concentrate "because of the pain" – but you name the problem by the vivid sensation in the tooth rather than by the lost pleasure. The combination of vivid sensation and no pleasure is the familiar pattern of pain, as well as of some aversive emotions like panic.

Thus "motivated" doesn't mean only deliberate or even pleasurable. Indeed, to say that all responses depend on their consequences, but that some unpleasant consequences like pain reinforce responses like attention, is to require some distinction between pleasure and whatever that reinforcement is. As I just noted,[14] it's now well known that you

60

can be trained to resist an urge to panic, or grieve, or entertain obsessions, or even respond with an aversive emotional pattern to painful stimuli like dental work or childbirth; but even after this training, something keeps drawing you toward these negatively valued responses. Drawing, not pushing. Giving in to these experiences must be rewarding in some sense, but it's obviously not pleasurable.

The spike of Figure 3B may depict the "hook," not only of pains, but of panic, grief, unsatisfied craving, and so on. As with pains, a vivid feeling that's hard not to explore is inextricably mixed with a variable amount of unpleasantness.

The best intuitive illustration of the relationship of reward and pleasure occurs at the borders of overindulgence in addictive habits. I once heard two smokers say that they smoked without pleasure until they cut down, then found that pleasure returned. Cigarette smoke was obviously a *reward* at both times, since it maintained a behavior; but when near-satiation reduced this reward, it ceased to be experienced as *pleasurable* at a level where it was nevertheless effective enough to be chosen over the alternative of no smoke. Similarly, human subjects have been observed self-administering morphine, but not placebo, at doses too low to be reported as pleasurable.[19]

Behaviors that are necessarily rewarding but are not pleasurable are actually common. People often work to avoid the opportunity for them. Someone who hallucinates or obsesses looks for distractions from these urges; a nail-biter coats her nails with something bitter; a hiker who didn't bring enough food tries to avoid thoughts that might provoke appetite. But such strategies are an anomaly for conventional utility theory. In conventional theory, biting your nails is either worth it or not; if panic is a choice, then panic is either worth it or not. There's no role for self-control. The possibility of rewards that aren't pleasurable gets swept under the rug, and the apparent choice of unpleasure is explained away by invoking classical conditioning: "It's not really a choice, it's a transferred reflex."

4.2 INTERESTS COMPETE FOR SELECTION

Herrnstein's matching law gives utility theory its missing piece: the hyperbolic discount curve that impels a person to form temporary preferences while still maximizing her expected, discounted utility at every step. This simple tool will let utility theory handle the longstanding mysteries of irrational and conflictual goals. And it turns out to need no internal homunculus – no ego or judge or other philosopher-king, no organ of unity or continuity, although it will predict how such an organ may appear to operate. In this model the person comprises a variety of interests – groups of reward-seeking processes – that have been shaped by a natural selection process. The selection is based on hyperbolically discounted rewards, and the interests compete strategically for selection in a marketplace that is almost as free as the natural selection of species. The competition of these interests moves Adam Smith's "unseen hand" inside the individual mind.

Hyperbolic discount curves predict competition among these incompatible reward-seeking processes, like that among animals in nature. The range where they're dominant is their niche, where they have the opportunity to get the rewards they're based on, and to evade the attempts of incompatible interests to keep them from getting these rewards. That is, just as with species of animals, there are surroundings where an interest is able to attack a competing interest and other surroundings where it's vulnerable to attack. This interaction produces characteristic experiences according to each reward's period of dominance.

If discounting were exponential, this kind of model would make no sense; a person would have only one unified interest and would never be motivated to limit her own future wishes. The popularity of allegories of mental conflict over the years would be puzzling: the fights among embodied virtues and vices in Renaissance times, moralists' parables of self-government, the separate personalities inside one fictional character. But hyperbolic discounting sets a person against herself and makes Ulysses hearing the Sirens the enemy of Ulysses setting out for home. The "interest" is what I'm calling the unit of this competition, the entity made up of all the behaviors that serve the same end.

Just as animals can be described as filter feeders or foragers or hunters, interests can be characterized as being relatively short-range or mid-range or long-range. Some of a person's short-range interests may lie in simply replacing her longer-range ones, as drug addiction beats out social reward-seeking in an addict's mental economy. More often, though, a short-range interest is not in killing but in parasitizing longer-range ones, like an addiction to credit card abuse that preys on a person's longer-range interest in saving money. In that case, the long-range interest provides money for the short-range interest to consume.

Interests of different durations form something like a chain of pre-

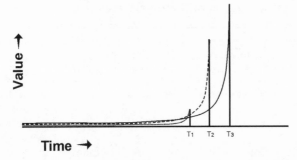

Figure 4. Discounted values of three alternative rewards with amounts in the ratio of 13:70:100. At these intervals, the first reward (available at time T_1) is temporarily preferred to the second (at T_2), and the second is temporarily preferred to the third (at T_3). If the first reward is a food binge and the second is feeling thin enough the next day, these values will cause the binge to be chosen over both feeling thin and the third, long-run optimal alternative, which might be a feeling of having risen above food obsessions.

dation, like the line of fish in the famous cartoon, each with its mouth open to eat the smaller fish ahead of it. But among interests, it's the smaller ones that prey upon the larger ones, or at least the shorter-range (and thus perhaps less "reasonable") interests that prey on the longer-range ones. Figure 4 shows how hyperbolic discount curves can make a succession of rewards, each later and larger than the one before it, dominant in turn. The alternative that winds up actually being chosen is the first one that isn't forestalled in advance by processes based on larger, later rewards.

In theory there could be continua containing any number of mutually incompatible rewards, but it's hard to distinguish more than the four I've just described, plus the category of longest-range rewards that are never regretted (Table 1). Take, for instance, a patient trying to overcome bulimia. Her longest-range interest is to eat flexibly, but she has a compulsion to strictly limit her intake. This compulsion arises from a perception that she has an addiction to eating, which periodically breaks out in the form of a binge. Let's say, to create a crude example, that her binging is sometimes preyed upon by an obsessional worry that her food is tainted, an itch-range urge that spoils the pleasure of eating – and that she then stubs her toe, and has such pain that she can't even entertain her worry; now we have what could be called a "chain of predation" containing each of the experientially distinct ranges of preference in Table 1: The pain interrupts the worry (itch range), which has in turn

Table 1. Zones of Temporary Preference Duration

Descriptor	Distinguishing Feature	Duration of Cycle	Time Until Recognized as a Problem	Examples
Optimal	Never aversive	No cycle	Never	Conflict-free satisfactions, "to love and to work."
Compulsions	Controlled by willpower; ambiguous feeling of aversion	Months to years	Decades	"Workaholism"; constrictions of personality like miserliness; anorexia nervosa
Addictions	Clear periods of pleasure and aversion	Hours to days	Days to years	Substance abuse, explosive emotional habits
Itches	Ambiguous pleasurable phase but conscious participation	Seconds	Minutes	Physical itches, obsessions, tics, mannerisms, hypochondria
Pains	Never pleasurable, no participation	Fraction of a second	Fraction of a second	Physical pain, panic

spoiled the binge (addiction range), which has undermined the rigid diet (compulsion range), which prevented her from eating rationally (longest range) in the first place. Shorter-range preferences attack longer-range ones in the same way that the urge to waste money could be said to parasitize the more prudent processes that accumulate the money.

There's no reason why interests in one range of payoff can't form alliances with interests in another, the way churches raise money by holding "casino nights," temporarily condoning gambling in order to overcome people's avarice. There are many ways that survival requires an interest to deal strategically with its competitors. A successful interest is therefore likely to include particular behaviors that take advantage of the time course in which its reward pays off, to forestall competing interests that are dominant over different ranges. I'll turn to this subject in the next chapter. First, we should look at how the concept of short-range rewards that aren't pleasures can be used to understand hungers and emotions.

4.3 EMOTIONS ARE A KIND OF APPETITE, BUT LACK OBJECTS

The implications of hyperbolic discounting free us from the need to invoke conditioning, and not only in the case of pain. Through the simple mechanism of seduction by short-range rewards, most of what motivates people in modern society – the huge category of appetite (hungers and emotions) – can be understood as motivated in turn, and subject to constraints that are altogether different from the releasing stimuli that conventional utility theory imagines. I'll return to this discussion several times; first, it will help to point out the essential sameness of hungers and emotions and their continuity with motives in general.

As named in common speech, emotions are a vast and heterogeneous array of experiences, ranging from three or four basic processes (fear, lust, and anger at least) that are governed by identifiable neuronal processes and are discernible in lower animals (the "core emotions"), through perhaps a dozen characteristic processes like joy and contempt that do not have an identified physiology but that are named in many cultures and are recognizable in photographs of faces from other cultures (call the additional processes "stereotyped emotions"), to potentially scores of subtle mood states like envy and irony that are identified mainly by describing the situations that elicit them and are apt to be peculiar to one culture or historic period (call the additional processes "subtle emotions").[20] Hungers are fewer, and are named by a stimulus that they move you to "consume" – food, warmth, a drug.

There are two conspicuous differences between hungers and emotions:

1. Hungers are more obviously controlled by the deprivation or supply of specific concrete stimuli. Even so, hungers for specific objects are extensively influenced by learned processes called "tastes" and thus have some of the culture specificity typical of emotions. To develop a taste for yak butter or blubber, you must learn to associate their fatty flavor with satisfaction; to develop a taste for an abused substance, you must come to associate the chemical taste of alcohol or the disgust and nausea of heroin injection with the euphoria of the high.

2. Emotions are more apt to stand alone, without leading to a distinct

consumption phase. Anger, for instance, may or may not demand vengeance; lust is just as often called a hunger as an emotion, and may be entertained for its own sake when there's no opportunity for physical gratification.

Hungers otherwise resemble emotions so extensively that an observer new to the topic would conclude that they are the same but for the happenstance of stimulus controllability. Jon Elster has reached a similar conclusion about emotions and the hungers that arise from addictions. He notes two differences: Addictions usurp the brain mechanisms that serve natural hungers (and perhaps emotions); and addictions are less "belief-dependent" than emotions, which seems to be another way of saying that they depend on concrete stimuli, the feature that I just called the defining characteristic of hungers generally.[21]

"Appetites" is probably the best word for hungers and emotions together, although it presumes an essential similarity that common speech doesn't recognize. Appetites seem to serve as a preliminary stage for some consumption modalities – like food, sex and drugs, and, when the preliminary stage is anxiety, pain. When the preliminary stage prepares for pleasure, appetites are the same thing as hungers. For emotions, appetite is arguably the only stage. Grief and joy lack a subsequent consumption phase. I'll speak of both hungers and emotions as appetites except where that particular distinction is important; in that case, I'll speak of hungers or emotions.[22]

Not only is the line between emotions and other appetites indistinct, so is the line between appetites and other reasons to seek or avoid things. Experts' lists of emotions differ enormously in extent and shade into what most people would call ordinary motives. Acting *in* fear of imminent death is accompanied by different physiological processes than acting *for* fear of looking sloppy, but is there any distinct point on the continuum between them where the fear ceases to be an emotion and becomes just a figure of speech for a motive? Is envy a special mental process or just a particular category of perceived want? What about curiosity?

The word "emotion" merely implies something that moves us, as if some of our behaviors were unmoved. But as we've just seen, it's likely that all behaviors are "motivated" – another word meaning moved. The only distinction between emotions and other motives seems to be their conspicuousness – some intensity or innate regularity that makes us notice them often enough to give them names. It looks as though the word "emotion" is to motivational science what the word "hill" is to topography: an identifiable feature that stands out from a less prominent background, but is made of the same stuff and may or may not be named as a unique feature, at the convenience of the observer. For purists, "emotion" is more like the word "mountain"; that is, purists demand greater contrast with ordinary motives before they'll use a special term, but they face the same problem of where in the foothills to put the boundary.

David Hume noticed this essential continuity 250 years ago:

> Now it is certain there are certain calm desires and tendencies, which, though they be real passions, produce little emotion in the mind, and are more known by their effects than by the immediate feeling or sensation. . . . When any of these passions are calm, and cause no disorder in the soul, they are very readily taken for the determinations of reason.[23]

4.3.1 Appetites Are Behaviors

Now we can return to my argument that seemingly involuntary processes, not just aversiveness but hungers and emotions generally, come from a particular time relationship of rewards, making them forms of seduction. The distinction between the desirable (chosen even at a distance) and the merely reward dependent is important because many theories, both scientific and commonsense, blame subjectively unwanted behaviors on unmotivated processes like the supposed mechanism of classical conditioning.

In Chapter 2 I pointed out why conditioning couldn't cause pleasure-seeking impulses (Section 2.2.1), but it has still seemed necessary as a way of imposing aversive experiences. If reward is defined narrowly as pleasure, some such mechanism seems indispensable; otherwise, what would make you pay attention to pain or entertain distressing emotions? With the recognition that very short-acting rewards can make what are on the whole aversive processes hard to resist, a much more parsimonious assumption becomes possible: that all substitutable behaviors and the mental processes that govern them are chosen strictly on the basis of their prospective results, that is, on the basis of the process I've been calling reward. All hypothetical prior causes that control behaviors in reflexive fashion (i.e., by pushing) turn out to be unnecessary.[24]

That is, the short-range rewards created by hyperbolic discounting provide a way around the need for a second selective factor to explain seemingly involuntary mental processes. In the two-factor theory of conditioning that I described earlier (Section 2.2.1), appetites must be elicited by stimuli that are outside of the person's control. If that theory's two assumptions about simple transferability of responses and about exponential discounting were true, the external-elicitation feature would be both possible and necessary. It would be possible because transferability implies that appetites are special kinds of processes that initially depend on innate releasing stimuli but can come to be elicited by arbitrary cues through pairing alone. It would be necessary, at least in the case of aversive appetites, because with conventional exponential discounting there is no other mechanism to make a person experience them. The easiest cure for fear would be to dismiss it – to stick your head in the sand – unless fear had peremptory control of your attention.

However, as we've seen (Section 2.2.1), the best evidence is that responses can't simply be transferred to new stimuli by pairing and that discounting is hyperbolic. Conversely, the short-range reward created by hyperbolic discounting offers a mechanism by which not only pain, but also panic and other emotions, hunger and other appetites, indeed all seemingly involuntary and sometimes undesirable mental processes can compete with pleasurable alternatives. The spikes on Figure 3 may depict the "hook," not only of pains, but of panic, rage, the rehearsal of grief, the urgings of hunger, or the pangs of unsatisfied craving. As with pains, a vivid feeling that's hard to ignore is inextricably mixed with a variable inhibition of reward.

Thus a good case can be made that appetites are behaviors – not voluntary, of course, but still goal-directed, shaped by (1) the increase in reward we get from consuming something with appetite versus without it or (2) an innate rewarding property of the appetite itself, in the same way that I suggested pain was innately seductive. Likewise, the stimuli that provoke appetites aren't turnkeys for some innate lock, but *occasions* that have been selected for their usefulness in predicting when the appetites will be differentially rewarding. Although it's usually hard to dissect apart the sequence of deprivation-leading-to-appetite-leading-to-consumption, it can sometimes be observed that deprivation leads to hunger only when hunger has some likelihood of leading to consumption.

People can learn to get hungry just when food is available, for instance at mealtimes. When food is never available, that is, under starvation conditions, people learn to avoid generating appetite entirely. Sailors learn not to crave cigarettes when the "smoking light" is not lit, and many

Orthodox Jews report no urge to smoke on the Sabbath, even though their level of deprivation would support a strong appetite. The same reward responsiveness has been observed for craving in opiate addicts in a program where opiates are available for consumption only on certain days; addicts have even been reported not to have withdrawal symptoms in a program where such symptoms are punished. Jon Elster has noted that "cravings are not only cue-dependent and belief-dependent [dependent on the belief that satisfaction is available], but 'cost-dependent.'" This practical property

> is also true of the more purely visceral urge to urinate, which may subside when there is no conventionally accepted way of relieving it and then intensify very rapidly when the agent knows that there will soon be an occasion to do so.[25]

It's certainly hard to think of hungers as goal-directed behaviors when those that don't seem to be rewarding in their own right may fail to extinguish after hundreds of occurrences where they weren't followed by their object. However, the arithmetic is probably no different than for a dog that wants to be fed. Begging is cheap compared to the value of the actual reward, and seems to be worth it even if food is almost never forthcoming at that time of day. Similarly, it's beyond most people's patience to convert an outdoor pet to an indoor pet: The sight of someone going out arouses the desire even after months of failure. So it seems to be with hungers as slight hopes appear.

Emotions, which aren't limited by the availability of consumption goods, are also experienced as involuntary. A discussion of what does limit them will have to wait until later (Section 10.1).[26] Here I'll note only that some features in common with voluntary behaviors suggest that they're ultimately reward-dependent – pulled, not pushed: Elster, who believes they're not reward-dependent, nevertheless points out that they can be fostered by cultivating dispositions for them, induced by thought alone, and deliberately aborted, and furthermore that we may sometimes feel guilty for having them, as if they had been deliberately chosen.[27]

4.4 SUMMARY

The temporary preferences caused by hyperbolic discounting are apt to be experienced differently, depending on their durations. Their most obvious manifestation is in activities that are strongly preferred for periods of minutes to days, but just as strongly feared in advance and regretted afterward. These are the thrills, only sometimes drug-based, that are preferred in what I call the addiction range of duration. Longer preferences have an avoidance phase that's less robust and are often experienced as compulsions. Preferences lasting only seconds are felt as urges (itches in my terminology) and are not usually desirable but still motivate participation. I hypothesize that still shorter urges that cycle rapidly reward only attention, not motor participation; this could explain why pains are vivid but aversive, and seduce you in a way that you can sometimes resist. These time ranges of temporary preference, along with consistent preference, shape five experientially distinct kinds of interest that compete for dominance in a motivational marketplace within each individual.

This model differentiates pleasures from the larger category called rewards, short-acting examples of which can lure you into decidedly unpleasurable activities. The concept of very briefly preferred rewards can explain many subjectively involuntary processes without resorting to dubious second principles of selection like classical conditioning. Such processes include not only physical pain, but also hungers (including cravings) and emotions, which seem to be members of a common category that I call appetites.

PART II

A BREAKDOWN OF THE WILL:
THE COMPONENTS OF
INTERTEMPORAL BARGAINING

CHAPTER 5

THE ELEMENTARY
INTERACTION OF INTERESTS

I have described a model of learned interests that compete freely on the basis of the time frames over which their rewards are preferred. The most important implication of such a model is an incentive within each interest to learn strategic behaviors that forestall competing interests.

If a person is a population of these kinds of roommates, each clamoring to control the use of the room, how does she make decisions? An interest can't eliminate a competitor simply by providing more reward than the other does, either at one time or on the average, since the competitor might undo the first choice when it became dominant at a particular time in the future. On the other hand, to continue to exist, each interest has to be the highest bidder at some time or it will extinguish; to achieve this, each may have to constrain others and can't be too constrained by them. Just because an interest is dominant at one moment in time doesn't mean it will get its intended reward; while an interest is dominant it has to forestall conflicting interests long enough to realize the reward on which it's based.

5.1 HOW ONE INTEREST BINDS ANOTHER

For long-range interests, this usually means committing the person not to give in to short-range interests that might become dominant in the future. Long-range interests don't usually conflict with each other, except in the trivial sense of being close choices, because the effect of distant rewards tends to be proportional to their "objective" size; the less well rewarded of two equally long-range interests tends not to survive, but there is no time when this interest includes an incentive to resist this fate, that is, no time when such resistance would increase your prospective discounted reward. I won't be examining this kind of choice-making.

For short-range interests, survival usually means evading commitments. However, short-range interests are also served by committing you not to act on other, incompatible short-range interests; and sometimes they can even commit you to disobey long-range interests. While on an eating binge, you avoid information about calories that might remind you of a diet, for instance, and you're incidentally forestalled from giving in to temptations that aren't compatible with absorption in eating, like having a sexual adventure.

There seem to be four kinds of tactics an interest can employ to commit future choice.

5.1.1 Extrapsychic Commitment

You can make it physically impossible to choose a future alternative or arrange for additional outside incentives that will influence a future self. Most examples involve a long-range interest controlling a shorter-range one.

Both the problem and the solution are basic. They're not the results of sophisticated human cognition. They can be shown to exist in birds: As I described earlier, pigeons can learn to peck a key, the only effect of which is to commit them to wait for a later, larger food reward.[1]

Examples of this elementary tactic persist in modern times. Many authors return to Ulysses' problem. The economist Robert Strotz, for instance, pointed out that apparently rational consumers pay to have their future range of choice narrowed. Movie stars pay financial managers to keep them from spending their own money, and many people used to put money in Christmas Club accounts that didn't pay interest in order to give themselves an extra incentive to save money. Jon Elster named a book after Ulysses' problem.[2]

Addiction therapists have been especially interested in disulfiram, a drug that changes the metabolism of alcohol so that drinking leads to nausea or even violent sickness. Disulfiram seemed to be a perfect solution to the temporary preference problem, but its results have been disappointing, probably because addictions can have some strategic value for long-range interests; we'll discuss these in Chapter 9.[3]

Some self-control devices make sense even in a world of purely exponential discounting – for instance, diet pills that act by reducing a person's appetite. If a rational planner decides that she ought to eat less, it's certainly easier if she can arrange not to be hungry. But devices that tie you to the figurative mast don't act by spoiling your appetite – for drinking or spending money, for instance. They keep you from acting when your appetite is strong. Such a plan makes no sense for conventional utility theory, which has people maximizing their prospects consistently over time. Hyperbolic discounting predicts a market for exactly this kind of commitment; and, as we saw, even pigeons will sometimes work to get it.

The availability and usefulness of physical committing devices are obviously limited. Even if you can get someone to hold your money until a certain time arrives, you may find that you really need it in the meantime. For that reason – or just because of the change of preference you originally foresaw – you may find yourself spending a lot of energy undoing the same plan you set up – for instance, by finding a way to borrow against your expectations of getting your money when your commitment has expired.

More often people find other people to influence them. We join groups that seem to be doing what we want to do – Weight Watchers or Alcoholics Anonymous, or a fitness club or even a discussion group. We may just let a friend know that changing a certain behavior is important for us, so that the friend will be disappointed if we don't actually change it. The tactic is to put your reputation in a community at stake. It was described by the sociologist Howard Becker as cultivating other people's respect or love so that this forms a "side bet," an additional incentive to avoid the impulses that these people would disapprove of.[4]

Social side bets are much more flexible than physical commitments, but they, too, are limited. For instance, they're useless against concealable impulses and against any impulse of which other people don't happen to disapprove; they would actually be counterproductive against an impulse to buy popularity. Furthermore, vulnerability to social influence has costs, especially in a cosmopolitan society, which multiplies a person's chances of meeting predators who would exploit this vulnerability. Despite these problems, it's a major strategy for people with strong social motivations. Carol Gilligan suggests that it may be more important in women than in men, a possibility I'll talk more about later.[5]

Short-range interests may use extrapsychic committing tactics against longer-range interests, too, but most examples are trivial. Getting drunk means that you can't be sober for a while, but there isn't much to say about this kind of commitment.

5.1.2 Manipulation of Attention

You can try to avoid information that would change your mind. If you already know that a seductive reward is available, you can try to avoid thinking about it: "If you speak of the Devil, he'll appear." This is the advice that was most respected in our culture before Freud pointed out the bad side effects of repression. A typical example appears in an early-twentieth-century book called *Right and Wrong Thinking and Their Results,* which advised the reader to "avoid discordant thoughts," by distraction if possible and if necessary by "the rule at Donnybrook Fair: 'whenever you see a head, hit it.' The least is not too small to be terminated if it is wrong." Behavioral writers even today advocate "stimulus control" as a useful way of avoiding impulses. It's a large part of what psychologists Janet Metcalfe and Walter Mischel suggests that people use to control passion. Even economists have begun to consider the "value of ignorance (in the form of not acquiring [even] free information)" for this purpose.[6]

Attentional tactics seem to be especially effective against very-short-range urges that require only a moment of attention to become dominant. In the previous chapter, I mentioned examples of structuring people's attention as a way of controlling dental or obstetrical pain. Similarly, I've known patients who have told of "fighting off" panic attacks, dissociative episodes, and even epileptic seizures by vigorously directing their minds away from the feeling that these events were about to occur.

There are obviously occasions when a blind eye at the right time keeps you from giving in to an urge. The trouble is that short-range interests may actually make more effective use of attention control than long-range interests can. When it's in your long-range interest not to realize that a temptation is available, it's also in your short-range interest not to get information on the long-range consequences of giving in. In the competition between long- and short-range interests, attention control is a two-edged sword. In fact, much of the psychotherapy developed by Freud and his followers involved teaching patients to catch themselves using suppression (deliberate avoidance of a thought), repression (unconscious but still goal-directed avoidance of a thought), and denial (avoidance of the implications of a thought). If a person could just avoid fooling herself, Freud thought, she would be simply rational.

Many writers besides the psychoanalysts have described how wishful thinking undermines people's long-range plans. Examples date back to Aristotle, who said that desire had the same effect on belief as being drunk, an observation often reported by people who have suffered lapses while trying to give up bad habits.[7] Motivated changes of perception are yet another phenomenon that makes no sense in a scheme where people discount the future exponentially.

Given temporary preference for present comfort, it isn't hard to picture a mechanism for repression. Many ways have been described whereby selective attention can systematically distort the information you collect. Experiments have shown that we tend to label our memories with their emotional meanings and retrieve them by these labels. What comes to mind first when I see someone walking toward me isn't her name or where I saw her last, but a sense of whether I'd like to see more of her or avoid her. The same is true of a book on the shelf or a place I have a chance to visit. If that first sense spells trouble, it's easy enough to steer in another direction without ever going into why I want to or whether I have an obligation not to do so. Economist Matthew Rabin has described how self-serving moral reasoning can occur in just such an unconscious way.[8]

5.1.3 Preparation of Emotion

You can cultivate or inhibit the motivational processes that have intrinsic momentum – generally the emotions. These processes can change how the expectation of reward influences your choice, at least in the near future. Once your appetite for a particular satisfaction is aroused, it has a committing effect that lasts for a while. It increases the rewarding power of its objects and may arouse distaste for things that interfere with it. The dessert cart comes, and suddenly the appeal of desserts is greater than it was. Or your anger is provoked, and suddenly it looms larger than the motives that had been present, possibly even including personal safety. Or you start to caress on a date, and sexuality looms in the same way, just as dating manuals for teenagers have always warned.[9]

In the previous chapter, I described examples where people learned not to have appetites when the rewards on which they were based were certain not to occur or when punishment for them would occur (Section 4.3.1). If this behavior were based on a fear of temptation, it would be an example of preparation of emotion. In fact, when someone is worried that her emotionality makes her vulnerable to other people's influence, she may learn to almost never entertain emotion, thus developing the alexithymia that I mentioned earlier. In a laboratory setting, children as young as five who are given the choice between a better, later food and a less preferred, earlier one can learn to guide their thoughts so as to avoid appetite and thus wait for the better, later food.[10]

These are forms of the impulse-controlling technique that the psychoanalysts call "isolation of affect." It requires single-minded consistency to work. Emotionality and other appetites have a relentless tendency to arise when there's even the slightest chance that they'll be rewarded, though some more so than others – remember Galen's observation that anger could be tamed like a horse, but that the "concupiscible" power (sexual desire) was like a wild boar or goat that had to be controlled by starvation (Section 1.1).

The psychoanalysts also describe cultivation of an emotion to forestall the development of a contrary one – "reaction formation" or "reversal of affect." If I were afraid I'd hate my mother, I might look for things to love about her; or if I thought my soft heart got me into trouble, I might look for ways to see people as my enemies. Again, the analysts only publicized what earlier writers had noticed. I've already quoted Francis Bacon, who wrote with approval about setting "affection against affection and to master one by another: even as we use to hunt beast with beast" (Section 1.1). In the eighteenth century this tactic was sometimes held out as the only practical committing device: The philosopher David Hume said, "Nothing can oppose or retard the impulse of passion but a contrary impulse."[11]

The short-range committing effect of emotion can serve both short- and long-range interests, just as external commitments and attention controls can. A long-range interest may cultivate emotions in order to achieve bravery or virtue, but it's at least as common that someone seeks refuge in a passion so as not to listen to reason.

5.1.4 Personal Rules

You can make a resolution. This may be the most common way that people deal with temporary preferences but also the most mysterious. What is there about "making a resolution" that adds anything to your power to resist changing motivation? This is just the will, the concept that Gilbert Ryle analyzed and found superfluous, and that conventional utility theorists like Gary Becker leave no place for.

Conventional utility theory doesn't suggest any role for a will – but of course, it doesn't recognize a temporary preference problem to begin with. Because of its assumption that people discount the future exponentially, it confounds two distinct meanings of will: a hypothetical element needed in dualistic philosophies to connect mind and body, as in "I willed my arm to move," and the faculty for resisting temptation that's commonly called willpower. If discounting is exponential, resisting temptation is a function just as superfluous as connecting mind and body; we'd be right to dispense with both.

By contrast, hyperbolic discounting can be expected to produce temporary preferences, which will in turn motivate the three committing tactics I've just talked about. The question now is whether these three tactics can account for the experience of willing things.

Most people I've talked with don't report using any of these devices while resisting temptation. When they've given up smoking or climbed out of debt, they mostly say they "just did it." Words like "willpower," "character," "intention," and "resolve" are often applied, but they don't suggest how people actually resist a temporary preference.[12] Some writers have described specific properties, however.

The most robust idea is that will comes from turning individual choices into a matter of principle. As early as the fourth century B.C., Aristotle proposed this idea (referring to dispositions to choose as "opinions"): "We may also look to the cause of incontinence [*akrasia*] scientifically in this way: One opinion is universal, the other concerns particulars. . . ." Galen said that passion was best controlled not by looking at individual opportunities but by following the general principles of reason; he noticed that impulse control was a skill that suffered disproportionately from failure to use it, and that habitual disuse made it especially hard for a person "to remove the defilement of the passions from his soul."

By Victorian times, the list of the properties of willpower had grown. The will was said to:

- come into play as "a new force distinct from the impulses primarily engaged";
- "throw in its strength on the weaker side . . . to neutralize the preponderance of certain agreeable sensations";

- "unite . . . particular actions . . . under a common rule," so that "they are viewed as members of a class of actions subserving one comprehensive end";
- be strengthened by repetition;
- be exquisitely vulnerable to nonrepetition, so that "every gain on the wrong side undoes the effect of many conquests on the right"; and
- involve no repression or diversion of attention, so that "both alternatives are steadily held in view."[13]

The property that stands out in this list is still Aristotle's universality: to unite particular actions under a common rule. Similarly, two researchers from the behavioral school have explored the idea that self-control requires a subject to think in terms of broad categories of choice rather than just seeing the particular choices at hand. Gene Heyman has found that pigeons can learn to make choices in an "overall" context instead of a "local" one if they are rewarded for following a cue telling them when they are doing this; they do not learn without this extra reward, however.[14] Howard Rachlin has said that self-control comes from choosing "patterns" of behavior over time rather than individual "acts." The former is "molecular" and myopic, the latter "molar", that is, global, an overview, based on a series of elements taken as a whole. In an experiment he did with Eric Siegel, pigeons made an impulsive choice significantly less often when 30 previous nonimpulsive choices were required than when the choice stood by itself.[15] These experiments don't model will specifically, but they do suggest that choosing categorically can partially undo the effects of hyperbolic discounting, even where the complexities of human culture aren't a factor.

Even cognitively oriented writers have noted the value of choosing in categories. Baumeister and Heatherton, for instance, speak of the need for "transcendence," which is "a matter of focusing awareness beyond the immediate stimuli," so that these stimuli are seen "in the context of more distal concerns." Similarly, some philosophers of mind have recognized the importance of making "a present choice in favor of a valued sequence of future actions or a valued policy to act in certain ways on certain occasions" in order to achieve "intention stability."[16]

There remains the question of how these categories of choice arise and what makes them recruit extra motivation. Baumeister and Heatherton imagine an ability characterized only as "one's strength to override the unwanted thought, feeling, or impulse." The philosopher Edward Mc-Clennen attributes "resolute choice" to "a sense of commitment to a plan initiated by [a prior] self." Using a more complex model, philosopher Michael Bratman argues that it is "rational to follow through with [a prior] plan in those circumstances for which one specifically planned" despite a current change of preference, not because of a commitment, but because of "a planning agent's concern with how she will see her present decision at plan's end." Both philosophers are describing a conflict of impulse and plan, but neither addresses the motivational dimension of the conflict.

Even Rachlin, a "radical" behaviorist, assumes that the necessary categories are intrinsically stable – that patterns of choice naturally hold together like the notes of a symphony, so that, once you're aware of the pattern, you'll be motivated not to break it up. For instance, if you see the pattern of "a healthy breakfast" as consisting of juice, cereal, a bran muffin, and skim milk, the reason you don't substitute apple pie for the bran muffin is that it would break up the pattern, just as not hearing the last notes of a symphony would spoil the experience of hearing the symphony. Likewise, a controlled drinker doesn't drink too much because it would spoil a pattern of temperance.[17]

There's something appealing about this viewpoint, and yet it doesn't ring entirely true. How do patterns like healthy breakfasts and temperance get decided on in the first place? And is it really true that we forgo the apple pie for the sake of consistency per se? Especially in potential addictions like overeating and drinking alcohol, people report that their urge is to break the patterns, not preserve them. Sticking to them feels effortful – quite the opposite of the case of listening to a symphony, where breaking away in the middle is what takes effort. What enforces a diet or a resolution?

Basic utility theory can provide an answer, but only if the form of the discount curve is hyperbolic. Assuming only that the discounted rewarding impacts of successive events add together, we can see that series of rewards will be chosen more in proportion to their objective sizes than will single rewards. The property of additivity hasn't been studied much, but a few experiments suggest that the hyperbolically discounted effects of each reward in a series simply add, at least in pigeons and rats.[18] Since this is also the simplest assumption, I'll adopt it from here on.

Consider a series of larger, later rewards and their smaller, earlier alternatives – for instance, philosopher Bratman's example of a pianist who throws his nightly performance off by drinking wine beforehand:[19] At a distance the pianist prefers to abstain and perform well, but every night at dinnertime he changes his preference to drinking the wine. However, as Figure 5A suggests, even at dinnertime he may prefer the prospect of abstaining every night to the prospect of drinking every night for the foreseeable future: The incentives for choosing between these categories of reward will be the summed expected values of the series of rewards. The incentives for choosing just for one night will be the curves from a lone pair, as we saw in Figure 2B.

In the schoonerlike picture of the summed discount curves from series of rewards, the "sails" get gradually lower as the choice point moves later in the series, for they comprise a decreasing number of curves added together. The last pair of sails are the same as a lone pair. If the series has no foreseeable end, which is the case for most real-life categories, the sails may be added forward to some kind of time horizon that stays a constant distance ahead, so that the height of the summed rewards stays roughly constant. In any case, summation of a series of rewards makes the first few sails higher than the sail drawn on a lone pair of rewards would be.

More importantly, the delayed rewards add roughly in proportion to their objective sizes, so that when their aggregate height is added in, the first sail in the series of smaller rewards doesn't protrude as high above the first sail in the series of larger rewards as it does in a solitary pair; with series of some amounts at some delays, the earliest sail doesn't protrude above its larger, later alternative at all. That would mean that when the pianist chooses categorically, he would always prefer to abstain, even at dinnertime. The choice of a whole series of rewards will be influenced by the rewards expected after the most immediate pair, and for all the subsequent pairs the discounted value of the larger, later alternatives is greater than that of the smaller, earlier ones. Only the nearest choice in a series is dominated by the smaller, immediate reward – although the nearest choice will obviously carry more weight than any single one of the later choices.

Two recent experiments confirm that choosing between whole series of small, early versus large, late pairs increases the preference for the large, late alternatives. Psychologists Kris Kirby and Barbarose Guastello found that undergraduates who preferred the small, early amount of money when choosing between one pair at a time regularly switched

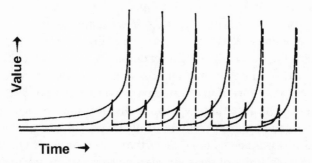

Figure 5A. Summed hyperbolic curves from a series of larger-later rewards and a series of smaller-earlier alternatives. At the beginning of the series, the period of temporary preference for the series of smaller rewards is about zero. The curves from just the final pair of rewards are the same as in Figure 2B.

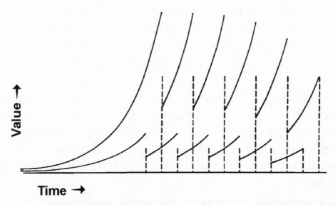

Figure 5B. Summed exponential curves from the two series of rewards shown in Figure 5A. Summing doesn't change their relative heights. (This would also be true if the curves were so steep that the smaller, earlier rewards were preferred; but in that case, summing would add little to their total height anyway, because the tails of exponential curves are so low.)

to preferring the large, late amount when choosing between series of five payoffs to be delivered at weekly intervals. The same switch occurred when amounts of pizza were offered rather than money. Similarly, psychologist John Monterosso and I have observed that rats choosing between squirts of sucrose prefer the shorter, earlier of a single pair of squirts but a series of three longer, later squirts over a series of three shorter, earlier alternatives.[20] The finding in rats suggests that the bundling effect comes from a basic property of the discount curves rather than from some cultural norm.

This property has to be a highly concave shape, such as that of hyperbolas. Exponential discount curves from a single pair stay proportional, and adding the whole series together doesn't change their relative heights (Figure 5B). Thus, bundling choices together wouldn't affect the direction of preference if discount curves were exponential rather than hyperbolic. The fact that hyperbolic discounting predicts the often-described – and now experimentally observed – increase in patience for bundled rewards seems to confirm that we're on the right track: The strategic implications of these curves may be central to whatever rationality human choice-making can achieve.[21]

5.1.4.1 Bundling Rewards That Extend Over Time. Most choices in real life aren't between brief moments of different intensity, but between extended experiences – the pleasure of a binge versus feeling fit and having intact prospects the next Monday, a venting of rage versus keeping a job and friends. Often the difference isn't between intensities of satisfaction-per-minute, but between different durations of comparable satisfactions. The pleasure of staying up for a couple of hours after midnight may be the same as the differential pleasure of not being tired the next day, but the latter pleasure lasts all day. However, if successive rewards are additive, it's easy to convert durations to total amounts. For instance, if you value the fun of staying up at one unit per minute and expect to lose one unit per minute of comfort from when you get up at seven the next morning until you leave work at 5 P.M., your discount curves from a day's aggregation of these rewards will look like those in Figure 6A.[22]

If you face a similar choice nightly and can make your choice for a long series of future nights at once (say 10), your incentives will be described by the curves in Figure 6B.[23] As with more discrete moments of reward, bundling these experiences into series moves your incentives toward the larger, later rewards.

So choosing behaviors in whole categories will lead to less impulsiveness, just as the philosophers have said. Here, then, is a fourth strategy to defend your long-range interest: the *personal rule* to behave alike toward all the members of a category. It's the equivalent of the philosopher Imanuel Kant's "categorical imperative": to make all choices as if they were to define universal rules. Similarly, it echoes the psychologist

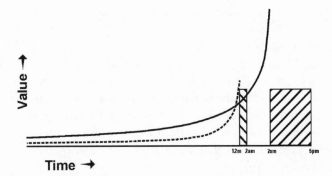

Figure 6A. Curves that are the aggregate of hyperbolic discount curves from each moment of time during continuing rewards – staying up from midnight to 2 A.M. versus feeling rested from 7 A.M. to 5 P.M.

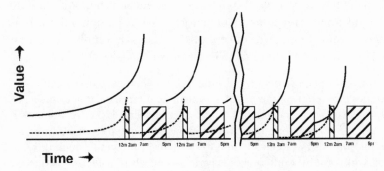

Figure 6B. Summed curves from ten pairs of the rewards depicted in Figure 6A. The effect of summation is the same as from the point rewards in Figure 5B.

Lawrence Kohlberg's sixth and highest principle of moral reasoning: deciding according to principle.[24]

5.2 THE WILL'S ACHILLES HEEL

The trouble is that this insight about choosing categorically doesn't eliminate the attraction of small, immediate rewards; it offers only a discipline that a long-range interest would benefit from at the expense of short-range interests *if only the person were consistently motivated to follow it.* So far I've described no reason why, when an inferior reward is immediately available, a pigeon or person shouldn't take it. When Rachlin and Siegel (Section 5.1.4) introduced a signal to remind their pigeons of the immediate availability of single rewards, the birds' apparent discounting shifted back from the exponential toward the hyperbolic.

People have more brainpower than pigeons and can probably perceive greater series of rewards, but short-range interests as well as long-range ones can use their enhanced reasoning skills. The bad news is that knowing the power of categorical decision making isn't enough. There's persistent pressure to backslide even after you've learned about molar or overall bookkeeping.

Ganging up on a short-range interest isn't the same thing as killing it. While acting in this interest, you're still motivated to learn anything that can evade the "universal principle" that dominates it. A quick mind can put together rules in any number of ways, so finding evasions is also easy. The trick is to differentiate between the choice at hand and the set of choices that are bound together by a rule. Just as the will is well described in history, so is our readiness to evade it. When William James wrote his pioneering analysis of "effort of will," he pointed out how a persons's "anti-impulsive conceptions" – that is, her molar conceptions à la Rachlin – are vulnerable to exceptions:

> How many excuses does the drunkard find when each new temptation comes! It is a new brand of liquor which the interests of intellectual culture in such matters oblige him to test; moreover it is poured out and it is a sin to waste it; or others are drinking and it would be churlishness to refuse; or it is but to enable him to sleep, or just to get through this job of work; or it isn't drinking, it is because he feels so cold; or it is Christmas day; or it is a means of stimulating him to make a more powerful resolution in favor of abstinence than any he has hitherto made; or it is just this once, and once doesn't count, etc., etc., *ad libitum* – it is, in fact, anything you like except *being a drunkard.*[25]

Even Aristotle went on in his description of "universal" and "particular" interpretations of choice to describe an ongoing competition between them.[26]

Thus people who have learned a "higher" or "richer" principle of choice aren't thereby freed from temptation. We aren't very old before our razor-sharp wits discover a perverse truth: If behaving according to categorical principles promises more discounted, expected reward than making isolated choices does, then making an isolated choice now and acting by rule in the future promises still more.

The problem is that there are many possible ways to define global categories. The ice cream at hand may violate one diet but not another; and even if it's so outrageously rich as to violate all conceivable diets, there's apt to be a circumstance that makes the present moment an exception, just as with James's drunkard: It's Thanksgiving dinner or my birthday, or a host has taken special trouble to get it, or I have cause to celebrate or to console myself just today, and so on. The molar principle that offers an exception *just this once* will be rewarded more than the one that doesn't, for it produces an aggregation of rewards, as shown in Figures 5 and 6, for all but the first larger, later rewards *and* the spike of reward at hand.

The tough question is not how molar bookkeeping recruits motivational support for long-range interests, but how this process defends itself from short-range interests, sometimes unsuccessfully. Acting in my long-range interest, how do I keep a short-range interest from repeatedly proposing an exception to my rule "just this once?"

Simple intuition offers the answer: Excuses that are too blatant lower my expectation of following the amended principle. I may be able to go off my diet on Thanksgiving without reducing my belief that I'll stick to it at other times; but if I try proposing other holidays, I'll probably notice that I'm starting down a slippery slope. The ability to take a drink at New Years or go off the diet on Thanksgiving provides flexibility to a potentially rigid commitment to a concrete rule; but the same principle that keeps Thanksgiving from setting a precedent might also work for my birthday and, with decreasing credibility, for the Fourth of July, St. Patrick's Day, Labor Day, Arbor Day, St. Swithin's Day, and Just This Once. This kind of logic can degrade a personal rule without my ever breaking it. Once I expect myself to find an exception whenever the urge is strong, I no longer have the credible prospect of the whole series of later, larger rewards – the cumulative benefits of my diet – available to choose.

In this way, hyperbolic discount curves make self-control a matter of self-prediction. This effect will be especially noticeable where self-control is tenuous. The hyperbolic discounter can't simply estimate whether she's better off dieting or eating spontaneously and then following the best course, the way an exponential discounter could. Even if she plans to eat less from a perspective of distance, she won't know whether or not she'll regularly prefer to eat ad lib when she's hungry. If she expects to eat ad lib, her long-range perspective will be useless to her unless she can use one of the first three kinds of commitments I described earlier – not a rich selection.

But what if she makes a new resolution to "decide according to principle" – to go on a diet – and starts off expecting to stick to it in the future if she sticks to it now? This condition may be enough to motivate sticking to it, but only insofar as she thinks it will be both necessary and enough. If she then violates the diet and loses faith in it, her principle will magically stop being enough. Personal rules are a *recursive* mechanism; they continually take their own pulse, and if they feel it falter, that very fact will cause further faltering.

Thus deciding according to molar principles is not a matter of making dispassionate judgments, but of defending one way of counting your prospects against alternative ways that are also strongly motivated. Your motivation to stick to a principle is not pure a priori reason – reason is not motivation – but the saving of your expectation of continuing to stick to it. It's the internal equivalent of the "self-enforcing contracts" made by traders who'll be dealing with each other for a long time, contracts that let them do business on the strength of handshakes.[27] This recursive process of staking the credibility of a resolution on each occasion when it's tested gives your resolve momentum over successive times. The ongoing temptation to commit a wrong act that will set a damaging precedent – and the ever-present anxiety that this may happen – is probably what makes this strategy of self-control feel effortful. It separates *intentions* from plain *expectations* and force of will from force of habit.

This model proceeds from hyperbolic discounting with almost no extra assumptions – only rough additiveness – and predicts credible weapons for either side in the closely fought contests that seem to occur as people make decisions about self-control: Long-range interests define principles, and short-range interests find exceptions.

5.3 SUMMARY

An interest that has survived in someone's internal marketplace must have included ways to forestall incompatible interests, at least well enough to sometimes get the reward it's based on. This need accounts for the examples of self-committing tactics that have long puzzled utility theorists. Three kinds are straightforward: finding constraints or influences outside of your psyche, sometimes physical devices like pills, but more often the opinion of other people; manipulating your attention, as in the Freudian defense mechanisms of suppression, repression, and denial; and preparing your emotions, as in the defense mechanisms of isolation and reversal of affect. A fourth tactic, willpower, seems to be at once the strongest and most versatile, but has hitherto been mysterious.

Hyperbolic discount curves from series of choices increase the preference for larger but later rewards when they're added together, which suggests a solution to the mystery: The device of choosing according to principle, which has been advocated since Aristotle's day, groups your choices into just such series. Principles of choice, or "personal rules," represent self-enforcing contracts with your future motivational states; such contracts depend on your seeing each current choice as a precedent that predicts how you're apt to choose among similar options in the future. Short-range interests evade personal rules by proposing exceptions that might keep the present case from setting a precedent. The will is a recursive process that bets the expected value of your future self-control against each of your successive temptations.

CHAPTER 6

SOPHISTICATED BARGAINING
AMONG INTERNAL INTERESTS

"Intentionality . . . is the most serious unsolved problem of modern philosophy."[1]

The implications of recursive self-prediction suggest an answer to the age-old question of what the will consists of: The will to stick to a diet has the same nature as the "will" of the nations in World War II not to use poison gas, or of those since not to use nuclear weapons. This will is a bargaining situation, not an organ. In fact it can be well described in terms of bargaining theory.

The relationship of bargaining agents who have some incompatible goals but also some goals in common is called "limited warfare." Countries want to win trade advantages from each other while avoiding a trade war; merchants want to win customers from each other while lobbying for the same commercial legislation; a husband wants to vacation in the mountains and his wife wants to vacation at the shore, but neither wants to spoil the vacation by fighting; a person *today* wants to stay sober tomorrow night and *tomorrow night* will want to get drunk, but from neither standpoint does she want to become an alcoholic. Whether the parties are countries or individuals or interests within an individual, limited warfare describes the relationship of diversely motivated agents who share some but not all goals.

When people find themselves in a limited warfare relationship, there's a strategy they can follow to prevent conflict in their area of common interest. Each will be suspicious of the others, of course; and one individual can't solve the problem by committing herself not to grab for advantage – unilateral disarmament – because the others will then be free to exploit her. However, among agents engaged in limited warfare with each other, there's a practical mechanism for peace: Their mixture of conflicting and shared motives creates the incentive structure of a well-studied bargaining game, the "prisoner's dilemma."

A detective arrests two men who've committed a burglary. The only hard evidence he has against them is their possession of burglars' tools, itself a minor crime. He interrogates them separately and offers each the following proposition:

> If neither you nor your partner confesses, I can't get you for the burglary, but you'll each get ninety days for the burglars' tools. If you confess and he doesn't, you'll go free and he'll get five years. If you both confess, you'll both get two years. If your partner confesses but you don't, he'll go free and you'll get five years. Don't you see that you're better off confessing, whether he confesses or not?

The dilemma is that, considered as a pair, they're better off if neither confesses; but unless they have some additional hold on each other's loyalty, each will optimize his outcome by confessing. They'll each get two years, even though, again considered as a pair, they had it within their power to get only 90 days.

A lot of bargaining situations turn out to have the same contingencies. Two or more parties do better if they all cooperate than if they all don't; but if only one *defects* against the others, she will do better still. Countries at war will do better by all not using poison gas than by all using it; but if one country surprises the others, it will do better still. Table 2 shows the values to country A of using poison gas at a given battle if country B does or doesn't use gas. If this will be the only battle, it seems to be in country A's interest to use gas, for A is better off using gas both if B uses it and if B doesn't. A similar payoff also faces B, so both will probably use gas and get a lower payoff than if both did not.

Why did no country ever use gas throughout World War II? How, in

Table 2. Prisoner's Dilemma for Gas Warfare: Outcomes for Country A

		If Country B Chooses	
		Gas	No Gas
If Country A Chooses	Gas	2	10
	No Gas	0	5

fact, does this situation offer a road to peace? The key fact is that in most conflicts the parties don't meet on the field of battle only once. In the poison gas example, if there will be several battles, each country would have some reason to avoid gas, as an offer to the other to cooperate on this aspect of the war and get a whole series of "5" payoffs instead of "2." Since following suit is both the most obvious strategy and the most successful one in repeated prisoner's dilemmas, each side could reasonably expect the other to do so, knowing only that the payoffs are in a prisoner's dilemma pattern. As long as using gas would set a precedent that predicts your disposition in future battles, and your opponent hasn't shown how she's disposed to choose, you have an incentive to avoid using gas.[2]

But how does this model apply to intertemporal bargaining, where the limited warfare is among successively dominant interests? Their situation seems different. For one thing, successive motivational states don't choose simultaneously, by definition. In a single game of prisoner's dilemma, it's important that both players move simultaneously, or at least that they move before they find out how their opponents have moved. The detective in the original game must have interrogated the prisoners one after the other, but made the second prisoner move before that prisoner found out how his partner had moved. But in the game with repeated moves, the two players don't have to make their decisions simultaneously for the prisoner's dilemma to arise. Each country will base its decision about using gas on the other's known moves, and the existence of a simultaneous, as yet unknown move will not affect the rationale for choice. Thus the choices made by a legislature that is dominated alternately by conflicting interests are also apt to follow a true repeated prisoner's dilemma pattern: One party may want to build arms, for instance, and the other to disarm, but neither wants to waste money. When each is in power, it must choose between cooperation – a middle level of armament – and defections, a series of which would mean alternately building and scrapping expensive weapons systems.

Successive motivational states also differ from individual negotiators in being transient; by the time you've entered a contrary frame of mind, you can't retaliate against the earlier self that betrayed you. Thus it has been objected that a person can't meaningfully be said to bargain with herself at a later (or earlier) time.[3] In interpersonal games, people deter even small defections by going out of their way to punish them, sometimes at a greater cost to their own interests,[4] but you have no way to reward or punish a past self. This is true, of course. But successively dominant interests do have stakes in each other's behavior that are very close to the ones in a literal prisoner's dilemma: The threat that weighs on your current self's choice in a repeated prisoner's dilemma is not literally retroactive retaliation by a future self, but the risk of losing your own current stake in the outcomes that future selves obtain.

Picture a lecture audience. I announce that I'll go along every row, starting at the front, and give each member a chance to say "cooperate" or "defect." Each time someone says "cooperate," I'll award a dime to her and to everyone else in the audience. Each time someone says "defect," I'll award a dollar only to her. And I ask that they play this game solely to maximize their individual total income, without worrying about friendship, politeness, the common good, and so on. I say that I will stop at an unpredictable point after at least 20 players have played, at which time each member can collect her earnings.

Like successive motivational states within a person, each successive player has a direct interest in the behavior of each subsequent player, and she'll guess their future choices somewhat by noticing the choices already made. Realizing that her move will be the most salient of these choices right after she's made it, she has an incentive to forgo a sure dollar, but only if she thinks that this choice will be both necessary and sufficient to make later players do likewise. If previous players have been choosing dollars, she's unlikely to estimate that her single cooperation will be enough to reverse the trend. However, if past choices have mostly been dimes, she has reason to worry that her defection might stop a trend that both she and subsequent players have an incentive to support.[5]

Knowing the other audience members' thoughts and characters – whether they're greedy or devious, for instance – won't help a person choose, as long as she believes them to be playing to maximize their gains. This is so because the main determinant of their choices will be the pattern of previous members' play at the moment of these choices. Retaliation for a defection won't occur punitively – a current player has no reason to reward or punish a player who won't play again – but what amounts to retaliation will happen through the effect of this defection on subsequent players' estimations of their prospects and on their consequent choices. So each player's choice of whether to cooperate or not is still strategic.[6]

These would seem to be the same considerations that bear on successive motivational states within a person, except that in this audience the reward for future cooperation is flat (ten cents per cooperation, discounted negligibly, rather than discounted in a hyperbolic curve depending on each reward's delay). Like an individual person trying to stick to a diet, the audience will either "have faith" in itself or not. It may forgive itself an occasional lapse, but once a run of defections has occurred, it's unlikely to recover its collective willpower without some event that gives it a new deal.

All means of connecting choices in a prisoner's dilemma pattern have the potential to succeed as principles of self-control. Any set of parties to a limited war – countries, groups, individuals, or successive motivational states within an individual – will seize upon such a grouping if it has this property: that all players can see it as dividing areas of mutually advantageous cooperation from areas where the hope of cooperation is unrealistic. The resulting tacit agreements about areas of cooperation constitute rules – in the intertemporal case, personal rules.

In effect, this committing tactic creates a side bet: The players stake their whole expectation of getting the benefits of cooperation on each choice where cooperation is required; this expectation is the kitty of the side bet, and it may be much larger than what was originally at stake in a given choice.

Public side bets – of reputation, for instance, or good will – have long been known as ways you can commit yourself to behave (see Section 6.1). What I'm describing are *personal* side bets, commitments made in your mind, where the stake is nothing but your credibility with yourself. They wouldn't be possible without hyperbolic discount curves, nor would they be of any use.[7]

6.1 BRIGHT LINES

Does the self we've always thought we had behave this way? Most of the time I don't feel like Ulysses, fearful of giving in to an irresistible impulse. If I'm tempted by something, I "make" a decision about it and expect to stick to my decision. If I want to change my mind about it, I look for a good reason, some rationale for change that I use in debating with myself. If the change turns out to have been a bad idea, I call my excuse a rationalization, but in either case the reasoning feels qualitative, not quantitative. I experience myself as judging reasons, not amounts. Furthermore, whoever it is that debates with me when I'm debating with myself, it feels like part of me, not a separate agent, certainly not an adversary.

But even these introspections fit much better with an intertemporal bargaining model than with the consistent choice model based on exponential discounting. With exponential discounting there would be no process that would underlie the sensation of making a decision, and changing my mind wouldn't feel like debate but simple recalculation. If hyperbolic discounting predicts enmity between some of my wishes and others, it's only partial enmity, since the reward or nonreward I experience affects all my recent choices alike, only discounted for elapsed time. Indeed, a de facto single reward center could represent whatever temporally unifying force there was among an otherwise diverse population of interests. The experience of being a whole self but having mixed feelings is just as compatible with this model of partially allied interests as with a model of a single, unitary but somehow flawed organ.

Furthermore, the intertemporal bargaining model predicts that a person's experience will change from judging amounts to judging reasons. This change follows from the recursive nature of intention. Incentives themselves may be measured in quantities, but whether or not you trust your future selves comes to hinge on litmus tests – key either/or decisions that you see yourself making. Once you've defined a prisoner's dilemma with an adequate personal rule for cooperation, you may think you've solved your problem for good. However, that will be true only if your options are divided strictly into "always defect" versus "always cooperate." As great as the prospect of reward may be for always cooperating, your prospect will be better still if you can expect to defect in the choice you face immediately and still cooperate in the future. If you're on a diet, for instance, you do better by always turning down dessert than by always accepting it, but if you can accept it once without otherwise going off your diet, that's the time that you'll be the happiest of all. Since any choice that looks like a defection will have the effect of a precedent, the trick is to make the present choice an *exception*, a choice that's outside of the game of prisoner's dilemma, however you perceive it.

As a solution to temporary preferences, intertemporal bargaining gets both its usefulness and its weakness from the openness to interpretation of what constitutes cooperation: what choices set precedents for what others and what choices are exceptions. Our lecture audience was a neat, circumscribed population who probably couldn't have escaped the notion that each member's choice served as a precedent for subsequent choices. Still, additional circumstances could make such an escape possible. If all the members were women except one man, or all grown-ups except one child, that loner might well reason that subsequent players wouldn't regard her choice as predictive of how the sentiment of the group was going, and she could take the dollar without much lowering her prospect of also collecting a subsequent stream of dimes. The same kind of reasoning is available to the person facing a choice about sticking to a diet, or getting drunk, or indulging her temper, or procrastinating: "If this choice is unique, it can stand on its own. I don't have to worry about how I'll look back on it when I face all those standard choices later on; it just doesn't look like part of what I bet myself I'd do."

This opportunity gives people some flexibility in their commitments: If we encounter a choice where the rules we set up seem to make us worse off, we can redraw those rules on the spot to leave this choice alone. But in the middle of a choice between a small, early reward and a larger, later one, the urge to see your way clear to take the early one is great, which leads people to gamble on claiming exceptions to their personal rules on shaky grounds.

The same problem exists in interpersonal bargaining: Cooperation between the countries in the choice about using poison gas is threatened by choices that are marginal in their aptness to be seen as precedents, such as the use of gas against a third nation or the use of an explosive that happens to give off toxic fumes. A country might hope to engage in such marginal behaviors without being seen as having betrayed its tacit agreement to cooperate. Because of this hope, there's more risk that the country will engage in them, and find it has hoped falsely, than that it will commit a clear betrayal.

Thus in the art of bargaining, finding lines between the good and the bad is not enough. To stabilize decisions against strong motivation to change them, you have to find lines that stand out from other lines – lines that can only be crossed or not, rather than exchanged for other lines that are more conveniently situated for the moment's purpose. Lawyers call them "bright lines."[8]

If two people will repeatedly divide up joint profits, they could decide on a 50-50 split, or 60-40, or 90-10, or any other formula, but the bright line will be at 50-50. If I'm trying to cut down on my drinking, I could limit myself to two drinks a day, or three drinks, or "until I start to feel high," but the only rule that stands out from other possible ones is no drinking at all. By contrast, if I'm trying to eat less, I can choose from a number of diets that try to anchor their instructions (no more than X calories; no more than X ounces of Y food group) at a bright line (only protein, only liquids, only fruit), but no really bright line exists. This may be why people recover from overeating less than from alcoholism.[9]

Whether agents in a limited war situation have to depend on a bright line to maintain cooperation – instead of being able to use less unique lines to gain more flexibility – depends on factors like their history and skill in that situation and the incentives at stake. For instance, war between the great powers since World War II may have been prevented by the widespread belief that even skilled policy making couldn't restrict it to conventional weapons.[10] Thus their very history of failing to avert the escalation of wars, added to the new threat of nuclear destruction, may have deterred them from venturing beyond the bright line between some war and no war at all. Similarly, alcoholics usually find that they can't engage in controlled drinking, and are advised by Alcoholics Anonymous (AA) to regard themselves as helpless against alcohol.

To be helpless means that you can't use your willpower flexibly in this area; that is, you can't successfully choose one principle of drinking or another, but can only hope never to be lured across the obvious bright line between some drinking and no drinking at all. Strictly speaking, these AA members are still using willpower; after all, their motivation to abstain comes from betting their expectation of sobriety against each urge to drink. But since they don't feel free to modify the terms of their bet, the experience is different from the experience of willing other things; it doesn't feel like their intention, but more like their surrender to an ultimatum. People for whom drinking isn't as rewarding, or whose wills haven't lost their credibility in the area of drinking, are able to obey less prominent lines or even their spontaneous preferences without losing control.

Poets and essayists and even psychologists have used the metaphor of a person as a population of interests. Sometimes this is only implied by their terms – "governing" yourself, for instance, or "blaming" or "punishing" or "rewarding" yourself. However, conventional utility theorists regard these popular metaphors as empty. Inside an organism that naturally maximizes its prospective rewards, who would govern whom, after all, and who would need to? In conventional utility theory, governance has to be a mere chain of command. If this theory has an interpersonal metaphor for decision making, it's a corporate hierarchy, with a CEO making the most rational choices she can and passing them down as orders to obedient subordinates. Despite how natural it has seemed to personify conflicting interests – from the "side of the angels" versus the "service of the Devil" to Freud's humanoid superego versus id – no one has been able to specify, in any way that withstands scrutiny, just what it could be that keeps a person's interests divided.

If the internal CEO just maximizes its prospects in a marketplace of choices, it shouldn't have to do any real governing. You could still call it a "self," of course, but this would just reflect the sum of the person's wishes and her plans for fulfilling them. This self wouldn't incite or restrain anything else, nor would it have any use for "coherence" or "boundaries" or any of the other regulatory properties that clinical writers say the self needs. Indeed, with the dominance of utility theory, the self has been in danger of following the will as a victim of Ockham's razor.

I reply that the allegorists had a point that shouldn't be dismissed; there are too many examples of self-defeating behavior that can't be explained as just bad calculation. In light of the strong evidence for hyperbolic discounting, it may be the unitary self that's fictitious. What we can observe is someone's behavior, or our own frame of mind, at single moments. How these moments come to look coherent over time is as much a matter of speculation as the nature of learning or memory. We now have good reason to believe that this process is innately programed to create diverse interests rather than a unique self-interest, and that there is a lot of scope for these interests to work out their differences in varied but imperfect ways.

The historic difficulty of specifying what the self consists of doesn't come from its superfluousness, but from the fact that it's a set of tacit alliances rather than an organ. The logic of limited war relationships naturally creates a population of cooperating processes, a fringe of outlaw processes, and a means of determining which will be which. And since limited warfare is conducted among individuals as well as within them, we can observe some of its properties in interpersonal examples.

Societies settle disputes with legal systems. Some depend on legislators – "lawgivers," individual or corporate, who lay down procedural principles. They've been the model for conventional allegorical theories of intrapersonal governance. But the most successful legal system in history, the English common law, has no lawgiver and no written constitution, only a tradition whereby the experienced users of the law cautiously try out new interpretations with an eye to seeing what precedents these interpretations set. Nor is the common law that different from what legislators create. Lawgivers really should be called "law guessers," since any government's power to force laws on an indifferent population is much less than the social power of the consensus that can be marshalled by a well-chosen line.[11]

Like the body of precedents that the common law has accumulated, a personal law develops within individuals. Lines that a person picked casually on first setting out to control a behavior – one particular diet, say, or a rule to eat nothing after dinnertime but fruit, or never to drink alone, or always to open all the mail the day it arrives – become bright lines after consistent repetition. What started out as one possible rule among many becomes *the* rule you've followed for the past year, or the past decade, and thus stands out in future negotiations with yourself.

Like the common law, this process doesn't require an executive function to steer it. Nevertheless, a person's efficiency at developing personal rules is probably increased by executive processes that find bright lines, or make lesser lines bright by virtue of their being the ones it has selected. Thus "ego functions" may be learned on the basis of how they improve intertemporal cooperation. But the power of these functions doesn't come from any authority outside of their own usefulness in serving one long-range interest or another. The ego isn't an organ that might sit in a central place like Descartes's pineal-based soul. It's a network server, a broker of cooperation among the interests, and, like interests, is itself engendered and shaped by differential reward – specifically, by the long-range reward that comes from better defense against short-range rewards.

I'm hypothesizing that intertemporal bargaining is what subjects your behavior to personal rules and makes it consistent over time, what creates its rankable goals and its procedures for consciously auditing your internal bookkeeping process. As we'll soon see, it can even motivate you to choose among some kinds of future goods as if you had *exponential* discount curves.

Ironically, this picture of the person mirrors what our picture of a corporate hierarchy has become. As economist Nils Brunsson has pointed out, people in corporations don't blindly follow orders, but act only when they're confident of each other's commitment to act. Executives don't function effectively so much by rationally analyzing facts as by finding facts that make good rallying points.[12] Even that model of strict command, the army, turns out to be held together by bargaining. As one pair of military analysts put it, "Armies must be analyzed as collections of independent individuals who are, in some senses, as much at war with one another and their own leaders as they are with enemy forces." Consequently, a commander's main task is to foresee and manipulate the prisoner's dilemma incentive structure that motivates his troops in battle.[13]

The concept of intertemporal bargaining makes it possible to see both why sophisticated authors have denied the will any substantive role in behavior and why they're wrong. Without the instability that comes from hyperbolic discounting, an organ that did nothing but intend things would be only a philosophical link between thinking and acting, and hence superfluous. If that were true, having a will that was strong or weak would have no meaning. But if intentions aren't stable, intertemporal commitment becomes a basic necessity. Skill in fostering it translates into willpower.

6.2 APPROXIMATING "RATIONAL" VALUATIONS

Thinking of a transaction as a member of a larger category dampens the fluctuations in spontaneous value predicted by the hyperbolas of Herrnstein's matching law. However, this kind of thinking is a bargaining ploy, not simple correction of an error: Insight into an error makes you not want to repeat it; staking the reward for consistent behavior against each impulse leaves you with a strong urge to obey the impulse, if only you can keep your long-run expectations intact.

However, this bargaining ploy can sometimes produce a semblance of exponential discounting, as shown in Figure 7. In the example in the figure, adding together the hyperbolically discounted values of 11 rewards (or slices of reward) that are each like the reward in Figure 1 produces a curve that's much closer to the exponential curve from that reward (or slice) than is the single hyperbolic curve in Figure 1.

Three bargaining factors make this semblance more likely to actually develop:

First, the set of interdependent choices needs to be both well defined and large. Money is the good that people are most apt to discount expo-

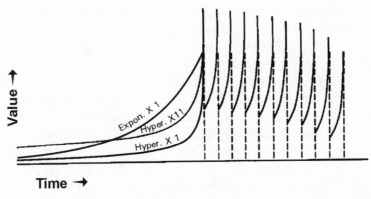

Figure 7. Summed hyperbolic discount curves from eleven rewards, compares with the exponential curve and hyperbolic curve from the single reward in Figure 1. The summed curves come much closer to exponential curve than the lone hyperbolic curve does.

nentially, probably because cash pricing makes a wide variety of transactions conspicuously comparable, and hence invites an encompassing personal rule about the value of money generally. It's easy to interpret any financial transaction as a precedent for all others. That is, if a person sees what she spends for food, clothes, movie tickets, toys, postage stamps, and so on all as examples of wasting or not wasting money, she'll add thousands of examples to her interdependent set of choices, each flattening her effective discount curve a little more. The ease of summing and comparing all financial transactions lets the value of purchasable goods fluctuate much less over time than, say, the value of staying up late versus getting enough sleep or of angry outbursts versus holding your temper. Accordingly, it's rare to see someone swayed by her immediate emotional comfort by only a tiny fraction more than by next year's, but common to see her behave as if her immediate wealth were worth only a tiny fraction more than next year's.

A second factor in creating spheres of exponential discounting seems to be some way of avoiding confrontation with most vigorous short-range interests. That is, you have to set up your personal rules so that your investment decisions aren't weighed against your strongest temptations. Two economists have recently pointed out that people assign their wealth to different "mental accounts" such as current income, current assets, and future income.[14] These accounts seem to represent personal rules that forbid dipping into capital for current expenses or borrowing to go to the movies but leave some money undefended to gratify whims. In effect, you find boundary lines for your thrift, selecting them where you think they'll never demand so great an act of abstention that you'll prefer to abandon them. You agree in advance to abandon your toughest whims to spontaneous valuation.

Finally, situations that put hyperbolic discounters at a competitive disadvantage create an extra incentive to simulate exponential discounting. For instance, money is essentially storable influence over other people's choices. This fact adds an additional stake to the goods involved in financial transactions. A person who can't control her urge to stay up too late isn't apt to fall behind other people because of it unless it gets so bad that she starts falling asleep at work. However, in buying and selling, you're not choosing simply in parallel with your neighbors, but in competition with them. As I noted before, if some of them are prudent enough to buy your overcoat every spring for $100 and sell it back to you every fall for $200, they'll soon wind up richer than you, and rewards in power over you, not to mention prestige, will be added to the goods that originally seemed to be at stake (Section 3.1). Of course, rivalry may also make people rash; but if you can follow your long-range interest, rivalry adds an incentive to get the motivational drop on other people and to keep them from getting the drop on you.

These three factors might supply you with adequate motivation to follow a personal rule for choosing according to exponential discounting.[15] Summed hyperbolic curves from all your expected financial choices might be enough to motivate you to observe a 6% rate, for instance. The amount of motivation that the summation effect must add is the difference in heights between the natural hyperbolic curve from each good in question and the chosen exponential curve, as in Figure 1. Close to a potential act of consumption, your rule must add incentive to reduce the effective discounting of the rewards it serves; at a great distance, your rule must motivate *less* saving than the high tail of the exponential curve impels.

The more common of these two situations is the need to evaluate an impulse "rationally." Your rule for exponential discounting must accumulate motivation from each of the rewards that your rule makes possible, and set this aggregate against any single impulsive spike, so that the summed curve of greater rewards is never (or rarely) pierced by such a spike. A rule to follow a low exponential rate is going to require more motivation and/or rule-making skill than a rule to follow a higher exponential rate. In theory such curves might motivate a rate of 3% or any other rate; but the lower the rate to be enforced, the less the amount of consumption at a given delay that you could succeed in deferring to a greater delay.

The social significance of different exponential rates shows how important the rivalry factor is in motivating these rates. People obviously differ in their ability to maintain low exponential curves, and differ even in their long-range motivation to do it. After all, "money isn't everything." But if your neighbor adopts a rate either much higher or much lower than yours, she'll be a problem for you. High discounters will seem to be needing help for their improvidence; low discounters will seem to be taking advantage of your human weaknesses to get ahead of you. Agreeing upon what is to be a community's "normal" discount rate is a highly charged social process. There's no bright line (aside from the motivationally impossible one of no discounting at all) that can define a good discount rate for an individual or provide a norm for a society. Thus the process of norm-setting is unstable; it lacks a site for a tacit truce in rate competition to form. In the long run, however, individuals or groups who accept a higher discount rate than the roughly consensual one tend to be ostracized as shiftless. Individuals or groups who achieve a lower rate, on the other hand, are seen as even more threatening; they're the ones who are accused of being misers, and often persecuted in the pattern of Western anti-Semitism or the attacks on Indians in Africa or Chinese in Southeast Asia.

Of course, a society often makes nonfinancial activities a basis of competition as well. Where people gain an advantage by staying hungry to attain stylish slimness or by cultivating sexual indifference to increase their bargaining power, the expectation of this advantage forms a stake for the relevant personal rules and can sometimes motivate heroic acts of abstention. As with money, people who are exceptionally successful are often accused of unfairness or psychopathology. However, just as cash pricing labels the largest number of a person's choices as comparable, it engages the largest number of people in social competition.

In all these areas, the intertemporal bargaining process sometimes lets people with fundamentally hyperbolic discount curves learn to choose as if their curves were exponential. None of the first three tactics discussed in Chapter 5 would let a primitive farmer starve herself during a hard winter to save her seed corn for the next planting. Community pressure could arise only if most individual farmers were so motivated; and control of attention and emotion commit only for short periods at a time unless they're systematically repeated, which would require an explanation in turn. But bundling whole series of choices together makes their summed discount curve look more exponential.

"Rational" calculation according to the laws of the marketplace seems to be a special case of choice-making within the encompassing matching law, analogous to the Newtonian laws of physics that operate for a limited range of values within Einsteinian relativity. Your ability to enforce exponential discounting on yourself will be limited by the amount that the required discount curve departs from the basic hyperbolic one that determines your actual motivation.

6.3 SUMMARY

Hyperbolic discount curves create a relationship of partial cooperation, or limited warfare, among your successive motivational states. Their individual interests in short-term reward, combined with their common interest in stability of choice, creates incentives much like those in the much studied bargaining game, repeated prisoner's dilemma. Choice of the better long-range alternative at each point represents cooperation, but this will look better than impulsive defection only as long as you see it as necessary and sufficient to maintain your expectation that you'll go on cooperating in the future. I argue that this intertemporal bargaining situation *is* your will.

Intertemporal cooperation – your will – is most threatened by rationalizations that permit exceptions to the choice at hand and is most stabilized by finding bright lines to serve as criteria for what you'll view as cooperation. A personal rule never to drink alcohol, for instance, is more stable than a rule to have only two drinks a day, because the line between some drinking and no drinking is unique (bright), while the two-drinks rule doesn't stand out from some other number and is thus susceptible to redefinition. However, skill at intertemporal bargaining will let you attain more flexibility by using lines that are less bright. You can even observe a rule to discount exponentially some relatively countable kinds of goods, like money, as long as you don't attempt too abstemious a rate. It is intertemporal bargaining skill, rather than some other cognitive ability, that determines how good your "ego functions" appear to be.

CHAPTER 7

THE SUBJECTIVE EXPERIENCE
OF INTERTEMPORAL BARGAINING

The hyperbolic discounting hypothesis has pushed us beyond both documented fact and common sense. Yes, the hyperbolas themselves are well-established facts, and yes, people do suffer from persistent motivational conflicts that conventional utility theory can't explain. We do talk sometimes about arguing with ourselves. Nevertheless, we experience ourselves as basically unitary; and if bundling choices into mutually dependent sets is central to the process of intending things, it has gotten amazingly little recognition.

In common speech "personal rules" don't mean the same thing as "willpower." They sound trivial, like guidelines for deportment – something a given person might not even have. I've applied the term to something much more central in human decision making. However, the very existence of personal rules as I've hypothesized isn't proven. So far the only evidence I've presented for them is that (1) hyperbolic discount curves predict a limited war relationship among interests, and (2) bundling choices together has been observed to increase patience.

Even our one robust experimental finding is counterintuitive: that the valuation process is based on hyperbolic discount curves, and hence is prone to extreme instability because of a tendency for decisions to reverse simply because time has passed. It's not that we don't observe the problems that these curves predict: The human bent for self-defeating behavior has been in the forefront of every culture's awareness. This, after all, is sin, or the weakness of the flesh, or the mistaken "weighings" of options that Socrates complained of. I've talked about the writers from Homer on down who've described people's attempts to overcome this bent. But something still feels wrong about the notion that we all have a distorted lens, that our weighing faculties are innately programmed to give disproportionate weights as a prospect gets closer.

Something may even feel wrong with the idea that motives, rather than cognitions, ultimately control our decisions. After all, to be caught "having a motive" is usually to lose moral force in an argument. Most of our ways of speaking about reasons to decide direct attention away from the decision maker and to the thing to be decided about. To say that something *is* good may imply no more than that we want it, but it sounds better.[1] To *be* good is rooted in the nature of the thing, while wanting it is just personal. Bypassing for the moment just why it should feel better when we have external reasons for our choices, this habit of projecting our motives onto external objects creates a problem: It leaves us unprepared to look at how our motives work.

In this chapter I'll look at the intuition problem – whether the intertemporal bargaining model of will really contradicts common experience; in the next chpater, I'll bring together existing evidence that what we call will is actually based on such a model.

The notion of interpersonal bargaining seems to offend intuition in three ways: (1) Pointing it out doesn't ring a bell. We have no recognition of intending things by such legalistic means, except perhaps for the small part of our decisions about which we've made conscious resolutions. (2) Subjecting every choice to bargaining might seem to require too much attention to be practical. (3) Most of our choices don't have the life-or-death quality that a recovering alcoholic's decision to take a drink has. However, I'll argue that there's no reason why people can't find bargaining solutions by trial and error, without an accurate theory of their function; expected values need not be reestimated continuously; and while the most rigid resolutions may include the atomic war or the helpless-against-alcohol contingency that we just discussed, in most cases such rigidity isn't necessary and may be counterproductive.

7.1 WHY DON'T WE KNOW WE'RE BARGAINING WITH OURSELVES?

Of course, you don't usually feel as if you're bargaining with yourself. You make a decision with all things considered, and later you make another decision where one of the things considered is the former decision, and so on. You don't make explicit trades, like cooperation now in return for cooperation in the future. But explicitness shouldn't be necessary.

In the most primitive form of barter, one tribe leaves its goods in a clearing and the other tribe leaves something else in exchange, constrained only by the concern that if it doesn't leave enough, there won't be repeat transactions. The participants may or may not have a theory of negotiation.

Theories of social rules developed long after people had a working knowledge of them. Until Renaissance times, laws were thought of as sacred mandates rather than pragmatic solutions to bargaining problems. The process of legislation involved "discovering" ancient laws rather than creating new ones. Even today, statutory law seems somehow less venerable than common law, the law that punishes *malum per se*. Similarly, Piaget described how grade school children think that rules have to be unchangeable.[2] If people experience personal rules in a similar way, either as the gift of some authority or as discoveries that work mysteriously, they will be apt to see them as properties of the external world rather than as practical expedients.

Furthermore, the personal rules that we do see as our own expedients are much more open to hedging – and hence less stable – than those that seem to have been given by something outside ourselves. Insofar as they seem subject to our wills, we feel free to modify them, declare exceptions to them, and attempt all the other bargaining maneuvers already described. But if we *believe* something about them that puts them beyond our power to meddle, then the extra value that comes from great stability is staked on this belief itself. To disobey this kind of rule is to act as if the belief weren't true, a decision that seems much more beyond our power either to limit or to repair – an act of nuclear brinksmanship. Thus rules that we perceive as external facts are apt to survive in preference to those we regard as just our personal legislation.

Let's look more closely at this possibility – specifically, that the process of attributing value to objects may include a tacit solution to intertemporal prisoner's dilemmas. Can simple "belief in" the value of an object function as a personal rule? The basic property of a personal rule is just that the benefits of the rule are at stake whenever you decide whether to follow it. You don't have to think of it as a rule, or think of what's at stake as your own credibility. Instead you can imagine a dummy stakeholder, however hypothetical or improbable, and interpret the precedents followed or broken by your choices as satisfactions or affronts to this stakeholder.

I want to attain a discipline x to overcome a temptation, and X is the patron saint of x, so I pray to X for strength. I've then added a stake to whatever incentive I originally faced to follow discipline x on any particular occasion: my expectation that X's help will let me follow it on all occasions. The more I then succeed in x, the more confident I feel of X's help, and the easier it is to follow x. If despite this help I give in to the temptation, I offend X and lose her help; sure enough, the next time it's that much harder to avoid the temptation. The X I've imagined is then my way of conceiving the stake of a personal side bet, the advantage to be gained through cooperation or lost through defection in a prisoner's dilemma. And while it may be hard for me at first to believe that a Saint X exists, the practical effect of a vow to her will eventually be noticeable – thus demonstrating her existence and leading me to vouch for it to others.

As a modern thinker, I'm more apt to say that there's no vow involved, but that my choice is dictated by the facts – but facts that, on closer inspection, bear some resemblance to Saint X. I may perceive what is in effect my rule to seek or avoid a particular situation as the fact that the situation *is* good or bad. The "facts" I respond to may have no ethical connotations at all; I may "know" certain objects to be dirty, unhealthy, or unlucky, even though my actual information about these objects is ambiguous. A person who fears drifting into procrastination may have some awareness that her housekeeping behaviors are precedents that predict the extent of this drift; however, she's apt to experience this awareness as the belief that a cluttered house is a health hazard, a belief she embraces despite the absence of any objective evidence that tells her it's true. When she shirks her cleaning she gets an uncomfortable feeling, which she'll describe as her distaste for clutter; but she probably can't report a sense that successfully ignoring the clutter would damage her rule. Similarly, anorectics may experience a rule not to give in to appetite simply as disgust for being fat. When beliefs do the job of principles, the facts believed in take on the role of Saint X.

Moral states often become translated into perceptions of external fact. Whether or not you were married was in past eras subjected to the same testing as whether or not you'd been vaccinated; marriage was once virtually a fact of physics, which, however surreptitiously contracted by an eloping couple, changed their inward natures and needed to be discovered at all costs. Likewise, virgins were a different kind of people from nonvirgins. Today the perceived moral wrong of eating animals often becomes disgust for meat, and the question of aborting fetuses turns on whether they "really are" people, as if further study of their well-known properties would prove a fact.

Similarly, people cultivate the belief that street drugs are always irresistible once tried, rather than just making an overt rule against trying them. This cultivation is apt to take the following form: An authority teaches that irresistibility is a fact; you encounter evidence to the contrary, for instance in statistics on ex-users who used only casually; you discount or somehow don't incorporate the contrary evidence, not because it seems to be of poor quality, but out of a feeling that it's seditious.[3] A belief that started out as a straightforward estimate of biological fact has at least partially changed to a personal rule that keeps the form of a belief. You can tell that this change has happened if you perceive the penalty for disbelief not as inaccuracy but as "softness on drugs."

Perhaps most of our personal rules started out as factual teachings or discoveries and remain rooted in them to a greater or lesser degree. I noticed a recent example in myself only after it had developed: I tend to "graze" during the work day rather than eat a well-defined lunch; accordingly, I'm at risk for eating more than I need. One day I discovered that some candied ginger I'd received as a present reduced my appetite for one or two hours after I ate a piece. I then began eating a piece in my office when I thought I'd eaten enough food. This was beneficial, but I noticed that I sometimes got hungry even after eating the ginger. The interesting observation was that I instinctively avoided eating anything after eating the ginger, even if I felt hungry, for fear that it would weaken the ginger's effect. That is, I realized later, I had come to use the spontaneous observation that ginger reduces appetite as the basis for a personal rule, "Don't eat again in the office after you've had ginger." It would now be impossible to say how much my reduced appetite after eating ginger comes from its direct effect, and how much from my reliable expectation that I wouldn't eat afterward even if I noticed hunger.

Many personal rules seem like that one. A wakeful child doesn't push her belief that her mother will come every time she's called for fear that she'll produce a counterexample. A person follows a belief that she's disgusted by violence to avoid war movies, lest she find that she isn't always disgusted; a person obeys a superstition to always clean up in a particular order, or create art with a particular ritual, or dress in a particular style, "for no reason" except a sense that *some* change would open the door to *more* change and thereby dissolve a comforting commitment.

Conscious resolutions may in fact be the palest of our personal rules, the ones that disturb our feelings the least if they don't succeed. The less someone's belief seems accountable for by the objective facts, the more it's apt to be the representation of an underlying personal rule. Indeed, most people rarely make personal rules in cold blood; as with societal rules, we experience their adoption as "going along with" or "believing in" a cultural assertion. That is, we think of the rule as a physical or social property of the world rather than of our will. Thus individuals and societies can conduct effective prisoner's dilemma–type negotiations without recognizing them as such.

The incentive for this kind of belief isn't accuracy or instrumental efficacy, but commitment to a standard of conduct. The punishment for moderately violating it is whatever forfeit the belief implies; the punishment for massively violating it is disillusionment with the belief itself, which means loss of the extra motivation against impulses that the belief recruits. This loss in turn portends a more arduous task of impulse control in the future. A person may explain her aversive feelings after moderately violating one of these rules as punishment inflicted by a supernatural being, or as guilt, the natural consequence of violating a universal moral law.[4] She may not feel wrong at all, but ill or contaminated. After a massive violation the feeling is more apt to be an unaccountable emptiness. I've known more than one war veteran, for instance, who said that their emotion after their first combat was elation at how easy it was to kill, but that after the war their perception of this ease made it unbearable to live among people. Having obliterated the rule that they previously experienced as a *belief in* the sacredness of human life, they have to struggle not to kill when they get angry.

Now we can make a guess at why the theory of hyperbolic discounting feels wrong at first: Most people *believe in* the rational value structure implied by exponential discounting, which we experience as consistent choice over time. We hold it out as a property of nature, which every normal person will discover in time. It may be just a quibble to say instead that exponential discounting is the inevitable equilibrium point that people largely learn to adopt in their long-range interest after they get experience bargaining with shorter-range interests. But bargaining is something we *do*. People want to characterize value as something we *discern*, for the very reason – my argument goes – that framing the rule as a belief will make it more stable.

To evaluate goods in terms of price, for instance, and to hold a belief that this price *is* what they're worth, is in effect to rule that you won't trade them for something cheaper when you have some spontaneous prompting to do so. Even though we recognize many factors that change a good's price – its scarcity or glut, its fashionableness, indeed its delay – these are social phenomena, barely influenced by my individual appetite. To focus on the objective price rather than on the subjective experience of consuming the good itself stabilizes my behavior toward it. Even allowing for psychological factors to change the price, there's an inertia to it that we find useful, and we're disturbed when a price becomes too responsive to the whims of situation. We think we shouldn't pay $10 for a hamburger when we're very hungry and it's the only one available, but only $3 otherwise, because some social process unresponsive to fluctuations in our appetite has determined that it's "worth" only $3. But sometimes we don't respect even the marketplace itself – when it doesn't reflect something relatively stable in the goods themselves. When the price of an airline ticket doubles with small changes that give the airline the upper hand, people get upset; and when a collectible with no intrinsic value is bid to a high price, we cluck our tongues. In the relatively inflation-free Middle Ages, people even believed that every good had a single, objectively "just" price. Whatever the role of price is in dealing with other people, we also use it as a discipline for our own impulses.

The strength of the cultural wish to let value inhere in goods themselves can be seen in the remarkably robust norm against any discounting at all. It's totally unrealistic, of course, but logic does seem to dictate that insofar as value inheres in things, it shouldn't "really" change with delay. Socrates' complaint that "magnitudes appear larger to your sight when near" assumed that any discounting was an error (see Section 1.1). In the Middle Ages, charging money for the use of money was a sin, according to the Catholic Church, and there have been economists down to the present time who say that we should value a delayed good as much as one that is present, allowance having been made for uncertainty.[5]

What I'm saying is that if you recognize your respect for prices as a mere rule – to act *as if* you discounted goods exponentially – instead of an insight that depends on the properties of the goods themselves, you weaken the very rule you're recognizing. Just as an alcoholic sometimes has to see herself as helpless against alcohol, and abstinence as something absolutely dictated by the fact of her disease, so we seem instinctively to see ourselves as helpless against irrationality and committed by an equal necessity to a belief in the external determination of worth.

I haven't encountered anyone making this argument against acknowledging the instability of worth – to make it would be to lose it,
after all, since it presumes just such an acknowledgment; but when
earlier writers pointed out that the "facts" on which people based moral
norms weren't found in nature, they encountered violent objections on
the grounds that these discoveries would undermine morality: Ockham's
arguments for nominalism got him accused of heresy, Galileo's demonstration of heliocentrism led to a sentence of life imprisonment, and
Darwin's theory of evolution provoked the Scopes "monkey trial" over
its immorality even half a century after his death.

The question of how much the value of a good is constrained by that
good's properties, and thus whether we should talk about the good as
"having" value, is a particular case of a larger debate about whether the
importance of things generally is rooted in their objective properties as
opposed to being constructed by the individual.[6] Hyperbolic discounting
turns out to offer a framework for this argument, which I'll discuss with
the limitations of the will in Chapter 11.

7.2 WOULD INTERTEMPORAL BARGAINING
ABSORB TOO MUCH EFFORT?

A continual process of negotiation would take up great amounts of time,
as compared to simply making a logical decision. However, there's no
reason why a person has to bargain with her future selves continuously,
any more than a corporation or legislature or any other group decision
maker does.

Social groups who regularly come to decisions through negotiation
don't spend most of their time on it. A legislature may debate one bill
through tedious proposals and counterproposals before deciding on it;
but once it has decided, it can leave the issue for years at a time. A new
kid or animal on the block goes through some testing before the old res-
idents decide on her place in the pecking order, but once established,
this place becomes routine. Just as hostile armies fight only a few of their
many possible battles, and merchants would rather divide up most mar-
kets than contest them, a person soon learns which of her motives are
dominant in particular situations and mostly accepts that order of things
thereafter. Once she has discovered which interest can dominate which
other interest in a given situation, she's most apt to take this as a fact and
not spend effort on further testing.

Interests can establish pecking orders just as the members of social groups can, although the person is apt to describe them in other terms, for example, as habit or a hierarchy of values. We get out of bed when a particular program starts on the clock radio, avoid reading magazines at work, or have a cigarette only after meals, not because we estimate freshly the impact of the precedent we would otherwise set, but because we've accepted the outcomes of bygone contests. We may be able to report no more reason than a set of "shoulds" and a vague uneasiness about *not* doing these things – what reason are we conscious of for not running red lights when no one's looking? – but ultimately it had to be intertemporal negotiation that set up that uneasiness. Even if a recovered alcoholic never seriously thinks about drinking, that fact has still been determined by a history of tacit bargaining with herself.

This means that choices don't have to be evaluated continuously, and alternatives that could no longer win a bid for adoption may continue to be chosen without question for some time. However, they'll be unstable and lose out once the person actually reweighs the choice in question.

Readiness to do this reweighing is also probably variable among individuals. Some people seem to feel confined by their plans and to be always looking for evasions. Others seem able to simply decide not to notice the Siren song of doubts and temptations, as if they had blinders they could put on. This latter trait is regularly found in good hypnotic subjects and has been studied under the name "absorption."[7] It's reasonable to assume that people who find it easier to confine their attention – the second of the four committing tactics described in Section 5.1.2 – are less lawyerly in their negotiations with future selves than others are. Nevertheless, the most compulsive doubter still makes most of his choices by "habit."

7.3 DOES ALL YOUR EXPECTATION OF SELF-CONTROL HAVE TO BE STAKED ON EVERY CHOICE?

As I've said before, intertemporal bargaining recruits the most long-range incentive if a whole category of reward is at stake whenever the person makes any choice within the category. The greatest committing effect comes from staking all rewards that are ever threatened by smaller, earlier alternatives against each of those alternatives – that is, by maximizing the size of the category of choices that serve as precedents in one vast intertemporal prisoner's dilemma. In practice, however, it seems to be only in extreme cases that a person stakes her very ability to intend actions at every choice-point. Recovered addicts facing their cravings may do this, as may countries facing the temptation to use a nuclear weapon; but usually there's room for interpretation – for arbitrage – and often the importance of choices as precedents is small compared with their value in themselves.

Of course, many choices are consistent over time because they have a steady incentive and aren't recursive at all – they don't depend on bargaining. Some people go to bed early just because fatigue makes staying up unpleasant. Likewise, consistent choice by members of a population may have nothing to do with a recursive process among them. A group may frequent a particular restaurant because they all like the food; they don't even notice the effect their choice may have on others in the group.

Again, many psychological processes are recursive for reasons other than a need for commitment. You may make it a point to notice where you spontaneously put your umbrella, and deliberately put it in the same place thereafter, just to avoid forgetting where it is. Similarly, you may try to meet other members of a group you're in by going where you've often seen them, knowing that others who are trying to meet you may rely on your doing just that.

However, many choices involve elements of personal or social impulse control mixed in with these nonconflictual motives – perhaps most choices do. A personal rule to put things "in their proper place" may involve self-prediction with regard to your laziness getting out of hand in addition to simply making it easier to find things; and group meeting places may evolve not just to make it easier for members to find each other, but so as to combat the lure of bad places – ones that are morally dubious or that threaten the group's identity.

Wall Street provides a good illustration of how the degree of recursiveness varies with people's strategies. Investors in the stock market are said to be "value-based" insofar as they buy stock according to the intrinsic worth of the company and "portfolio insurers" insofar as they buy on the basis of how they think its price will be affected by the crowd psychology of the market.[8] The motives of most investors are a mixture. A large component of trading based on market prediction per se will make the market volatile because it will "decide" purchases recursively, leading to sudden rises and even sharper crashes, just as the personal

114

decisions that are important mostly as precedents will be subject to sudden "losses of control." By contrast, value-based decisions have little importance as test cases and aren't affected by them either.

For an addicted gambler, a resolution not to go to casinos again may stake her whole expectation of future happiness on never once seeing herself cross the fatal threshold; but the same person's intention to keep her room neat is apt to be highly negotiable from one day to the next. It may retain some influence beyond her momentary, spontaneous wish to neaten the room even if she has had frequent episodes of rationalization, procrastination, and downright failure. Not much is riding on such an intention, but if there's not much resistance to it, it may still play a modest role in her life. Even where the outcomes are very important, for instance where an addicted overeater wants to cut down, the unavailability of a bright line to divide good and bad choices may prevent a large, credible stake from ever forming. As we saw earlier, there's no obvious boundary for eating as there is for drinking some alcohol versus none or using any atomic weapon versus not using it. Without both strong incentives and a believable rationale for testing what precedent is being set, people don't develop the kind of atomic brinksmanship with themselves that gets called an "iron" will.

The greatest incentives to develop iron wills are surely the social norms that elite groups in a society hold. The social codes that these groups teach their children contain specific criteria for good and bad; they teach that not only group acceptance but also personal self-esteem will be lost by any breach. Illustrations are the Calvinist businessmen who saw their expectations of salvation at stake, the various monastic ascetics who saw any physical pleasure as the start of depravity, and the noble Junkers or samurai who were prepared to kill themselves over small losses of honor. These are examples of making all of your important expectations ride on every choice you make. When individuals carry will strategies this far without social support, they're apt to be called pathological, as with compulsive personalities and anorectics; but when social support is added to personal motives, the combination is just esprit de corps.

In more forgiving environments – where there's less social rigidity and no fear of a major addiction – people are more apt to tolerate lapses. We become more like "value-based investors" in that predicting and influencing our intertemporal bargaining climate is a smaller portion of our motive for choice.

An atmosphere of brinksmanship can be dangerous to a personal rule. High stakes can decrease the chances of a personal rule's eventually succeeding. Decades ago, psychologist Alan Marlatt and his coworkers pointed out that failed resolutions get in the way of many alcoholics' recoveries – the "abstinence violation effect."[9] Thus addiction therapists try to tread a middle path, both encouraging resolve and arguing that failure is not disastrous; they recommend guidelines like "one day at a time." But they are confined by the inescapable equation that putting less at stake means having less resolve.

7.4 SUMMARY

Analyzing an activity that's usually second nature does what most observation processes do – distorts it by enlarging some features and factoring out others, so that the resulting picture seems foreign to familiar experience. The way I've presented the intertemporal bargaining model of the will may make it sound more deliberate, more effortful, and more momentous than casual introspection tells us it is: (1) Bargaining is usually thought of as requiring explicit consciousness of its contingencies; but the tacit bargaining that I've hypothesized to engender the will may take place under a number of rubrics – from appeals to the supernatural to the process of belief itself – rubrics that by chance or design disguise the nature of your participation. (2) Bargaining might be thought to require continual alertness; but bargaining may have its most important effect by establishing and only occasionally testing a dominance hierarchy of interests, which then governs choice without much further thought and which may feel just like habit. (3) The most conspicuous examples of bargaining (which I've called "atomic") stake huge incentives on all-or-none choices, as when an addict faces an urge to lapse; but many transactions can be small and largely focused on intrinsic incentives while still having a recursive component. The only faculty you need to recruit the extra motivation that forms willpower is a practical awareness that current decisions predict the pattern of future decisions.

CHAPTER 8

GETTING EVIDENCE ABOUT A
NONLINEAR MOTIVATIONAL SYSTEM

Motivational theory hasn't paid much attention to recursive decision making, possibly because it's hard to study by controlled methods. If a phenomenon is determined by the interaction of A and B, then studying the influence of each while the other is held constant won't reveal the outcome. People who demand to know *the* causes of behavior will be unhappy with a recursive theory, one that says that the sum of individual causes explains little – that outcomes aren't proportional to any input or mixture of inputs, but to the volatile results of their interaction.

However, analysis of recursive decision making should greatly broaden the field that can be studied. That's what happened in economics when analysts moved beyond behaviors that were continuous functions of other variables and began studying decisions as the outcomes of bargaining games.[1] However difficult it is to study nonlinear systems, such systems probably determine the most important features of choice. As one chaos theorist remarked, "nonlinear systems" may be about as extensive as "non-elephant biology."[2]

The best way to study recursive systems is to compare what is known about their behavior with models built of specified mechanisms. Direct experimentation may help, but only in verifying the operation of particular mechanisms. In the case of the will, as with the economy, parts that can be controlled are inseparable from a larger whole that's too complex and weighty to be controlled.

In this chapter I'll compare how the intertemporal bargaining model compares with four other models of will that can be discerned in modern writings, which I mentioned before in the section on private rules (Section 7.1). These models come from widely different intellectual traditions and often leave mechanisms unspecified, but they can be

117

compared at least in their positions on whether or how extra motivation is recruited:

- the "null" theory, that there is no extra motivation, and that will is therefore a superfluous concept.
- the "organ" theory, that the will is an entity characterizable as strong or weak in general and directed rather like a muscle by an independent intelligence.
- the "resolute choice" theory, that the will maximizes conventional utility by a rational avoidance of reconsidering plans but (probably) involves extra motivation.
- the "pattern-seeking" theory, that the will consists of an appreciation of pattern that is intrinsically motivating.

These models contrast with the intertemporal bargaining theory developed here, which bases will on the differential expectations of whole categories of rewards versus single rewards; this, of course, presumes hyperbolic discounting.

The null theory is held by some philosophers, represented in this book by Ryle, and by conventional utility theorists, for whom I've used Gary Becker as the standard bearer. The organ theory is implicit in many of the cognitive psychologists, among whom I've mentioned Baumeister and Kuhl. Resolute choice has recently been proposed by other philosophers, represented by McClennen and Bratman. Intrinsic pattern-seeking seems to be unique to behavioral psychologist Rachlin.[3]

The phenomenon being modeled, will, has suffered from being so familiar that modern authors haven't taken the trouble to define its properties or even work out a common terminology. None of the authors whose theories I'm comparing with intertemporal bargaining even use the word, "will"; I impose it on them because they write about how people make their behavior consistent in the face of temptations, which might be taken as most people's core understanding of what will means.

However, as I mentioned earlier, the Victorian psychologists analyzed what they took to be this common understanding into specific components (Section 5.1.4). I'll use these components as the properties that a theory of will must model. I've added two observations on the variability of two of these properties, making a total of eight characteristics to be accounted for. In addition to these straightforward properties of will, some philosophers have argued extensively about hypothetical situations that amount to thought experiments specifying properties that aren't obvious at first glance. I'll discuss three of these controversies at length, because they seem to give the most dynamic picture of what will must be. First, however, I'll match our five models with the basic eight. The following straightforward properties have been described:

1. The will represents "a new force distinct from the impulses primarily engaged"; that is, it recruits additional motivation beyond what seems to be physically at stake in a given behavior. This would certainly be the effect of choosing in whole bundles, which all theories but the null theory seem to accept.

2. It seems to "throw in its strength on the weaker side . . . to neutralize the preponderance of certain agreeable sensations." If the side that's opposed to the agreeable sensations is the weaker one, then the will throws its strength toward the long-range interests, again not controversial.

3. It acts to "unite . . . particular actions . . . under a common rule," so that "they are viewed as members of a class of actions subserving one comprehensive end." Choosing in molar or global patterns has been the property of will that is most often described. All non-null theories take notice of it, but only hyperbolic discounting explains *why* it should have an anti-impulsive effect (see Section 5.1.4).

4. It is strengthened by repetition. The organ model asserts this, by analogy to exercising a muscle, but it doesn't follow from either the resolute choice or pattern-seeking models. In the bargaining model, repetitions strengthen will by adding evidence predicting cooperation.

5. It is exquisitely vulnerable to nonrepetition, so that "every gain on the wrong side undoes the effect of many conquests on the right"; thus the effects of obeying and disobeying a personal rule aren't symmetrical. Baumeister and Heatherton mention this effect, but don't say why their organ model should predict it; rationality and pattern-seeking models don't mention or predict it. By contrast, the bargaining model is innately asymmetrical, because impulses need become dominant only briefly to cause a defection that greatly reduces your confidence in future cooperation.

6. It involves no repression or diversion of attention, so that "both alternatives are steadily held in view." Organ models often mention controlling attention as a mechanism but also refer to self-monitoring. The other models all accept it; indeed, the null model says that the *only* thing self-regulation requires is a clear view.

7. Resolve doesn't depend precariously on each single choice except where stakes are high and well defined, the case that fits the atomic bargaining pattern that I discussed previously. This variability in how much a person's will tolerates rationalizations and lapses doesn't seem to have been described elsewhere. None of the other theories predicts it.

8. The tendency of a failure in one sphere to precipitate failure in others is also variable, ranging from a spectacular domino effect to a picture of enduring weaknesses coexisting with an otherwise strong will. The organ theory specifically contradicts this frequent contrast, predicting that, since the will is a unitary resource, depletion of its "strength" in one area will lead to failure in others. Rationality and pattern-seeking theories neither contradict nor predict cases of circumscribed weakness. As we'll see, bargaining theory predicts their frequent occurrence (Section 9.1.2, "lapse districts").

8.1 EVIDENCE FROM DIRECT EXPERIMENTS

Experimental evidence that might suggest how these properties arise is scanty but not absent. Interdependent, possibly recursive processes that can operate without observable signs and occur only in humans are particularly difficult to observe. Will is hard to describe by introspection and self-reports about the process of willing, intending, vowing, and so on are always open to alternative interpretations.

Animal models confirm that uniting actions into a common class (property 3) increases the preference for larger, later rewards. Rachlin and Siegel's experiment (Section 5.1.4) showed that pigeons can learn to make their choice consistent when rewarded for doing so, and even keep this trait for a while after the differential reward is no longer in force. This is some of the evidence that Rachlin offers for his pattern-seeking model, but the mechanism for this residual consistency remains unclear. The work of Mazur and others has demonstrated the summation property of hyperbolic curves that's necessary for the intertemporal bargaining theory, and its implication that bundling choices into series will increase the preference for larger, later rewards was verified by my experiment with Monterosso (see Section 5.1.4 and note 20 in Chapter 5).[4]

As for tempting human subjects directly, it would be hard and probably unethical to deploy enough incentive to overcome their willpower experimentally. However, people seem not to bring willpower to bear in small amount-versus-delay experiments, making it possible to study how the contingencies of reward can create will-like patterns. The experiment by Kirby and Guastello that I described earlier (Section 5.1.4) shows that undergraduates prefer larger, later alternatives more when offered bundled series of them than when offered them only singly. Furthermore, when these subjects faced repeated single choices, even suggesting to them that their current choice would predict their future choices produced a modest increase in their preference for larger, later rewards.[5]

These findings in animal and human subjects match property 3 and contradict conventional utility theory (see Figure 5B). The increase in patience that Kirby and Guastello saw when they suggested to their subjects that current choice predicts future choice specifically supports intertemporal bargaining. Furthermore, while none of these findings disproves the other three alternative theories, they all argue for the greater parsimony of intertemporal bargaining: Only intertemporal bargaining *needs* the summation effect to account for why choosing in bundles should lead to self-control. Furthermore, the summation phenomenon offers a way that your will can arise from simple discounting, given only the perceptual acuity to notice your own choices as precedents. The other theories all rely on additional principles – that there is an organ of will or some kind of innate aversion to either reexamining or disrupting your plans.

8.2 EVIDENCE FROM AN INTERPERSONAL ANALOG

A further advantage of an intertemporal bargaining theory is that some facets can be tested in interpersonal bargaining games to see how well these facets predict the properties analogous to will. The interaction of internal interests will have many of the same components as the interaction of individual people or even corporations. To the extent that successive frames of mind pose the same strategic problems as separate bargainers, it should be possible to study the logic of this choice-making by looking at interpersonal bargaining.

Can a repeated prisoner's dilemma give a small group or pair of negotiators something like a shared will? That is, can it give them a pattern of choices that improves their payoffs over what they would get in one-shot prisoner's dilemmas and that has the properties that the Victorians named? In research that I'm now doing, two to four adult male volunteers take turns choosing between a larger number of points (exchangeable for money at session's end) just for themselves and a smaller number of points that each player would get equally. This game doesn't model the intertemporal discounting mechanism as well as the single pass through a roomful of people that I described earlier (Section 3.2), but it is much more practical for controlled experiments.

Typically, player A chooses between 100 points for herself and 70 points each for herself and player B. Then B makes a similar choice, then A again, and so on, for an unpredictable number of turns that varies between 100 and 250 in each game. Choosing the smaller amount for everyone could be called cooperation, and choosing the larger amount just for oneself defection, although in the explanation to the subjects it's called "going it alone." The players don't know each other and never meet; they play on computer terminals in separate buildings and are told that they should try to maximize their individual earnings. The same pair plays five games a day, for three or four days in a row, before breaking up. No subject is ever used again, so that each pair starts with no prior experience of the game.

Of course, the crucial element of intertemporal bargaining – the element that makes it necessary, after all – is the effect of delay, and delay can't be a meaningful factor in these games. However, the reward that player A gets for player B's cooperation is smaller than the reward that A gets for her own defection, thus modeling the intertemporal bargainer's discounted interest in each future choice. Player A clearly does better the more she can get B to cooperate. She does best if she can get B to cooperate while currently defecting herself, but her defections endanger B's continuing cooperation. Her incentive to try occasional defections models the options facing the intertemporal bargainer who is always tempted to defect "just this once."

If the players faced these contingencies only once and never expected to meet again, they would have a strong incentive to defect, as in the standard single-play prisoner's dilemma (introduction to Chapter 6). Thus the mere introduction of repetition creates properties 1 and 2 from our list: The expectation of possible cooperation adds extra incentive to cooperate, and adds it to the hitherto weaker side, which is in each player's longer-range interest.[6]

Furthermore, the game creates these properties by means of establishing property 3, uniting actions under a common rule: The most important incentive that now faces the players at each choice is to make sure that the other player(s) see them as following suit in a series of related cooperations; when the players cooperate, this incentive must have been enough to overcome the spread between the outcomes that are literally at stake in a given choice: 100 for the self-only option but only 70 for the cooperative option.

Property 4, strengthening by repetition, is observable in the interpersonal situation, although it's hardly surprising. In an experiment I did with Pamela Toppi Mullen, Barbara Gault, and John Monterosso, the computer waited until pairs of subjects showed a consistent preference by cooperating on five successive pairs of moves, and then sometimes told each that the other had defected on the last move. Sometimes the computer repeated this false information for two pairs of moves, or three, or four, so that the effect of zero to four reported defections on the subjects' real choices could be studied. We looked at how breaking up the runs of reported cooperation by a partner reduced the likelihood of a subject's cooperating on her next turn. The results are shown in Figure 8A. The more ostensible defections by the partner, the more likely the subject was to defect himself.[7]

Property 5, that lapses have more impact than observances (cooperations), is also testable, and the outcome is less intuitively obvious. In the experiment just described, the effect of opposite moves was studied not only on a cooperative tendency but also on a tendency to defect. When subjects had defected on five pairs of turns in a row, the computer reported from zero to four false cooperations (Figure 8B). Subject pairs were much less likely to return to their previous levels of cooperation after reported defections than to return to a pattern of defection after reported cooperations, and this effect endured after the false reporting had stopped. That is, property 5 seems to be true of bargaining in pairs of players: One defection undoes the effect of several cooperations.[8]

Property 6, that the increase in self-control doesn't depend on incomplete information or deception, is clearly true of intertemporal bargaining.

Property 7, variable sensitivity to lapses depending on the stakes, was also seen, by observing at the low-motivation end of the spectrum. These experiments have a novel, gamelike atmosphere and low stakes; accordingly, a subject usually forgives single defections. He does so even though he has no basis for choosing other than what he concludes from the other subject's behavior.

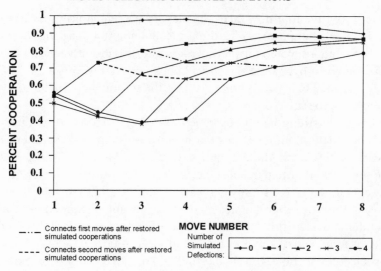

Figure 8A. Rates of cooperation after false information that the player's partner has defected on 1, 2, 3, or 4 successive turns, or not at all (continuation of baseline), followed by false information that the player's partner has cooperated on 7, 6, 5, 4, or 8 turns, respectively. The player makes a total of eight moves based on false information.

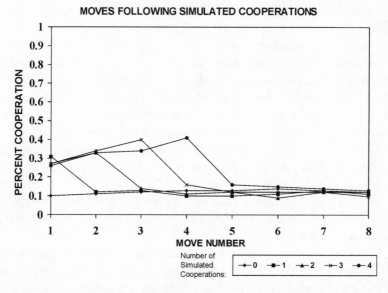

Figure 8B. Rates of cooperation after false information that the player's partner has cooperated on 1, 2, 3, or 4 successive turns, or not at all (continuation of baseline), followed by false information that the partner has defected on 7, 6, 5, 4, or 8 turns, respectively. The player makes a total of eight moves based on false information.

Table 3. Properties of Will: Fit with Observations

	Null	Organ	Resolute	Pattern	Bargaining	Match
New distinct force	C	P	P	P	P	Y
Strength to the weaker side	C	P	P	P	P	Y
Unites under a common rule	C	?	P	P	P	Y
Strength through repetition	C	P	N	N	P	Y
Asymmetrical vulnerability	C	?	N	N	P	Y
No diversion of attention	P	?	P	P	P	Y
Variable effect of a lapse	N	N	N	N	P	Y
Circumscribed weaknesses	N	C	N	N	P	?
Rational to drink toxin	C	N	C	N	P	
Sensitive dependence	C	C	C	C	P	
Diagnosis becomes cause	C	C	C	C	P	

Null = null theory of will; Organ = organ theory; Resolute = resolute choice theory; Pattern = pattern-seeking theory; Bargaining = intertemporal bargaining theory; Match = whether interpersonal bargaining behavior matches a property of will; C = contradicts; N = no prediction; P = predicts; ? = unclear from the theory; Y = yes, i.e., bargaining results show this property.

Property 8, a variable tendency of lapses in one area to cause lapses in other areas, is testable in principle but hasn't been explored in our bargaining experiments.

Observations of interpersonal bargaining behavior reveal a similarity between cooperation in repeated prisoner's dilemmas and the properties that have been ascribed to the will. This similarity supports the intertemporal bargaining hypothesis of will and opens the way to exploring some aspects of the will with interpersonal analogs.

These predictions, and the limited testing of intertemporal bargaining, are listed in Table 3. So are three more intricate tests, which I'll discuss presently.

8.3 EVIDENCE FROM THOUGHT EXPERIMENTS ON INTENTION

While some direct experimentation seems to be possible, Jon Elster's recent comment on another elusive phenomenon, emotion, seems also to be true of will-like processes: "I do not by any means exclude controlled studies or systematic observations as sources of knowledge about the emotions, yet if we want to understand the emotions as *the stuff of life* . . . they take second place."[9] However, ordinary introspection hasn't advanced our understanding of the will beyond what the Victorians described. Fortunately, it's possible to define special cases related to will that bring out revealing inconsistencies in common assumptions about it. This has been the genius of philosophy. Philosophers' discussion methods turn out to be uniquely valuable for exploring the implications of limited warfare among successive motivational states. Their convention of finding a thought experiment that can be agreed upon as expressing the major properties of a problem, and confronting different theories of the problem with this experiment, has been especially useful for clarifying the necessary elements of will.[10]

Philosophers repeatedly push the conventional model of intentionality (= will) to its logical limits and have thus condensed its problems into a few concise paradigms. Three are particularly illustrative: Kavka's problem, the question of free will, and Newcomb's problem.

8.3.1 Kavka's Problem

In Kavka's problem a person is offered a large sum of money just to intend to drink an overwhelmingly noxious but harmless toxin. Once she has sincerely intended it, as verified by a hypothetical brain scan, she's free to collect the money and not actually drink the toxin.[11] Philosophical discussion has revolved around whether the person has any motive to actually drink the toxin once she has the money and whether, foreseeing a lack of such motive, she can sincerely intend to drink it in the first place, even though she would drink it if that were still necessary to get the money.

Kavka's problem poses the question: Are the properties of intention such that a person can move it about effortlessly from moment to moment, the way she raises and lowers an arm, and if not, what factors constrain changes of intention? Wholly unconstrained changes would make intention seem no different from the imagining of intention. The problem makes it clear that intention must include a forecast of whether you'll carry it out; but this would seem to make it impossible to intend to drink the toxin, since mere forecasting leaves the intention powerless against a sudden change of incentive, even one that's entirely predictable. In that case, Ulysses couldn't intend to sail past the Sirens unaided, and Kavka's subject couldn't intend to drink the toxin, since they couldn't expect to fulfill their intentions.

This outcome doesn't make sense, however. Not only do we sometimes intend things when we don't expect the intention to succeed – a hopeless alcoholic can still intend to stop drinking – but also the intention itself feels like part of what determines whether it will succeed. In common speech, intention is an active process, not just observation, although it may sometimes be too feeble to achieve its ends. And yet, if a person were an exponential discounter, what role beyond forecasting could a process like intention ever play?

A conventional utility theorist can't solve the toxin problem, since she must regard intention, like will, as a fanciful concept, and thus believe that only her self-prediction will show on the brain scan. She'd have to accept the seeming paradox that it may be impossible to intend an act that, at the time of intending (= forecasting), is strongly motivated. Philosophers have sometimes balked at this conclusion, but have been able to come up with little rational incentive to drink the toxin: only "savings with respect to decision-making costs" and the promising but vague "need to coordinate" successive decisions.[12]

However, if will is an intertemporal bargaining situation, an answer is at hand: Intending is the classification of an act as a precedent for a series of similar acts, so that the person stakes the prospective value of this series – perhaps, in the extreme, the value of all the fruits of all intentions whatsoever – on performing the intended action in the case at hand. Thus the person could meaningfully intend to drink the toxin, but only because she couldn't subsequently change her mind with impunity.

If I resolve to donate bone marrow painfully to a friend with leukemia but then renege, I haven't gotten away with stealing altruistic pleasure during the period that my resolution was in force. My failure to go through with it has reduced the credibility of my intending and hence the size of the tasks I can subsequently intend. My willpower has suffered an injury, perhaps a costly one. Thus Kavka's subject does have an incentive to follow her original intention once she has the money: preservation of the credibility of her will; whether this incentive is adequate to overcome the approaching noxiousness of the toxin doesn't matter for purposes of the illustration. Will, in short, is a bargaining situation where credibility is power. How a person perceives this bargaining situation is the very thing that determines how consistently she'll act over time.

We can make the thought experiment more realistic by using an example where something like Kavka's brain scanner really exists: when a person's estimate of what she herself is about to do occasions emotions. Say you're a mediocre movie actor, and a director casts you, with some misgivings, to play a pipsqueak who gets sent down a terrifying toboggan run. You don't have to go down the run yourself – the director is perfectly happy to have one of his stunt men do it – but you have to play a scene right beforehand in which you're frightened out of your wits. You realize you can't fake the necessary emotion, but also that you are genuinely terrified of the toboggan run. The role is your big break, but if you can't do it convincingly the director will fire you.

Under these circumstances, you think it's worth signing up to do the run yourself in order to ace the previous scene. But if, after playing this scene, you find out that you can still chicken out of the toboggan run, is it rational to stick to your plan? There are two reasons why it might be:

- If the panicky anticipation scene might have to be shot over, and you had chickened out of the run the first time, it would be hard for you to believe any intention to go through with it next time. That is, you'd inescapably see this choice as a precedent predicting your own future choices.
- Even if you knew that the scene was a wrap, but you had resolved to go through with the run unconditionally, you'd weaken the credibility of your resolve if you chickened out. There might be similar scenes in the future, or just equally big challenges to your resolve, and your most reasonable expectation (assuming that the toboggan run was the most salient example so far) would be that your resolve would wilt. Of course, the cost of this loss of credibility would have to be assessed separately from the value of keeping this movie role; your credibility might or might not also be worth the agony. This is another instance of a single two-way choice creating something of an atmosphere of brinksmanship.

Kavka's contribution has been to create a conceptual irritant that can't be removed until we supply a piece that is missing from conventional assumptions about intention. The piece I suggest is credibility, the stake that you add to a mere plan to keep yourself from reneging on it. To add a piece like this may be cheating; I imagine that Kavka envisioned philosophers working with only the elements he gave. But the theoretical problem may not have been a Chinese puzzle with a hidden solution, but a card game that we have been playing without a full deck.

The fact that an intertemporal bargaining model can fill out the deck provides empirical support for its importance in will.

As we've seen, drinking the toxin is irrational under the null theory and the resolute choice theory. The organ and pattern-seeking theories seem to make no prediction about it. Only intertemporal bargaining makes it affirmatively rational.

8.3.2 Freedom of Will

Freedom of the will is a much more venerable puzzle. Its continuing provocativeness has come from our discomfort with both the idea that our choices are entirely caused by conditions that existed from the beginning of time and the idea that something can be uncaused. Modern positions called "compatibilism" have tended to fudge the obvious impossibility of rejecting both of these ideas. Like the cognitivists and the conventional utility theorists we discussed in Chapter 1, the two sides each seem to suffer from a missing piece.

Advocates of free will have been reduced to appealing to the physical indeterminacy of subatomic particles to give it a place in a generally causal universe, although unpredictability at that level has no obvious relationship to the experience of free will. As the philosopher James Garson put it:

> A conception of freedom that entails personal responsibility is badly served by loosening the bonds between reasons and actions.[13]

On the other hand, advocates of determinism fail to supply an intuitively believable way to account for the experience of making a free choice.

Again, I'll suggest that intertemporal bargaining can supply a practical piece to fill the gap. In fact, the argument between determinism and free will seems to be an example of the reward-versus-cognition debate, which may have dragged on for lack of a rationale for intertemporal bargaining. In the free will debate, the missing piece would be the recursive self-predictive process that makes us unable to predict even our own minds with certainty.

This unpredictability has often been held to be the crux of free will. In William James's famous example, for instance, it was *not knowing* what his own behavior would be in advance – for example, whether he would walk home on Oxford Street or Divinity Avenue – that characterized his decision as free. Yet most proponents of free will would require that a free choice be unknowable *in principle* from external determinants. They depict choices that are knowable and merely unknown as unfree. Doubtless this call comes partly from the eerie implication that, if your choice is knowable, someone else *could* know it – an evil genius, say, or an omniscient God, or a perfected science of psychology. Another part of the reason for rejecting determinism has been that, if your choices are foreknowable even in principle, they seem to bypass you; you have no apparent role in forming them.[14] These are the objections that a recursive self-prediction theory must answer.

This is the same dilemma that has dogged strict utility theory. If your choice is entirely determined by your estimated utility, you never really *decide* anything; you only discern incentives. By contrast, a basic characteristic of cognitivism is the reservation of ultimate choice to an imponderable ego. Some cognitivists acknowledge that cognitions must act by brokering emotions, as the philosopher d'Holbach first described it two hundred years ago: "Reason . . . is nothing but the act of choosing those passions which we must follow for the sake of our happiness." But this still requires that part of the psyche that is the broker to move passions but to be unmoved by them. This ego is like a sailor or canoeist, who navigates by balancing forces stronger than her own, but still does so with some force not derived from the wind or current.[15]

If I'm shooting rapids in a canoe, the force of the water is much stronger than my arms. I can choose only which current will bear me along.[16] But the strength I steer with is still my own and is unrelated to the force of the water. To model strict utility theory, a canoeist would also have to steer by the force of the rushing water, which would mean that the rationale of the steering choices would somehow have to use the logic of rushing water, not the extraneous wishes of a person floating on it. The ultimate dilemma of the utility theorist is how to describe such a steering mechanism without making it seem improbable that the person whose will it represented would feel human – that she would experience authentic doubt, self-esteem, and other subtle feelings, particularly the one we're now discussing: freedom of will. Such a description has, in effect, to evoke the feeling of being a canoeist from the logic of the water – a challenge perhaps as great as proposing how life itself arose from inorganic matter.

Going on conventional assumptions, any maximizer seems like a mere calculating machine, a throughput.[17] However, in an intertemporal bargaining model, will is a recursive process. This idea supplies an answer both to the need for unpredictability in principle and to the participation of the self in the process of determination. The person herself can't be absolutely sure of what she'll do in the future and makes her present choice based on her best prediction. But this choice also affects her prediction, so that before she has acted on her choice she may predict again, and may then change her previous prediction and thus her choice. A recovering alcoholic may expect to resist taking a drink, but this expectation surprisingly disappoints her, and when she notices this she loses some confidence in her expectation; if her expectation falls below being enough to stake against her thirst, her disappointment is apt to become a self-confirming prophecy. But if this prospect is itself daunting enough in the period before it becomes preferred, she'll look for other incentives to oppose her thirst before it becomes too strong, and thus raise her expectation of not drinking, and so on – all before she's actually taken a drink. Her choice is doubtless determined in advance, in the same sense that all events have strict causes that have causes in turn; but what immediately determines her choice is the interplay of elements that, even if well known in themselves, make the outcome unpredictable when they interact recursively.

Hyperbolic discounting makes decision making a crowd phenomenon, with the crowd made up of the successive dispositions to choose that the individual has over time. At each moment she makes the choice that looks best for her; but a big part of this picture is her expectation of how she'll choose at later times, an expectation that is mostly founded on how she has chosen at previous times. At any given moment she's thus both free to choose, in the sense that she can follow her current inclination, and unfree, in the sense that she *must* follow this inclination. Given this constraint, she'll usually follow the crowd – that is, follow the path beaten by her own previous choices. However, she may sometimes lead the crowd, by finding a new principle of choice that she can expect herself to follow in the future if she follows it now, despite a history of contrary choices.

Participation in the acts of this crowd of successive choice-makers is an extremely self-referential process, hidden from the outside observer and even from the person herself facing it in advance. She can never be sure how she herself will choose as she tries to follow this crowd and also lead it from within; she may read a small sign of faltering as her cue to bail out – that is, to stop cooperating with later selves on a given plan – just as investors may see a small hike in interest rates as

131

a signal to start a massive selloff. Or she may not. She won't know until it happens.

The recursive prediction process might seem too time-consuming to be the basis of decisions that are made in split seconds. To review my past choices and then take an introspective reading on my own behavioral tendency, then to forecast what this predicts for the future and to revise my current wish – and then perhaps to repeat the process to correct for this revision – sounds like it would occupy congressional periods of time. But this process certainly doesn't take place at the verbal level; if it did, it would be more reportable. It doubtless takes place in the mind's short-hand, the thing that you're aware of knowing at moments when you "can't find the word for it," the code that, if the mind were a computer, would be called "machine language."

A recursive process among people provides an example: Members of an audience may want to applaud a performance at certain places, but no one wants to be caught applauding alone. Before starting to applaud, each member must predict whether other members will applaud at this particular moment; a bold member may even estimate whether, at a borderline occasion, they will applaud *if* she applauds. Each person then either begins to applaud or does not. The audience as a whole makes this recursive, self-referential decision in a fraction of a second. And it does so efficiently; it's uncommon, though not rare, to hear individuals start to applaud alone. Similarly, strangers passing on a walk decide recursively whether to acknowledge each other or not, perhaps in scores of examples on a single excursion. Forecasting your own future choices should need no more time than this, and no other process besides a recursively updated estimate of your disposition to choose.

The will maneuver – intertemporal bargaining in a prisoner's dilemma framework – makes behavior "chaotic" in the technical sense of the term. Several authors have suggested that the analysis of internally fed-back events known as "chaos theory" might be applicable to psychology, but they haven't found a central example of the phenomenon.[18] Intertemporal bargaining seems to be the process in which such internal feedback becomes important. It creates shifting combinations that couldn't be predicted from mere summation of the relevant motives. Behavior becomes like the weather – often predictable in the immediate future if you have a good knowledge of its driving forces, but subject to sudden shifts that can't be predicted from a distance. As Garson says, "chaotic events are unpredictable not because they are arbitrary, but because they are information-rich."[19]

Of course, mere dependence on internally fed-back processes doesn't create the feeling of being a self:

> If chaos-type data can be used to justify the existence of free will in humans, they can also be used to justify the existence of free will in chaotic pendulums, weather systems, leaf distribution, and mathematical equations.[20]

That is, even information-rich processes that don't somehow engage what feels like our self will still be experienced as random, "more like epileptic seizures than free responsible choices."[21] So far, chaos theory has not been given an element that internalizes the process.

I'm arguing that intertemporal bargaining supplies that extra element: that your own motivation – in many cases emotion – is what you're predicting. In conventional accounts, will is an irreducible process that doesn't need to predict itself, and indeed couldn't:

> Making a decision and predicting that decision are mental states that exclude each other in the same mind, since making a decision implies, by the very meaning of the term, uncertainty as to what one is going to do.[22]

But hyperbolic discounting turns predicting a decision into an integral part of making that decision. Indeed, the only thing that differentiates *making* decisions from following whims becomes discernment of the self-referential consequences that are at stake, that is, your expectations of future reward. In the words of chaos theory, free decisions are those that are "sensitively dependent" on the steps taken by the person herself toward deciding.

It's the prominence of the person's recursive intertemporal bargaining process that reconciles free will and determinism. Although clearly pulled by identifiable motives, a person's choice in such a process can't be predicted with certainty, even by the person herself. Nevertheless, choice is as strictly determined as the weather and, like the weather, must depend on causes that reach back infinitely far:

> The first morning of creation wrote
> What the last dawn of reckoning shall read. (Omar Khayyam)

This is the onrushing stream that must generate the canoeist as well as push the canoe. The feeling of responsibility that you have for your choice but not for the weather comes from the fact that the causation of your choice is mediated by genuine intertemporal bargaining, and your own future selves will punish defections before society even begins to debate your guilt.

The fact that intertemporal bargaining can produce the experiential elements of free will without violating strict determinism doesn't prove that it *is* the mechanism of free will. Conversely, its ability to reconcile these two of our most heartfelt but seemingly inconsistent beliefs doesn't prove that it occurs. Nevertheless, the properties of free will that have emerged from the numerous introspections on the subject provide a test for parsimony if nothing else, a test that favors the intertemporal bargaining solution. All the other theories of will seem to have no place for the sensitive dependence of future choices upon the present one.

8.3.3 Newcomb's Problem

The difficulty of reconciling free will and determinism in the absence of a rationale for recursive decision making is well summarized in another seeming paradox of choice. The philosopher Robert Nozick named it "Newcomb's problem" after the physicist, William Newcomb, who suggested it to him. As he recently summarized it:

> A being in whose power to predict your choices correctly you have great confidence is going to predict your choice in the following situation. There are two boxes, B1 and B2. Box B1 contains $1,000; box B2 contains either $1,000,000 ($M) or nothing. You have a choice between two actions: (1) taking what is in both boxes; (2) taking only what is in the second box. Furthermore, you know, and the being knows you know, and so on, that if the being predicts you will take what is in both boxes, he does not put the $M in the second box; if the being predicts you will take only what is in the second box he does put the $M in the second box. First the being makes his prediction; then he puts the $M in the second box or not, according to his prediction; then you make your choice. (Nozick, 1993, p. 41)

Since the money is already in place before you make your choice, orthodox decision theory says that you should choose (1) – both boxes – and get $1,000 more than if you chose (2), whatever the being had decided. The problem is that you believe the being to have anticipated this and to have left nothing in B2; since you feel perfectly able to choose B2 alone, and can believe the being to have anticipated this as well, you may increase your present expectation by choosing B2.[23]

By positing a being that can predict your choices, this problem again raises the question of predestination, the most unsettling implication of determinism. If all events, including your choices, are strictly determined by the events that have gone before, then both belief in free will and efforts to exert willpower may be superstitious – just self-deceiving efforts to make yourself more optimistic about outcomes that are out of your hands. In a world without hyperbolic discounting and hence without recursive choice-making, this conclusion seems inescapable. However, the recursive nature of the volition process bridges the distinction between diagnostic and causal acts.

Diagnostic acts are symptoms of a condition but don't cause it, as when smoking is a sign of nervousness; causal acts bring on the condition, as when smoking causes emphysema. Acts governed by will are evidently both diagnostic and causal. Smoking may be diagnostic of inadequate willpower; but seeing herself smoke causes further smoking when the person, using it to gauge how strong her will is, gives up trying to stop. Like most of the great philosophic paradoxes, Newcomb's problem isn't an idle exercise but puts a major psychological problem in a nutshell. In fact this problem had already been described, and on a grander scale.

The great sociologist Max Weber puzzled over how Calvinist theology could have increased its adherents' self-control when it preached predestination, that is, when it held people to be helpless as to whether they would be saved or damned. His solution was, in effect, that the doctrine of predestination transformed a person's array of individual choices about whether to do good into a single, comprehensive personal side bet, the stake of which was her whole expectation of being saved:

> [Good works] are the technical means, not of purchasing salvation, but of getting rid of the fear of damnation. . . . [The Calvinist] himself creates his own salvation, or, as would be more correct, the conviction of it. But this creation cannot, as in Catholicism, consist in a gradual accumulation of individual good works to one's credit, but rather in a systematic self-control which at every moment stands before the inexorable alternative, chosen or damned.[24]

Under such a belief system, orthodox decision theory would hold doing good to be a superstitious behavior, in that it's purely diagnostic, so that doing it for the sake of seeing yourself do it is fooling yourself.[25] It would be like choosing only box B2. However, the authors who have pointed this out don't consider an important possibility: that the motive to get a good diagnosis was itself part of the mechanism by which destiny worked – that God's grace *consisted of* a strong motive to believe you were saved. In other words, good works were actually a causative factor of your predestined fate, but only the continuing fear that you were destined to be damned motivated enough works to save you, and only some people were given the capacity for this fear. If extra good works constituted cheating on the test, they did not invalidate it; in fact, only those who had it in them to cheat this way could do well enough to be saved. It was a recursive system: Diagnosis → behavior → diagnosis, where giving up on the good diagnosis led to giving up on the behavior, which made the bad diagnosis correct.[26]

A higher power will grant sobriety to some alcoholics, and that acknowledgment of your helplessness against alcohol is a sign that you may be one of those who'll receive this favor. Such a shift in your concept of causality is not casuistry. It marks the formation of a wider personal rule – staking your expectation of salvation itself against each temptation. Furthermore, the shift from seeing it as a matter of willpower – "good works" – to seeing it as mere diagnosis of a preexisting condition – your destiny – strengthens your resolve rather than weakens it: Your concern with diagnosis isn't superstitious but rational, as we've just seen, since diagnosis has causal effects; and furthermore, interpreting this concern as without causal efficacy rather than as an element of bargaining deters the arbitrage that usually compromises conscious exercises of will.

The celebrated James–Lange theory of emotion also seems to have been based on the observation of recursive decision making: When a person is in doubt about whether she'll succumb to a negative emotion (or achieve a positive one), the appearance of a physical manifestation of the emotion will be evidence that the emotion is gaining ground, evidence that may, like the alcoholic's first drink, throw the decision beyond the zone of balance. "He anticipates certain feelings, and the anticipation precipitates their arrival." Darwin had said the same thing:

> The free expression by outward signs of an emotion intensifies it. On the other hand, the repression, as far as this is possible, of all outward signs softens our emotions. He who gives way to violent gestures will increase

his rage; he who does not control the signs of fear will experience fear in greater degree.[27]

That is, the person does not emit a simple behavior, either an emotion followed by physical signs or physical signs followed by an emotion, but rather makes a series of predictions about the apparent strength of an emotion vis-à-vis his controls – predictions that tend to be self-confirming.

Muscle behavior itself may be governed recursively. Neurophysiologist Benjamin Libet has observed that a "readiness potential" in the brain not only precedes voluntary movement, but precedes a person's awareness of her intention of voluntary movement, by 550 milliseconds and 350 milliseconds, respectively."[28] As Libet points out, her awareness of the intention occurs long enough before the action that she could modify or abort the action, so that the effect is genuinely voluntary. Nevertheless, the whole process appears as an unconscious instigation followed by a perception that could be called a self-prediction, which may be followed in turn by one or more responses to this self-prediction – a sequence exactly analogous to the James–Lange theory of emotion.

Here again, passive perception and active choice are blurred into a single process that gives some of the experience of each. The seemingly farfetched premise of Newcomb's problem grabs our interest because it's another way of zeroing in on that large and mysterious stake we sense to be operating during volition. Several writers have pointed out that Newcomb's problem has most of the features of a prisoner's dilemma.[29] Like the prisoner's dilemma, it's easily solvable in a repeated format, but seems to demand a counterintuitive move analogous to mutual defection – choosing both boxes – when presented as a single play. The condition of Newcomb's problem – that an omniscient being knows "what kind of person you are" – is just another way of representing the mysterious stake of expectation that makes choice consistent over time.

If you're the "kind of person" who takes one box – that is, if taking one box would consistently be your intention in this circumstance – but then you manage to step out of character and take two, you'll win bigger, but something feels unaccountably wrong with that choice. I suggest that it's the same thing that would feel wrong if the problem were changed to Kavka's format: To put the million in box B2 you must only intend to take the single box, but having fully intended to do so, you can take both boxes and get $1,001,000. The question of whether you can intend fully under those expectations is almost the question of whether you can defeat a truly omniscient being; but in the Newcomb form you project the contingencies onto an outsider, and thus make the "cooperative" move seem superstitious while not really believing that it is. In both cases you feel that you need to cooperate, but lack a rationale for this to make sense under utility theory. Indeed, all of the other theories of will say this would be irrational.

Newcomb's offer has the same arithmetic as the temptation to hedge on a personal rule: If you're the kind of person who sticks to her rules, you'll have faith in the presence of the $M and also avoid the temptation to try for both the sure $1,000 *and* the $M; likewise, on a diet, you'll have faith that sticking to it will make you thin (cf. the $million), and avoid the chance to claim an exception "just this once" (cf. the $1,000), which, if well justified, could give you the present food *and* the expectation of being thin. On the other hand, if you're a chiseler, you'll try for $1,001,000, and the exception to your diet. Furthermore, your realistic view of yourself probably tells you which kind of person you are, so that the single-box solution leads to continued rule-following and the two-box solution leads down the slippery slope to no will. This view is apt to be one that you don't acknowledge to yourself (see Section 9.1.3). Attribute it to an omniscient power and you have what feels like personal predestination.

This equation of Kavka and Newcomb ignores some of the distinctions present in the original problems, but from the picoeconomic point of view, these puzzles have done their work: to show up the awkwardness of the assumptions on which these problems were based, which led to these very distinctions. These puzzles start with our common-sense assumption that intention is an irreducible, impenetrable black box, the properties of which must be deduced by its input and output; but this process of deduction produces absurdities and thus calls this very assumption into question. If we also know about hyperbolic discount curves, we can use these thought experiments to conceive something very different from a box – more of a brokerage process – which is hard to dissect, not because it has impenetrable walls but because it's recursive.

Kavka and Newcomb express opposite ends of the spectrum of how the will can be experienced: Kavka expresses how a significant precedent can set your will on a course upward or downward. Newcomb expresses the suspicion that despite the seeming freedom of your choices, they're actually driven by expectations of your own conduct that have already formed and hardened. We experience both poles from time to time and mostly hang ambiguously in the middle.

This spectrum of willfulness is created by differences in the degree to which your own behaviors, and thus your expectations of your behaviors, are fed back into the process of evaluating your options: from mere expectation ("I'll probably A, but I'm open to whims") to intention ("I'll try to A, but at this point I don't care if I change my mind") to effort ("I'll try to keep from changing my mind, but it won't be a disaster if I do") to resolution ("I'll stake much of my expectation of being able to resolve things on my doing A"). This is not a smooth continuum, but depends on the topography of the choice involved – where there are possible distinctions that could be used for rationalizations.

8.4 SUMMARY

If we regard as will whatever it is we do to make our choices more consistent in the face of temptation, it's possible to find five distinct models of it in the literature of motivational science – mostly in philosophy and psychology. I match the implications of each model with eight properties that characterize the common experience of will, using experimental findings where these exist. I also see how these models handle three controversial thought experiments that have pinpointed problems with conventional assumptions about will.

The null model, in which will is superfluous, is contradicted by almost all evidence. The organ model, which rather vaguely depicts the will as a faculty deployed by a person like an arm or leg, is silent on most tests but is contradicted by observations that weakness of will can be specific to particular kinds of choice and by evidence of recursive choice-making. The resolute choice model, in which the will acts just by inhibiting reconsideration of plans, and the pattern-seeking model, which similarly says that people are innately averse to breaking up long-range motivational patterns for the sake of short-range ones, are at least consistent with the eight properties but are contradicted by evidence of recursive choice-making. The intertemporal bargaining model that I have been describing actively predicts the eight straightforward properties of the will and the ability of interpersonal bargaining analogs to re-create them. Intertemporal bargaining not only predicts but depends on the increase in preference for larger, later rewards that comes from summing hyperbolic discount curves, and suggests definitive solutions to the seeming paradoxes in the three thought experiments.

PART III

THE ULTIMATE BREAKDOWN OF WILL:
NOTHING FAILS LIKE SUCCESS

CHAPTER 9

THE DOWNSIDE OF WILLPOWER

My mind seems to have become a kind of machine for grinding general laws out of large collections of facts, but why this should have caused the atrophy of that part of the brain alone, on which the higher tastes depend, I cannot conceive.

Darwin, *Recollections*

If your morals make you dreary, depend upon it they are wrong. I do not say "give them up," for they may be all you have; but conceal them like a vice. . . .

Robert Louis Stevenson, *A Christmas Sermon (Part II)*

All self-control devices can impair your reward-getting effectiveness: If you have yourself tied to a mast, you can't row; if you block attention or memory, you may miss vital information; and if you nip emotion in the bud, you'll become emotionally cold. Unfortunately, personal rules, which are the most powerful and flexible strategy against the effects of hyperbolic discounting, also have the greatest potential for harming your longest-range interests.

9.1 SIDE EFFECTS OF WILLPOWER

Suspicions of the will are fairly recent. Recognition of a will-like process that can oppose the promptings of impulse goes back to the classical Greeks, but until modern times it was regarded as an undiluted blessing. For example, Aristotle described not only passions that could overcome people suddenly, but also countervailing "dispositions." These are forces that develop through consistent choice (habit) in one direction and subsequently impel further choice in that direction. He was clearly rooting for these dispositions to win out.

Later generations shared Aristotle's mistrust of passion and opted for maximal controls. At the end of the eighteenth century, Kant was still saying much of what Aristotle had said. He depicted an egolike part of the will, the *wilkur,* which can let itself be led in one direction by impulses and in the other by personal maxims for conduct (the content of the *wille*). He said that choice in either direction creates a disposition that impels further choice in that direction, and that the best course was to use the *wille* to embrace an inflexible moral law.

Even in modern times, willpower is often valued uncritically. For instance, both Piaget and Kohlberg, the two authors who most studied the development of moral judgment in children, thought its highest stage was an ability to choose the principles that will bind you.[1] Many writers have recognized two opposing forces that coerce the ego, but they've endorsed the "higher" coercion, by principles, as a complete solution to the problem created by the lower.

However, a number of modern writers have warned that your sense of will may decrease rather than increase if you bind yourself too extensively to rules. Kant and Hegel had barely finished describing how people should make all particular choices according to universal, rational standards when Kierkegaard began to point out how this kind of rationality could erode the vitality of experience. Kierkegaard's ideas developed into existentialism. A perception that gives your current choice more importance as a precedent than as something in itself threatens existential values such as authenticity and living in the present. Existential therapists have called it an "idealistic orientation" – an overly theoretical approach to life. They've rated this as an improvement over the pursuit of transient pleasure, but say that it's still inauthentic because of rules' legalistic side effects. In the same vein, Victorian novelists such as Hardy and Chekhov said that "obedience to [moral] prescriptions may constitute moral weakness."[2]

Theologians have long known of the dangers of "scrupulosity," the attempt to govern yourself minutely by rules. The philosopher of religion Paul Ricoeur has pointed out that freedom of will is encroached upon not only by sin but also by moral law, through the "juridization of action" by which "a scrupulous person encloses himself in an inextricable labyrinth of commandments."[3]

Psychotherapists have also embraced this insight. Freud said that the goal of psychotherapy was not only to expand the functioning of the ego at the expense of the id, but also to "make it more independent of the superego." Most of the schools of therapy that developed in Freud's wake made overgrown personal rules their chief target. Frederick Perls's Gestalt therapists blame the person's sense of estrangement from self on following "cognitive maps" rather than noticing the emotional immediacy of a situation. Carl Rogers's client-centered therapists fault the person's setting up artificial "conditions of worth" that stake her self-esteem on every choice. The cognitive therapy of Aaron Beck, Albert Ellis, and others purports to use the tools of logic to stop your perception of precedents in your own behavior from running amok in the form of "overgeneralization," "magnification," and "arbitrary inference." Eric Berne's transactional analysis blames psychopathology on a "parent" ego state, whose rigid opposition to a "child" state locks the person into repetitive "scripts" for behavior.[4]

For many writers self-government by rules is still a good, but not the greatest good. William James said, "the highest ethical life . . . consists at all times in the breaking of rules which have grown too narrow for the actual case." Psychologist Jane Loevinger put conscientiousness ("the internalization of rules") high in her sequence of ego development but below an 'autonomous' stage characterized by "a toleration for ambiguity." Even Lawrence Kohlberg, after some years of advocating his six-stage model, suggested a stage of moral development beyond his highest, 'principled' stage; but he defined it only vaguely as having to do with existential integrity. Howard Rachlin acknowledged that the "elevation of value by elaboration of pattern" sometimes motivates overly rigid behavior like workaholism or teetotaling instead of a "higher," subtler mixture of rule and relaxation. The philosopher Alfred Mele described "*errant* self-control – that is, an exercise of self-control in support of behavior that conflicts with a consciously held decisive better judgment." Martin Hollis's recent criticism of Economic Man raised the same concern:

> A Rational Economic Man . . . must be able to reflect on whether the upshot of his calculations is truly the rational course of action. This is to raise a query about the base of the calculation. . . . A person may find himself locked into his preferences against his real interests.

These writers' message is that plans can become prisons.[5]

From one viewpoint, this warning is hard to fathom. Personal rules are something we create for ourselves – if not deliberately, at least under the influence of relatively long-range incentives. There's nothing we've discussed so far that suggests why a rational person, realizing at some level that she discounts the future hyperbolically, can't come close to maximizing her long-range rewards by bundling her choices into categories. This, after all, has been the solution trusted alike by the classical Greeks and modern writers like Heyman and Rachlin.

From another viewpoint, it isn't surprising that personal rules can backfire. They're certainly a novelty in nature: Intertemporal bargaining seems to be a rather artificial process unlikely to have arisen in lower animals.[6] It was the human race that vastly expanded an individual's scope of choice and discovered that free choice often serves us worse than bald necessity. Indeed, confrontation with temporary preference might have been the "knowledge of good and evil" described in the biblical story of Adam and Eve, knowledge that made the pair aware that they were naked.[7] In the absence of any protections inherited from past eras of evolution, we apparently used the same intelligence that created this impulse problem to find a way around it – which was the discovery that adding the prospect of distant options to imminent ones stabilizes choice. When we looked for cues that predict long-range reward, we noticed that our own current choice was one of the best of those cues. Hence, according to this schematic account, the human will was born.

Unfortunately, a person's perception of the prisoner's dilemma relationship – and the willpower that results from this perception – don't simply cure the problem of temporary preference. Willpower may be the best way we know to stabilize choice, but the intertemporal bargaining model predicts that it will also have serious side effects, side effects that have in fact been observed by clinicians. Cobbled together from properties of hyperbolic discounting that apparently didn't affect evolution much before humans appeared, willpower remains something of a stopgap. Intertemporal bargaining hasn't restored us to a prelapsarian state of consistent preferences. Rather, it has formalized internal conflict, making some self-control problems better but others worse.

These side effects need to be discussed. Where they're recognized at all, they aren't seen as the consequence of using willpower. In a dangerous split of awareness, we tend to see willpower as an unmixed blessing that bears no relation to such abnormal symptoms as loss of emotional immediacy, abandonment of control in particular areas of behavior, blindness toward one's own motives, or decreased responsiveness

146

to subtle rewards. I will argue that just these four distortions are to be expected to a greater or lesser extent from a reliance on personal rules. They may even go so far as to make a given person's willpower a net liability to her.

9.1.1 Rules Overshadow Goods-in-Themselves

The perception of a choice as a precedent often makes it much more important for its effect on future expectations than for the rewards that literally depend on it. When this is true, your choices will become detached from their immediate outcomes and take on an aloof, legalistic quality.

It's often hard to guess how you'll interpret a current choice when looking back on it. Did eating that sandwich violate your diet or not? Where there's a lot of ambiguity, cooperation with your future selves will be both rigid and unstable. Unless you can find clear lines to use as boundaries, it may be hard to tell whether, facing a choice in the future, you'll look back at your current choice and judge it to have been a lapse.

The difficulty of estimating this depends on the topography of the choice, as I described earlier. A person trying to give up a heroin habit at least benefits from the bright line between some heroin and no heroin at all; but if you're trying not to overeat, you have to make judgment calls continually about what food to allow yourself, even if you've committed yourself to one single diet.

Consequently a short-term interest can usually claim a believable exception to the diet, and may escalate its claims by degrees until it has rendered your diet useless without ever inducing you to clearly violate it. Your diet may go so far as to make you weigh each portion, but it can't say how much fat "lean meat" can actually have; and besides, it can look ridiculous to weigh food when you're at a restaurant and be bad manners to do so when eating with other people; and "eating with other people" can include times when you're on the phone with them; the zero setting of your scale may wander a bit below zero without your being obliged to fix it; and if you break or lose your scale, it may take you a while to find another one of just the right kind; and so on like this. Where the boundaries aren't inescapable, making choices about self-indulgence is risky.

Under the influence of an imminent reward you may claim an exception to a rule, but later think you fooled yourself, that is, see yourself as having had a lapse. Conversely, you may be cautious beyond

147

what your long-range interest requires for fear that you'll later see your choice as a lapse. This rationale exacerbates compulsiveness. Every lapse reduces your ability to follow a personal rule, and every observance reduces your ability *not* to. Errors in either direction impose costs that would never result from the exponential curves of Economic Man, since those curves wouldn't make choice depend on recursive self-prediction in the first place.[8]

As we've seen, personal rules may arise without your active participation; they can make large categories of differential reward hinge on decisions of little intrinsic importance; and they may be hard to modify once established. If you're aware of this growing confinement, you may even try to nullify a rule by violating it. For instance, you may deliberately break a perfect attendance record, or "discard" your virginity, just so as not to have the incentives that have collected along those boundaries as forces in your future decision making. Arnold Bennett, a popular novelist and advice giver early in the twentieth century, warned against the way arbitrary rules seemed to grow and solidify in some people by a process he called "fussiness." His remedy was to break these rules systematically before they acquired a force greater than the person's other motives could counteract:

> [If the fusser has developed a rule never to wear black clothes,] let him proceed to the shopping quarter at once. Let him not order a suit-to-measure of black. Let him buy a ready made suit. Let him put it on in the store or shop, and let him have the other suit sent home. Let him then walk about the town in black. . . . He is saved!

What Bennett seems to have been pointing out is that a rule can grow larger than the other motives that bear on a particular behavior, and that a person has some opportunity to encourage or thwart this growth.[9] Sometimes a rule grows in strength like a tree or a sand bar; it can become an unopposable compulsion if this process is undisturbed for a long time.

9.1.2 Rules Magnify Lapses

When you violate a personal rule, the cost is a fall in your prospect of getting the long-range rewards on which it was based. But this prospect is what you've been using to stake against the relevant impulses; a lapse suggests that your will is weak, a diagnosis that may actually weaken your will in the recursive, James-Lange-Darwin pattern I described earlier.

To save your expectation of controlling yourself generally, you'll be strongly motivated to find a line that excludes from your larger rule the kind of choice where your will failed, so that you won't see your lapse in this setting as a precedent for choices in all other settings as well. This means attributing the lapse to a particular aspect of your present situation, even though it will make self-control much more difficult when that aspect is present in the future. It may even mean that you abandon attempts to use willpower where that aspect is present. For instance, you may decide that you *can't* resist the urge to panic when speaking in public, or to lose your temper at incompetent clerks, or to stop a doughnut binge once begun. Your discrimination of this special area has a perverse effect, since within it you see only failure predicting further failure. If you no longer have the prospect that your rule will hold there, these urges will seem to command obedience automatically, without an intervening moment of choice. At the cognitive level, your belief that the urge is bad (irrational, immoral, unhealthy, etc.) may be joined by a belief that it's irresistible, which will be good news for your short-range interest.[10]

Just as personal rules don't have to be consciously formed (see Section 9.1.1), exceptions don't require deliberate rationalization; an exception can impose itself on your intentions in the most awkward places, wherever a lapse has foretold a broad loss of impulse control. I've called this area, where a person doesn't dare attempt efforts of will, a "lapse district," by analogy to the vice districts in which Victorian cities tolerated the vice they couldn't suppress. Where the encapsulated impulses are clinically significant, a lapse district is called a "symptom" – for instance, a phobia, an explosive character disorder, or a substance dependence.[11]

Thus the perception of repeated prisoner's dilemmas stabilizes not only long-range plans but lapses as well. Cognitive models of self-control failure based on exhaustion of "strength" or some sort of accumulating backlash (an "opponent process") don't account for failure that continues over time in a specific modality of reward.[12]

9.1.3 Rules Motivate Misperception

Personal rules depend heavily on perception – noticing and remembering your choices, the circumstances in which you made them, and their similarity to the circumstances of other choices. And since personal rules organize great amounts of motivation, they naturally tempt you to suborn the perception process. When a lapse is occurring or has occurred, it will often be in both your long- and short-range interests not to recognize that fact: Your short-range interest is to keep the lapse from being detected so as not to invite attempts to stop it. Your long-range interest is also at least partially to keep the lapse from being detected, because acknowledging that a lapse has occurred would lower the expectation of self-control that you need to stake against future impulses.

After a lapse, the long-range interest is in the awkward position of a country that has threatened to go to war in a particular circumstance that has then occurred. The country wants to avoid war without destroying the credibility of its threat, and may therefore look for ways to be seen as not having detected the circumstance. Your long-range interest will suffer if you catch yourself ignoring a lapse, but perhaps not if you can arrange to ignore it without catching yourself. This arrangement, too, must go undetected, which means that a successful process of ignoring must be among the many mental expedients that arise by trial and error – the ones you keep simply because they make you feel better without your realizing why.[13] As a result, money disappears despite a strict budget, and people who "eat like a bird" mysteriously gain weight.

Clouding of consciousness in the face of temptation has been familiar to observers from Aristotle to the present day.[14] Here's a motivational pattern that could easily create a black market, indeed an underworld, of those interests that can control attention so as to block your notice and recollection. To get past your various interests in manipulating your own fund of information, a perception has to be somewhat acceptable to those interests. Just as a society stipulates agreement to propositions that individual members could find strong evidence against if they tried – myths of history, urban legends, and what is "politically correct," to name a few – so an individual develops a canon of official beliefs that she wouldn't stake her life on if it came to that. It's like the congressional practice of physically stopping the official clock when members want to continue deliberating after a time limit that they themselves have set. Evidence from all the watches and clocks in the world won't be enough to get the members to act as if their time were up. The more the bargaining of interests can select beliefs in this fashion, the more beliefs take on the properties of behaviors (see Chapter 11).

Barriers to attention are especially noticeable in some people, who are apt to be good hypnotic subjects. A few years ago the psychologist Ernst Hilgard showed that these people harbor a "hidden observer," an elicitable mental state whose knowledge is much more accurate than what they can otherwise report while trying their best. Hypnosis – or an emergency – seems to bypass whatever has been constraining their consciousness. It seems that among perceptions, just as among behaviors, there's a systematic kind that differs from the spontaneous kind in that it's governed by some consideration other than accuracy. This consideration is apt to be how this perception affects the bargaining of interests.[15]

9.1.4 Rules May Serve Compulsion Range Interests

Just because a decision comes to be worth more as a precedent than it is in its own right doesn't necessarily mean it's the wrong decision. On the contrary, you'd think that judging choices in whole categories rather than by themselves would have to improve your overall rate of reward. Whenever it doesn't, you ought to be able to call off the side bet that motivated the rule. How, then, can self-enforcing rules for intertemporal cooperation ever become prisons? Why should anyone ever conclude that she was trapped by her rules and even hire a psychotherapist to free her from a "punitive superego"?

It might seem from the logic of summing discount curves (Figures 5A and 6B) that cooperation in a repetitive prisoner's dilemma would have to serve the players' long-range interests, or else they'd never adopt this strategy. In my bargaining games, if I offered pairs of subjects a choice between just 50 points for each player versus 100 points for themselves alone, the tendency to cooperate would disappear in a flash. But those games mark off a series of choices as inescapably similar. In everyday life a person can discern many possible prisoner's dilemmas in a given situation; and the way of grouping choices that finally inspires her cooperation need not be the most productive because of two factors – the selective effect of distinctness and the mathematical properties of aggregated hyperbolic discount curves themselves.

First, personal rules operate most effectively on distinct, countable goals. Thus, as I noted earlier, the ease of comparing all financial transactions lets cash prices fluctuate much less over time than, say, the value of an angry outburst or of a night's sleep. The motivational impact of a series of moods has to be much less than that of an equally long series of cash purchases.

The impact of having rewards marked by discrete stimuli can be seen in experiments where the cost of bad choices is lower payoffs, as opposed to experiments where the cost is longer delays to payoffs. In the melioration experiments described in Section 3.1, the subjects learned not to make bad choices when the consequence was less money per turn, but not when the consequence was longer delays between turns, which cost just as much in a game of fixed duration.[16] Amounts are eminently countable; delays are a matter of intuition unless someone specifically measures them. Accordingly, subjects achieve "rational" behavior to amounts much more readily than to delays. By the same logic, when compulsion range interests are based on well-marked rewards and their richer, longer-range alternatives are harder to specify, the compulsions may win out because they offer clearer criteria for personal rules. The personal rules of anorectics or misers are too strict to promise the greatest possible satisfaction in the long run, but their exactness makes them more enforceable than subtler rules that depend on judgment calls.

Rules that will prove too concrete from a long-run perspective may still be attractive if you're trying hard to avoid your impulses, especially if you've had a conspicuous addiction range interest – for instance, the person who diets to the point of anorexia nervosa to end a history of overeating. It's easier to enforce specific rules about diet than more subtle rules like "eat what you need" or "eat what you'll be glad of in retrospect," though if the latter were adequate rules they'd permit the most reward in the long run. When you seek the comparative safety of having the most clear-cut criteria for your personal rules, you may be forestalling not only short-range impulses but also your chances for the richest reward in the long run. Furthermore, we'll see in the next chapter how obviousness per se may sometimes have a perverse effect – that is, how concrete rules for pacing emotional rewards may *necessarily* serve compulsion range interests.

Second, a look at the simple combination of discount curves tells us that relatively long-range temporary preferences can combine against interests of both shorter and longer duration. Figure 9 shows that the hierarchical preferences depicted in Figure 4 may combine in intertemporal bargaining to make the series of middle rewards dominant over not only the smallest, earliest rewards, but also over the largest, last

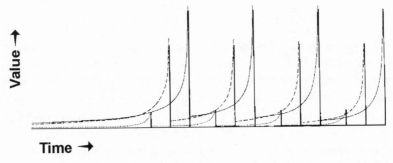

Time →

Figure 9. How personal rules can serve midrange interests: summed, discounted values of three alternative series of rewards (13:70:100, as in Figure 4). With this bundling, the smallest-earliest rewards no longer temporarily dominate the middle rewards, but the series of middle rewards temporarily dominates the series of largest-latest rewards. If the largest-latest rewards couldn't be summed, the dominance of the middle rewards would become even greater. If the rewards are binges, feeling thin enough, and rising above food obsessions, the concern with thinness is apt to win out.

ones. This dominance is temporary: From a distance the series of largest, last rewards is preferable; but if the rewards are constituted so that there's often the opportunity for one of the middle rewards to be chosen in the relatively near future, the middle series may dominate choice most or all of the time.

For instance, the bulimia that someone seeks treatment for is clearly a trait that the person herself cultivates, but seeking treatment implies that she perceives it not to serve her longest-range interest. Leave out, for the moment, the possible role of short-range appetite in this perception. The compulsion to diet is a midrange interest and is probably maintained by personal rules for maintaining appearance – which, as Figure 9 suggests, are maintained by motivation not only to outlaw the overeating but also to resist the antibulimic therapy treatment that's in her longest-range interest. That is, bundling each of the three series of incentives may transfer dominance from the spontaneous wish to eat more not to the longest-range interest but to the dieting. Under the terms of the problem, this would be a victory for a compulsion range interest.

So cooperation among successive motivational states doesn't necessarily bring the most reward in the long run. The mechanics of policing this cooperation may produce the intrapsychic equivalent of regimentation, which will increase your efficiency at reward-getting in the categories you've defined but reduce your sensitivity to less well-marked kinds of reward.

9.1.5 There's No Formula for Rationality

Both hyperbolic discounting and the personal rules that compensate for it have distorting effects. Therefore, there can be no hard and fast principle that people should follow to maximize their prospective reward. Thus "rationality" becomes an elusive concept. Insofar as it depends on personal rules demanding consistent valuation, rationality means being systematic, though only up to the point where the system goes too far and we look compulsive. Even short of frank compulsiveness, the systemization that lets rules recruit motivation most efficiently may undermine our longest-range interests, as we'll soon see.

The attempt to optimize our prospects with personal rules confronts us with the paradox of definition: that to define a concept is to alter it, in this case toward something more mechanical. If you conclude that you should maximize money, you become a miser; if you rule that you should minimize your openness to emotional influence, you'll develop the numbing insensitivity that clinicians have named alexithymia; if you conclude that you should minimize risk, you become obsessively careful; and so forth. The logic of rules may come to so overshadow your responsiveness to experience that your behavior becomes formal and inefficient. A miser is too rigid to optimize her chances in a competitive market, and even a daring financier undermines the productiveness of her capital if she rules that she must maximize each year's profit. Similarly, strict autonomy means shielding yourself against exploitation by others' ability to invoke your passions; but alexithymics can't use the richest strategy available for maximizing emotional reward, the cultivation of human relationships. Likewise, avoidance of danger at any cost is poor risk management.[17]

In this way, people who depend on willpower for impulse control are in danger of being coerced by logic that doesn't serve what they themselves regard as their best interests. Concrete rules dominate subtle intuitions; and even though you have a sense that you'll regret having sold out to them, you face the immediate danger of succumbing to addictions and itches if you don't. If you haven't learned ways of categorizing long-range rewards that permit them to dominate systematic series of midrange rewards, your midrange interests will prevail.

This situation seems to be exactly what is described by the term "compulsion," both in clinical and everyday speech, with one important exception: Compulsions are the diametric opposite of impulses, which are temporary preferences of short duration. "Compulsive" drinking is then a misleading use of the term unless someone has a personal rule that demands drinking, the way she might have a compulsion to eat health foods or be a teetotaler.[18]

I'll spend the last two chapters talking about the implications of the compulsion problem. They go far beyond the pathogenesis of character flaws and turn out to be the most serious limitations of the will.

9.2 PRACTICAL CONSEQUENCES OF WILL'S SIDE EFFECTS

Modern culture has been slow to recognize the dilemma of personal rules: that we're endangered by our willpower as well as by our impulses. For instance, modern writers wring their hands both about the average citizen's rising body mass index and about the prevalence of dieting in the young, without noting the implication that the enemy is now approaching from two opposite directions.[19]

In the interpersonal realm the dangers of rules are much better known. The English long ago established courts of equity to correct distortions that arose from laws, and the great social rule-maker Jeremy Bentham cautioned that rules shouldn't be fully binding. A recent review by the legal scholar Cass Sunstein makes it clear that social control by rules creates side effects analogous to my problems 1, 3, and 4: The need to preserve precedents makes rules too rigid; this rigidity "drives discretion underground" into transactions that aren't a matter of record; and the need to use available bright lines between what is and isn't permissible both forbids innocuous activities and licenses cleverly defined harmful ones.[20] This last side effect is by no means confined to the realm of law: Quality assurance programs that focus doctors' motivation increasingly on measurable indicators of quality are reducing their clinical intuitiveness.[21] Problem 2 also is evident in the interpersonal sphere. For instance, some potential drug addicts may be protected by legal deterrence, but many who are not deterred become identified criminals who are worse off than they would be if drugs weren't illegal.

Within the individual, these four problems with personal rules sharpen the basic conflict of successive motivational states and raise its stakes. Rules we create in our long-range interest may or may not wind up advancing this interest against shorter-range ones. After the need for clarity has taken its toll on subtlety, and overcaution has reduced flexibility, and misplaced caution with its consequent lapses has eroded resolve and corrupted self-observation – in short, after the makeshift nature of our attempt at deciding according to principle has caught up with us – our wills may wind up getting in the way of our longest-range interests.

The robustness of suboptimal rules may sometimes make addictions more attractive. Better to be fat, someone might think, than anorectic. Your will may become so confining that a pattern of regular lapses actually makes you better off in the long run. The lore of addictionology often attributes binging to a patient's inhibitedness in the other areas of her life; her general overcontrol is said to set up periodic episodes of breaking loose. The model of intertemporal bargaining predicted by hyperbolic discount curves provides a specific rationale for this pattern: Rules that eliminate any large source of emotional reward will create a proportional motive for you to bypass or break the rules. If these rules have, in James's phrase, "grown too narrow for the actual case," even your long-range interest will lie in partially escaping from them. Thus personal rules that serve compulsion range interests can create alliances between long- and short-range interests. The person's occasional binge comes to serve as a corrective to the comparative sterility of such rules, a means of providing richer experiences, while its transient nature still limits the damage it does. The longest-range interest of an alcoholic who is too rigid when sober may be to tacitly foster the cycle of drunkenness and sobriety rather than be continuously imprisoned by her rules.

Alcoholics are sometimes described who become nicer, or more genuinely creative, or more fully human when drunk. Furthermore, some addicts plan binges in advance. Such people may believe that their binges are undesirable – indeed, rationality will almost certainly dictate such a belief – but the therapists they hire find them mysteriously unresponsive to treatment. The patient who arranges to drink several days in advance – goes off the disulfiram that commits her to sickness if she drinks, for instance, or brings bottles to her rehabilitation program for later use – can't simply be yielding to a short-range impulse. This is behavioral evidence that she experiences a rational plan like giving up drinking as a compulsion that, even at a distance, appears to need hedging, although she may be unable to report any such thing.

This phenomenon suggests why a simplistic policy of "the more willpower, the better" contradicts the experience of many addicts. To them, more willpower just means less of the human qualities they value most in themselves. They're able to listen to reason only when reason, represented by personal rules, stops starving their own longest-range prospects for emotional satisfaction.

Modern culture may be part of the problem. That is, it may be offering more pervasive incentives for personal rules than it used to. Overblown personal rules can arise in response not only to extraordinary temptation or ineptness in dealing with temptation, but also to an environment's extraordinary demands for systematic decision making. An argument can be made that as society develops a complex, interdependent economy, it generates both better means for individuals to maximize their efficiency and more pressure to do so. Not that you have to be more obedient or otherwise narrow your choices; on the contrary, the range of choosable behaviors has grown enormously. But if you choose on a basis that ignores what the common wisdom accepts as your economic advantage, it's harder and harder not to notice the cost.

Even as modern parents and rulers have less control, the logic of an increasingly comprehensive marketplace has more. The implications of our choices come to extend beyond particular contexts within which generalization is natural – from our choices involving one friend, or lover, or customer to others in the same category – to most of our choices over long periods of time. To list three of the many manifestations of this progression: (1) Cash prices and wages, which make disparate decisions comparable, have penetrated choice-making ever more minutely, so that goods and services that used to be bartered informally as part of relationships are increasingly paid for. It's telling that the smallest unit of money in use was half a day's wages in medieval times but is now barely worth picking up from the floor (ironically, the penny in both cases).[22] (2) Similarly, the long-term records that result from your behavior, which once consisted (beyond a few major documentations like births, marriages, and deeds) of neighbors' memories, are now automated, quantified, and increasingly collated. The consequence is greater comparability of past and current choices; a job report, credit rating, or traffic ticket that was issued a decade ago is increasingly available and is used to predict your behavior. (3) Formal acculturation by schooling is increasingly lengthy and increasingly audited according to standards. Your performance in one subject or at one time can be compared to your performance elsewhere, or to another person's, with increasing precision, and these comparisons are apt to determine your career choice, your advancement, or at least the self-estimates that govern your morale. In these and many other ways, each of your choices is made comparable to, and thus predictive of, a range of other choices. Attention to this aspect of choice is rewarded by greater efficiency in any systemizable endeavor; but, as we've just discussed, it may lead to less productive occasioning of reward in the long run because of the compulsiveness it engenders. We'll see even more problems with systemization in the next two chapters.

The vogue for quantifying and comparing doesn't feel forced upon us by alien interests. On the contrary, these are means to the ends we ourselves have defined, means that are increasingly selected for efficiency by the competition of the marketplace. We freely adapt our personal rules to be compatible with them, but these rules may nevertheless serve compulsion range interests.

Extensive reliance on personal rules is probably necessary in cosmopolitan societies. Granted, there have been non-Western societies that didn't show signs of using them. The Indians of the Great Plains, for instance, are said to have had no word for will or willpower, but experienced motivation as a force of nature. The same may have been true of the Bushmen of South Africa.[23] But people in these societies have cultivated an openness to social influence that causes motives to be averaged not over time but across persons. One member may take up a drug of abuse or surrender to a passionate rage, but her neighbors will have much more influence over her decision. This arrangement is obviously volatile, since crowd psychology can lead a group of hyperbolic discounters to agree in unison on decisions that are in none of their long-range interests. However, the rasher heads are at least mixed with wiser ones, so that individuals get some protection against individual impulses.[24]

Reliance on a community for personal self-control was evident in medieval times even in Europe, where the law held small groups to be responsible for the behavior of each member; but since then, people have shown a consistent taste for escaping the intrusiveness of intimate groups. The history of Western society has been a relentless march toward individual autonomy and privacy, and away from collective action at the neighborhood level. Milestones include individual beds in individual bedrooms, detached houses, farms that stand alone rather than being interlaced around a village, the popularity of reading as entertainment followed by personal television sets and Walkmen with headsets and the current development of individualizing the plots of video games and even movies to suit individual viewers.[25] Early in this progression the individual became the unit of accountability. Around the turn of the nineteenth century, English society realized that spontaneous emotionality weakened a person's bargaining stance with others,[26] and the resulting race toward stiffness of the upper lip further eroded people's skill in listening to their neighbors.[27]

In the resulting society, you impair your competitiveness by leaving yourself open to social influence. Even altruism comes to be regulated by a process that shields you from social pressure. In Western philosophy the highest moral thinking has been held to comprise solitary feats like Kant's categorical imperative – that you should always choose as if your choice set the precedent for a universal rule. Even though the highest ethical goal is to advance the welfare of the people around you, you aren't supposed to do this by staying open to pressure from those people themselves: The most demanding charity may not be the most deserving, and a beggar may spend your money on drugs. The philanthropist who's most praised is autonomous, a dispassionate judge of how her choices serve her principles.

During most of his career studying moral thinking, Lawrence Kohlberg placed the categorical imperative at the top of a child's progression toward ethics, his sixth stage of development, while responsiveness to social influence was only the second stage. Responders to his work pointed out that a taste for absolute autonomy in decision making was a particularly male trait – his girls seemed to "arrest" at a lower stage than his boys – and that this taste didn't necessarily lead to the best self-control.[28] Nevertheless, men have actually held a competitive edge in Western economies. Indeed, men have conventionally specialized in having iron wills, which, besides giving them a competitive edge, protected wives while the latter cultivated the social arts requiring vulnerability; wives in turn were expected to assuage the side effects of motivational autonomy that their men incurred – rigidity, social inhibition, emotional isolation[29] – an arguably symbiotic specialization of self-control styles. However, many people now see systemization as granting such an overwhelming advantage that they tell women either to cultivate it or to work toward its cultural devaluation – "pod" and "difference" feminists, respectively.[30]

Attuned as we are to modern efficiency in the developed world, we don't recognize the oppressiveness of an environment so rationalized that much of our natural idiosyncrasy has been anticipated and either harnessed or selected out. But newcomers accustomed to more backward economies find our relationships superficial; and our own fictional heroes are increasingly those who rage against systems. The costs of basing decisions only on countable outcomes never appear in cost/benefit analyses; indeed, they are recognized only obliquely, as anomie or other imponderable morale problems, part of the "X-inefficiency" of workers that somehow limits their responsiveness to monetary incentives.[31] Only in the last two decades has there been retrenchment where systemization is most advanced – in large corporations – in the form of decentralization, quality circles, self-directed work teams, and other retreats from the conventional approach of time/motion efficiency.[32] Any large retreat may be motivationally impossible. Even the Bushmen, who seem so much less happy after they join the fringes of civilization, show no tendency to return to the simplicity of their former lives.[33]

9.3 SUMMARY

Seeing your current choice as a precedent predicting similar future choices can reduce your tendency to form temporary preferences; but you can expect it to produce four serious side effects that make your behavior more compulsive.

- When an option is worth more as a precedent than as an event in its own right, you're less able to experience it in the here-and-now and your choice-making becomes rigid.
- A lapse that you see as a precedent reduces your hope for self-control in similar situations in the future, a reduction that recursively reduces your power of self-control in those situations.
- The incentive not to recognize a lapse may lead to gaps in your awareness of your own behavior.
- Explicit criteria for defining lapses will tend to replace subtle ones, making your choice-making overly concrete. The increasing systemization of society both encourages and reflects a shift of emphasis from social controls to personal rules as people's predominant self-control strategy.

CHAPTER 10

AN EFFICIENT WILL
UNDERMINES APPETITE

The poor man must walk to get meat for his stomach, the rich man a stomach for his meat.

Franklin, *Poor Richard's Almanac*

Our relative overvaluation of nearer experiences does a lot more than make us prone to addictions. It literally throws a curve into many experiences for which our norms are linear. In a culture where one of the basic properties of rationality is consistency, it makes us irrational at the outset.

I've discussed how the seemingly mystical idea of a will – free, more or less powerful, and somewhat brittle – describes the crux of our strategic response to temptation. The elusiveness of the will as a concept has historically come from the fact that it isn't an organ but a bargaining situation. Its brittleness comes from the often perverse inventiveness of sequential negotiators – each one the self, evaluating prospects from a shifting perspective – who are trying to maximize their prospects in a never-ending prisoner's dilemma. But however complicated the mechanism of willpower may seem, it's a neat little package compared to the other expectable consequences of intertemporal bargaining.

The most important departures from conventional utility accounting probably don't come from preference in the addiction range of durations – the urges that last for minutes to days and create the need for personal rules – and they don't come from the side effects of those personal rules themselves, even though these are considerable. The most pervasive failure of linear accounting seems to occur at the speed of attention: It's the operation of the matching law on short-latency responses that must make experience seem most puzzling, at least when judged by the proportional lines of conventional theory.

We encountered the first of these puzzles while examining temporary preference itself: that pain seems to attract attention and deter approach at the same time. As we saw, hyperbolic discounting offers at least a starting hypothesis about how this can occur – that pain is a recurring cycle of seductions too close to resist and micro-satiations too brief to be satisfying, a rapid version of an itch that is in turn a rapid version of addiction, with the phases of indulgence and aversion occurring so rapidly as to fuse in conscious perception (see Section 4.1.3).

Several other phenomena, which I'll detail presently, are equally puzzling for a strict utilitarian model, as long as that model uses conventional discount curves. However, these experiences are so pervasive that behavioral science has treated them as givens, just "the way things are." As with the case of pain, utility theory habitually sidesteps the questions that they raise, sometimes with the excuse that there's no accounting for tastes. However, they're amenable to analysis with a hyperbolic model. Although they seem disparate at first glance, I'll argue that they all stem from a property analogous to the seductiveness of pain – the seductiveness of premature satiation – and the singular inability of will to deal with this seduction. Ultimately, they're what limit the scope of the will.

- *The limitation of emotion puzzle.* The experiences that people value most are usually emotional ones. But it isn't hard to generate emotions voluntarily. People usually don't do this because daydreamed emotions are less satisfying than the kind that have proper occasions, but that fact in itself lacks an explanation. Recall that this need for external occasions was the remaining fact about appetites that seemed to require classical conditioning to explain it (see Section 2.2.1). How do emotions come to function like the limited goods of commerce, those that you have to get from the outside world?
- *The construction of fact puzzle.* Writers since Plato have noticed that people's beliefs about the world don't correspond entirely to the measurable facts and sometimes barely resemble them at all. Yet we experience beliefs, like passions, as obligatory, things that our observations force us to have. It has lately been fashionable to assert the contrary, that there's no objective basis for beliefs. Social constructivists say that beliefs and fictions share the status of "texts,"

strings of possible interpretations that people choose because of the rules of a language game.

It has become clear that belief is at least partially a goal-directed activity, and thus classifiable as a behavior, rather than a passive consequence of incoming stimuli. However, propositions that are overtly goal-directed are experienced as different from beliefs; they're experienced as "make-believe." Insofar as belief is a behavior, what constraints make it different from make-believe?

- *The vicarious experience puzzle.* Other people are especially valuable as sources of emotional experience. Conventional utility theory calls this a simple putting-yourself-in-the-other's-place and regards it as natural whenever social distance is short.[1] But moving social experiences don't depend precisely on distance, or even on the existence of a real other person as opposed to a fictional character; and in many cases, one person's experience is obviously different from her vicarious object's – at the extreme, for the sadist and for the victim. How do other people move us, and what are the constraints on that process?
- *The indirection puzzle.* Some goal-directed activities can't effectively approach their goals by direct routes. Trying to sleep may inhibit sleep, and trying not to panic often induces panic. Trying to be dignified makes you ridiculous; trying to laugh inhibits laughter; happiness has also been said to elude people who strive to attain it.[2] At first glance, this problem seems to strike at the heart of any motivational model, not just one that assumes exponential discounting. How can any goal-directed activity be undermined by striving toward its goal? How can a reward-dependent activity not be strengthened by reward?

In many cases, an answer comes from consequences I covered earlier of our tendency to form temporary preferences. Direct routes to goals may take you too close to short-range urges: Trying hard is arousing and will compete with sleep; noticing that you're trying not to panic may seem like a bad sign and undermine the conditional expectation of control that your will relies on. However, in other cases, will itself seems to ruin the outcome it seeks. The desired outcome may be just the appearance of being unwilled, as in the case of dignity. But why should this appearance be desirable, and why should experiences like laughter and happiness be spoiled by will?

These four puzzles are beyond the reach of conventional utility theory; but they don't imply that human nature is too complex or too mysterious to analyze, a conclusion that's been popular among writers with a more romantic bent. They can be accounted for as further consequences of the hyperbolic discount curves that describe the value of delayed reward. I believe that picoeconomics, the study of these curves and their consequences, can go a great deal further in detecting regularities in such seeming chaos in human nature. However, I have space only to suggest how the implications of these examples are exacerbated by, and ultimately defeat, the will.

These four puzzles all turn out to be aspects of the same phenomenon, the fourth side effect of willpower discussed in Chapter 9. The greatest limitation of the will comes from the same process as its greatest strength: its relentless systemization of experience through attention to precedent. This systemization braces it against temporary preferences but also makes it unable to follow subtle strategies to keep the reward mechanism productive.[3]

Let's look at the first of these four puzzles more closely; the solution will provide a key to the other three as well:

10.1 THE LIMITATION OF EMOTION PUZZLE

As I noted in Chapter 1, a society that has largely satisfied its physical wants spends most of its effort on obtaining emotional experience. Emotional rewards of one kind or another seem to be a large part of most people's day-to-day incentives. We may decide to climb mountains, or become an object of envy, or achieve moral purity, or accomplish any number of other feats that aren't necessary for our physical comfort. We could ignore these tasks without any obvious penalty; but we somehow become committed to them, occasionally to the point of dying for them.

However, emotional reward is physically independent of any particular turnkey in the environment, a fact that confronts conventional utility theory with a serious inconsistency. To function as a reward according to that theory, a good has to be limited in supply or accessibility; if it's available unconditionally, it will never induce significant motivation to obtain it. As Adam Smith originally observed, this is just the reasoning that makes air have less market value than diamonds, although air is more necessary.

To avoid the counterintuitive implication that maximal control over your feelings will optimize self-reward, utility theory has had to assume that emotions and other appetites are unmotivated reflexes which must be released by turnkey stimuli and that then "drive" a person;[4] and the most stirring emotions do seem to require some sense of necessity, so that we experience them not as spontaneous choices but as responses to an external provocation, such as an emergency or a vivid stimulus. However, emotions require no specific turnkey from the outside world. As any actor knows, they can be cultivated to appear, if not exactly on demand, at least as a reliable result of deliberate effort.

When actor Emma Thompson has her half-minute-long paroxysm of joy in the movie *Sense and Sensibility,* her tear ducts and other involuntary muscles are clearly behaving the same way as in someone who is having the emotion spontaneously. The emotion is false only in the sense that she doesn't believe that the occasion for it in the script has really happened to her. Just as clearly, she's having the emotion intentionally, and may have had to have it several times in a row before the director was satisfied with the scene. But once she had learned to have it, she almost certainly didn't go home and have it repeatedly for her own entertainment, instead of going to a good restaurant, say, or paying to see someone else's movie. Even when a person learns to have an emotion on purpose, she has it only on limited occasions, in this case while enacting a script.[5]

By the same token, when we see this scene in the movie we have the emotion vicariously; that is, we reconstruct it with our own physiologies. We feel as if we needed the movie in order to do this – that's why we paid our money, after all; but all we got from the movie was information – text, if you will – nothing that might unlock a reflex. We, too, might be said to have learned the emotion, at least insofar as we could then rehearse the memory of the scene at will and produce part of the feeling. But again, although the experience comes more readily with repetition, the accompanying feeling has diminishing impact.

Although emotions are physically available, something makes them less intense in proportion as the occasion for them is arbitrary. To the extent that someone learns to access them at will, doing so makes them pale, mere daydreams. Even an actor needs to focus on occasions to bring them out with force; one benefit of acting as a vocation may be that it provides these occasions on a satisfying schedule.[6] But what properties does an event have to have in order to serve as an occasion for emotion? The fact that there's no physical barrier opposing free access to emotions raises the question of how emotional experiences come to behave like economic goods that are in limited supply. That is, how do you come to feel as if you have them passively, as implied by their synonym, "passions"?

10.1.1 Avoiding Premature Satiation

The basic question is, how does your own behavior become scarce? I'll divide it into two parts: Why would you want a behavior of yours to become scarce, that is, to limit your free access to it? And given that this is your wish, how can you make it scarce without making it physically unavailable?

The answer to the first part can provide a basis for resolving all four of the seeming paradoxes I've just described: All kinds of reward depend on a condition that's outside of your arbitrary control, your *potential* for reward. Even those rewards that are widely recognized to be self-rewards, like daydreaming or letting yourself partake of an inexhaustible supply of chocolates, depend on a potential to be rewarded in those ways, and this potential follows its own unchangeable laws. The older biologists called it "drive."

Drive is an unfortunate term because it implies that this potential is necessarily unwelcome, something that drives you to get rid of it. Some writers still make this assumption,[7] but there are many situations in which people recognize this potential for reward as a desirable resource. All kinds of reward depend on a readiness for it that's used up in the course of the reward and can't be deliberately renewed. It's often called "appetite," the term I've been using for an arousable preparation to consume the reward. Since this arousal isn't possible without the underlying readiness, its inclusion within the concept doesn't change the meaning much, but sometimes it will be useful to distinguish potential or *available* appetite from the aroused appetite itself (see note 22, Chapter 4).

The important thing about appetite is that some ways of consuming its reward reduce its potential at a far greater rate than others; this means that some ways permit you to get a lot more reward than others from a given amount of appetite. People are familiar with a number of common mistakes that waste appetite: To go from the more concrete to the less: Filling up with food too rapidly spoils the pleasure of a meal; premature orgasm reduces the pleasure available from sex; looking ahead to the outcome of a mystery story wastes the suspense that's been built up; coming to the punch line too fast reduces the effectiveness of a joke; and people generally become bored with tasks that allow their minds to anticipate their completion, that is, that contain no elements of surprise or ambiguity.[8] All decisions to harvest appetites that are close to the satiation point are probably misguided. As ethologist Konrad Lorenz said, "to expend any joy down to the point of full exhaustion is downright bad pleasure-economy."[9]

The concept of wasting available appetite isn't novel, but it's usually looked on as a trivial problem. Conventional utility theory says that it should arise only when you're unfamiliar with a particular kind of appetite. An adept consumer should simply gauge what the most productive way to exploit a potential appetite will be and pace her consumption accordingly.

However, in practice this seems to be hard to do. People look for techniques that constrain their rate of consumption rather than leaving themselves free to pace themselves ad lib. Concrete examples of these techniques include going to banquets with many courses that pace the rate of eating, eating lobsters or crabs out of the shell, and retarding orgasm with anesthetic creams or bondage techniques. The existence of a market for self-committing devices suggests that rate of consumption is an area of conflict between smaller, earlier and larger, later rewards.

That's just what hyperbolic discounting predicts. The consumption mistakes I just listed all involve going too fast. If the properties of appetites are often such that rapid consumption brings an earlier peak of reward but reduces the total amount of reward that the available appetite makes possible, then you have an amount-versus-delay problem. Where people – or, presumably, any reward-governed organisms – have free access to a reward that's more intense the faster it's consumed, they'll tend to consume it faster than they should if they were going to get the most reward from that appetite. In a conflict of consumption patterns between the long and pleasant versus the brief but even slightly more intense, an organism that discounts the future hyperbolically is primed to choose brief but more intense consumption.

This problem makes no sense in a world of exponential discounting. In an exponential world, an adept consumer should simply gauge what the most productive way to exploit an appetite will be, and pace her consumption accordingly. People could sit in armchairs and entertain

themselves optimally by generating just enough appetite and then satisfying it. There are actually people who attempt this, but with disastrous results: Two kinds of psychiatric patients try to take their sources
of reward into their own hands and withdraw their investment from
risky activities. Schizoid characters feel threatened by social give-and-
take and often contrive to live entirely in their rooms or in a shack in
the woods. Insofar as they succeed in doing this, their solitary activities
mysteriously become stale, and they often fall prey to irrational worries,
fears, or rituals. Similarly, narcissistic characters, who seemingly function
at a much higher level, choose their activities and companions so that
continual success is a foregone conclusion. They, too, report a mysterious reduction in satisfaction that can't be accounted for by any confrontation with reality; their problem is that they've managed to get
reality to obey them almost as well as their fantasies do. Thus, the
harshness of reality doesn't seem to be the factor that limits arbitrary
emotional reward. On the contrary, common experience teaches that
emotional reward, indulged in ad lib, becomes unsatisfactory for that
reason itself.

So how can someone resist the urge for premature satiation? To some
extent resistance should develop spontaneously, by the same process of
learning that causes the problem. Where the reward is physical, like
sex or exercise, occasions that are continuously available extinguish as
cues for seeking it, so that adults usually have little urge to masturbate,
and people who pay to go to gyms may still avoid walking on errands.
Likewise where the reward is entirely mental, behaviors that keep appetite nearly satiated become unattractive even in the short run, so that
people tire of checking their odometers frequently on trips or reading
quickly gratifying literature like joke books for any length of time. Insofar as particular combinations of occasion and behavior keep significant appetite from becoming available, they seem to be experienced
as innately unattractive. It's rewards based on the middle range of appetites – those that have grown to be worth harvesting from a moderately short-range perspective – that provoke the learning of counter-
measures based on long-range reward.

This learning should be easiest for physical rewards: You can make a
personal rule to consume them only in the presence of adequately rare
criteria; but with emotional rewards, the only way to stop your mind
from rushing ahead is to avoid approaches that can be too well learned.
Thus the most valuable occasions will be those that are either (1) un-

certain to occur or (2) mysterious – too complex or subtle to be fully anticipated. To get the most out of emotional reward, you have to either gamble on uncertainty or find routes that are certain but that won't become too slick.

To restate this pivotal hypothesis: In the realm of mental reward – the great preponderance of the reward that well-off people pursue – possible behaviors must compete on the basis of how well they can maintain your available appetite. Ready access extinguishes the common ruck of self-generated emotion. Processes that are rewarded by emotion compete for adoption on the basis of the extent to which their occasions defy willful control. Direct paths to reward become progressively less productive, because insofar as they become efficient they waste your readiness for reward. Conversely, if there's a factor that delays consumption from the moment at which this consumption could, if immediate, compete with available alternatives – the moment it reaches what could be called the "market level" of reward – that factor may substantially increase the product of (value × duration) before the appetite satiates (Figure 10).

As we discussed earlier, when a puzzle becomes familiar your mind leaps ahead to the ending, dissipating the suspense and poorly repaying the cost of attending to it in the first place. The times in the brackets in Figure 10 become shorter and shorter as you learn to solve the reward-getting problem it depicts. You then have to search for new puzzles or gamble on finding more than just new things of the same kind. Durable occasions must either (1) change so that they remain novel (new problems, new faces, new plots, new decor, or, as the style of puzzle becomes familiar, new styles) or (2) be intricate or subtle enough to defy total comprehension. This is the quality a work of art must have to save it from the obsolescence of fashion,[10] and maybe too the quality needed by an enduring personal relationship.

In short, durable occasions for emotion have to be surprises, so that you don't have to restrain your attention from jumping ahead. Thus it's usually more rewarding to read a well-paced story than to improvise a fantasy. Accordingly, surprise is sometimes said to be the basis of aesthetic value. And the mystical quality that existentialists' pronouncements have always had can now be seen as a way of recognizing the premature satiation problem: "The world is ambiguous . . . [this] is the reward for being human because it adds challenge, variety and opportunity to existence." Furthermore, "as long as man is an ambiguous

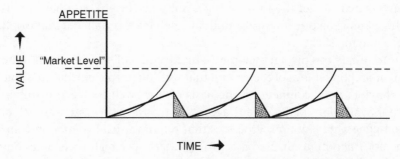

Figure 10A. Cycles of growing reward potential (rising straight lines) and actual consumption (gray areas) leading to satiety. Consumption begins when the total value of expected consumption reaches the competitive market level. Hyperbolic discount curves of the total value of each act of consumption decline with delay from its anticipated onset.

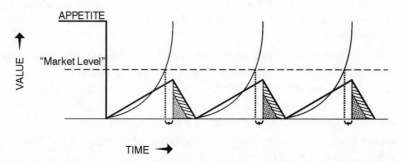

Figure 10B. Increased reward (stripes) resulting from increased appetite when there is an obligatory delay in consumption from the moment of choice (brackets); the choice to consume occurs when the discounted value of the delayed consumption reaches the market level.

creature he can never banish anxiety; what he can do instead is to use anxiety as an eternal spring for growth into new dimensions of thought and trust."[11] In modalities where an organism can mentally reward itself, surprise is the only commodity that can be scarce.[12]

To repeat satisfactions that were once intense, you have to at least structure them as fantasies involving obstacles in order to achieve a modicum of suspense; but as a fantasy becomes familiar and your mind jumps ahead to the high points, the fantasy collapses further into being just a cursory thought – an irritant if it retains any attractiveness at all and a disregarded, empty option if it doesn't. In the absence of new challenges, punishing scripts start to get selected because they don't habituate as much; and so the psychic life of people who live in fantasy degenerates into a recurring state of emergency or paranoid delusion.

Most people develop intuitions about how to foster sources of surprise, for example, a rule not to read ahead, without ever making an explicit theory. As you grow up and become too efficient at daydreaming, you discover other activities that provide unpredictable occasions for reward. That is, you do things that contain conspicuous moments, which, taken as occasions for an emotional reward, let you feel in a pattern that replenishes your available appetite for that feeling. You explore new territory, or race with a competitor, or leave yourself open to fall in love. You learn that, in the absence of these conspicuous moments, generating an emotion won't usually be worth the effort.

These limits on emotion aren't always personal rules. Indeed, they couldn't be; the habituation of ad lib self-reward must occur by an elementary process, since emotion apparently occurs in lower animals as well as in people. The only limits needed come from learning about what kind of occasion predicts that an emotion will be rewarding. This is self-prediction in the elementary sense described by Darwin, James, and Lange (see Section 8.3.3), not the interpretation of behaviors as precedents that is necessary for willpower, which is probably restricted to humans.

Although there are wide variations in the equilibria people find between gratification at a whim and strict dependence on external occasions – the fantasy-prone seem to have emotions that are more robust than other people's despite equally free access,[13] while sociopaths can usually imagine very little, even with effort – everyone learns limits to her self-induction of positive emotions. By a similar logic, people avoid in advance occasions for entertaining the horrible, and if they can't – for example, in cases of overwhelming trauma, like posttraumatic stress syndrome – they dissociate the recollection into a circumscribed experience, just as if it were a binge or other major lapse of control (see Section 9.1.2). People – and presumably lower animals – wind up experiencing as emotion only those patterns that have escaped the habituation of free access, by a selective process analogous to that described by economist Robert Frank for the social recognition of "authentic" emotions: Expressions that are known to be deliberately controllable are disregarded, as with the false smile of the hypocrite.[14] By this process of selection, emotion is left with its familiar guise as passion, something that has to come over you.

171

10.1.2 The Adaptiveness of Learned Habituation

We can now say more about how hyperbolic discounting might be more adaptive than an exponential kind, even though it seems less rational (see Section 3.1). Why, in other words, should nature have selected occasions for emotional reward as the goods we value, rather than a turnkey system of reward that must literally be controlled by outside stimuli? We do know that lower animals have been found not to be entirely dominated by concrete rewards. Hungry monkeys have been observed to prefer exploration tasks to tasks that obtain food; and even in small-brained animals like rats, the power of visceral rewards such as food and sex is modified by factors like variety, which are wholly unnecessary to the physical consumption of those rewards.[15]

Perhaps the explanation is something like this: The tendency of vivid rewards to fade away into habit as you get efficient at obtaining them may keep you motivated to explore your environment, both when you're young and inept and when you've become a master problem solver. If reward were strictly proportional to how much of some external stimulus you could get, then a reward formula that was sufficient to shape your behavior when you were a beginner would lead you to rest on your laurels once you'd solved that particular problem. But instead, as you become increasingly skilled in an activity, the reward it generates increases only at first, and then decreases again because your appetite lasts decreasingly long.

> The paradox is that it is just those achievements which are most solid, which work best, and which continue to work that excite and reward us least. The price of skill is the loss of the experience of value – and of the zest for living.[16]

However, the satiation of familiar rewards may be less adaptive in wealthy societies. In the absence of some factor that refreshes available appetite, as Lorenz said,

> The normal rhythm of eating with enjoyment after having become really hungry, the enjoyment of any consummation after having strenuously striven for it, the joy in achieving success after toiling for it in near-despair – in short the whole glorious amplitude of the waves of human emotions, all that makes life worth living – is dampened down to a scarcely perceptible oscillation between scarcely perceptible tiny displeasures and pleasures. The result is an immeasurable boredom.

This is because

> the mechanisms equilibrating pleasure and displeasure are thrown off balance because civilized man lacks obstacles which force him to accept a healthy amount of painful, toilsome displeasure.[17]

Failure of appetite is familiar enough, but without hyperbolic discounting to explain why people don't accept that "healthy amount of painful, toilsome displeasure" it has not made motivational sense.

For simplicity I've been talking mainly about positive, or pleasurable emotions. Negative emotions aren't the opposite – by the same line of reasoning that pains aren't the opposite of pleasures – but, like pains, they differ from positive experiences in seducing only your attention. That is, they're vivid but aversive. They're avoided in the longer-latency behavior patterns that are experienced as intentional or deliberate. However, the distinction between positive and negative is less distinct in emotions than for the more concrete incentives. True, we mostly seek joy, although the existential philosopher Sartre warned us that all emotions degrade experience; and we mostly avoid terror, although we may pay to experience it at the movies or on a roller coaster. But many emotions, like anger, nostalgia, awe, and pity, are "mixed," meaning not that they're neutral but that they're compelling without being clearly either pleasurable or aversive. And all emotions attract us rather than imposing themselves without any participation on our part; as we have seen, even inducements to panic, an emotion that sometimes makes people dysphoric to the point of suicide, can be disregarded with practice.[18]

Emotions that are negative or mixed are as seductive as positive emotions, but the value of their occasions disappears with the perspective of distance. A horror film may occasion a negative emotion, anxiety, in the timid in the same way that it occasions a positive emotion, thrill, in the adventurous; and the urges toward thrill or anxiety may be equally strong in their respective populations when the occasions are at hand. But in advance, the people who get thrilled will buy a ticket to the film, and the people who get anxious won't. By the same logic, just as a person learns techniques to defer satiation when she finds an emotion pleasurable, she learns to hasten satiation or remove the drive (e.g., to get punishment over with) for aversive ones.

So here the will meets its most restricting limitation yet: It can make you more rational and hence more efficient at getting reward, but it can't control the learning that pushes toward premature satiation. Even when the will is doing its best – that is, when the system it creates is not too rigid or too evadable and when it moves you to its purpose in a direct line – even then it's still apt to impair reward by wasting available appetite. This suggests that you're best off using willpower in activities that are means to something else, rather than when you're doing things that are an end in themselves. However, the picture becomes complicated when you need to protect the activities that are ends in themselves from your own efficiency by regarding them as means to some other end. I'll discuss this last situation in the section on indirection in chapter 11.

10.2 SUMMARY

The value of willpower is limited not only by the four side effects discussed in the previous chapter, but also by two ways that immediately rewarding options seduce attention: in pains/itches and in premature satiation. Itches and pains were discussed in Sections 4.1.2.1 and 4.1.3, respectively. Premature satiation seems to be the limiting factor for emotional reward, with the following logic:

- Rewards that are freely available will be limited by how much and how long you have appetite for them.
- Hyperbolic discounting makes you innately impatient to reach peak consumption of a reward, which often moves you to satiate your appetite for it prematurely.
- To the extent that you can't keep your attention from anticipating a familiar sequence of events, this familiarity alone will dissipate your appetite. The only protections from anticipation are for the events to be incomprehensible or surprising.
- Premature satiation weeds out emotions not cued by events that are adequately rare and outside of your control.

The will is not only powerless to interfere with premature satiation because of the pervasiveness and immediacy of opportunities for attention-based reward; it may accelerate satiation by its very efficiency. For people who want utility theory to prescribe orderly progress toward maximal satisfaction, this is an even more unfortunate downside of willpower – actually a ramification of the compulsiveness that I described in the previous chapter.

CHAPTER 11

THE NEED TO MAINTAIN
APPETITE ECLIPSES THE WILL

[Knowledge] is good just by being knowledge; and the only thing that makes it knowledge is that it is true.

Tom Stoppard, *The Invention of Love*

What greater superstition is there than the mumbo-jumbo of believing in reality?

Christopher Fry, *The Lady's Not for Burning*

We're now at the heart of a central human paradox: that the better the will is at getting rewards, the less reward it will finally obtain. The paradox arises because the will only works – given its nature as a bargaining situation, we could say "only *forms*" – in tasks that have regular, clear-cut steps. This clarity fosters anticipation, which increasingly wastes available appetite through premature satiation and which the will is powerless to prevent in any direct way. Although this mechanism provokes solutions that must disappoint anyone seeking a recipe for rationality, it removes the apparent absurdity from three of the most basic human activities, which I'll now discuss: the construction of beliefs, empathy with other people, and motivated indirection in approaching goals.

11.1 THE CONSTRUCTION OF FACT PUZZLE

It's now common knowledge that people's beliefs about the world around them are heavily influenced by their own tacit choices, both "innocent" assumptions and wishful thinking. We have to decide so much about attending to or ignoring information that some "social constructivists" have put fact and fiction on a par, under the name "text."[1] To a great extent, belief does seem to be a goal-directed activity. However, it can't be based simply on rewardingness and still be experienced as belief. Belief differs from make-believe in depending on the ruling of some external arbiter, some test that's beyond your direct influence, rather than simply being chosen.

Beliefs could be viewed as dispositions to choose one particular text over its alternatives. Often these dispositions are shaped by environmental contingencies: My belief that a dropped object will fall rather than rise comes easily and consistently; any urge to reexamine it has long since extinguished. Such "instrumental" beliefs – those that are differentially rewarded by their practical effects – have little room for social construction. But for other beliefs there's either no such shaping or it's delayed, leaving the present motivational impact of the belief to depend on the way it occasions emotion. Such beliefs may concern the past or future (Was there a conspiracy to assassinate JFK? Will my pension be big enough?), or refer to present facts that can't be discovered with certainty (Does my spouse really love me?), or are meant to be assertions rather than descriptions (Is abortion murder?). Instrumental beliefs may also occasion emotions in major ways, of course (Are my brakes failing?), but in the instrumental realm self-deception is punished by experience.

Where the consequences of beliefs are emotional rather than instrumental, the constraints on them haven't yet been explored. However, the pervasive urge for premature satiation discussed in the previous chapter is a likely limiting mechanism. That is, there should be an incentive to cue emotions by facts in order to optimize available appetite. Emotions tied to beliefs that can shift as convenience dictates will become daydreams, just like emotions that aren't tied to beliefs at all. The texts that get selected as noninstrumental beliefs will be those interpretations of reality that serve as effective occasions for emotions.

By this hypothesis, accuracy per se is only one selective factor for belief in a fact, and not an indispensable one at that: Beliefs that foster suspense will reward us more than beliefs that merely have internal consistency or match stimulus patterns, regardless of what appetite is available for them, and will thus divert emotional investment from those beliefs. Suspense requires facts to be unpredictable – the solutions to puzzles, the conquest of a mountain, the discovery of historical data, or a gamble on someone else's behavior. The facts that are important for emotional rewards aren't selected for their instrumental properties, but for how well they support some variety of gambling: Does my interpretation make the puzzle, or mountain, or historical problem, or human relationship tough enough without being impossible?

Nevertheless, there have to be rationales for keeping the propositions that we authenticate as facts unique; otherwise, our beliefs would be too fluid, too obedient to our wishes. Indeed, this effect often makes the beliefs shaped by instrumental needs the best occasioners of emotion. Thus our "construction" of facts is far from arbitrary; even when practicality isn't a factor, it's a process of finding those texts that are not only desirable but well enough anchored to limit emotional self-indulgence.

Realism is a matter of degree. In general, the occasions that elevate texts from the arbitrariness of make-believe are:

1. Outside of your control. Even fiction, if written by someone else, has more emotional impact than your own daydream with the same content.
2. Rare. A situation in a sports event that comes up only once in a decade is more moving than one that happens every week, which is in turn more moving than one that happens several times in a game. This factor makes cues better pacers in proportion as they are:
   a. Current rather than historic – since current events of a given kind are rarer than those that may have happened in the past generally. There may have been only one major earthquake this year, but six in the past decade and scores before that.
   b. Occurring near rather than far, including to nearer relatives rather than more distant ones. You can have only one spouse and two parents but any number of cousins.
   c. Verifiably true. Events seen as facts have more impact than those seen as fictions. This, too, is because of their relative rarity; and veridical truth isn't necessary, as long as your belief stands up to some well-disciplined test for truth. An entrenched historical myth or urban legend may serve as well as a fact.
   d. Consistent. Potential beliefs that are consistent with beliefs already held are fewer than those that could be formed ad hoc from immediate circumstances.
3. Surprising, as just described. Rarity is necessary but not sufficient to maintain occasions for emotion.[2]

Beliefs that occasion negative emotions compete by a similar logic, modified by the fact that we try to avoid them but that they habituate less than positive emotions.[3] Part of growing up is cultivating a will to resist the promptings of phobia, performance anxiety, hypochondria, paranoid jealousy, or the fear that an oncoming driver will steer into our lane. We give in to one of the corresponding beliefs not only when they are realistic – after a positive test for cancer, for instance – but also when we have a strong appetite and one of these factors selects a unique occasion for it. If I'm the nervous type and I notice a pain I never had before right after my best friend is diagnosed with cancer, I may not be able to resist the urge to panic. Once my expectation that I can ward off such a fear falters, the lesser habituation of fears may make my belief that I have cancer a far more intrusive lapse district than could be based on a positive temptation.

I'm hypothesizing that noninstrumental beliefs are selected for how they pace emotions according to particular kinds of occasions. An awareness of taking arbitrary control of such beliefs comes to predict loss of emotional force.

This issue is a lot like the choice of how much importance to invest in a movie. You're usually not conscious of this choice, but it becomes evident when a movie starts to be too punishing and you reduce its importance. You say to yourself, "This is only a movie," and yet you aren't discovering new information; you've never ducked when guns pointed to the audience. Rather, you're announcing your disinvestment: "This movie shall no longer be important to me. I won't reward myself any longer according to the events in its plot."

Where there's no instrumental need, the penalty for badly placed beliefs isn't some practical failure, but a failure to occasion emotional reward as effectively as possible. The person who withdraws her investment during the scary part of the movie loses her chance to be rewarded by the parts that follow; to some extent, she will lose her ability to keep her investment in subsequent movies when they tempt her to disinvest.

It's noteworthy that we perceive such changes of rule as changes of fact – "This *is* only a movie." Indeed, beliefs are almost always perceived as keyed to facts; even when they are "leaps of faith," the faith is still "in" some external situation. We don't see these beliefs as dependent on our following rules. Indeed, the reverse is more apt to be true: Rules are seen as facts, as in my example of believing in the appetite-suppressing power of ginger, and other examples in Section 7.1. Parents teach a child rules in declarative sentences, the kind that describe facts about the world: Crime doesn't pay, sleeping late is unhealthy, the Devil finds work for idle hands. We sense the same dangers in seeing personal rules as just practical that Piaget's ten-year-olds did when they insisted that rules for games were eternal or that early legislatures did when they "discovered" laws rather than writing them (see the same section).

To sum up: Facts that are adequately rare and surprising become goods, commodities in limited supply that reward us in ways not necessarily connected with their instrumental value; and we protect the uniqueness of these commodities by not noticing our participation in assigning them value. The threat that people often feel from the social constructivists is the nihilism or solipsism that looms when this uniqueness is endangered. However, the constructivist point doesn't require us to regard belief as arbitrary, any more than an awareness that the rules of a game are socially agreed upon would make 10-year-old boys disregard these rules. It removes only a final and probably unnecessary protection, a sacred ignorance of our participation in assigning significance to external cues. The identification of robust motivational constraints on this assignment should give constructivism an acceptable framework.

11.2 THE VICARIOUS EXPERIENCE PUZZLE

Especially puzzling for utility theory is the way we take on other people's experiences, both pleasant and unpleasant, as our own.[4] Economic Man is supposed to maximize his own prospects, and help others only insofar as doing so will accomplish this. However, you find counterexamples all the time, from people who leave tips for waiters they'll never see again to heroes who give their lives to save strangers in fires and accidents. People also have the potential to derive satisfaction from others' pain; examples range from laughter at others' misfortune (in previous centuries the main theory of humor),[5] to sadists who specifically inflict pain for the sake of their own pleasure, to the many societies that have used human sacrifice to relieve various kinds of emotional malaise – often by specifically trying to maximize the pain of the victim. The Khonds of Orissa, for instance, raised victims especially for torturing to death, in which ceremony "the more tears he shed, the more abundant would be the supply of rain." Even at the height of Christian influence in Europe, richer towns bought condemned criminals from poorer towns for the spectacle of executing them.[6] Instrumentality again aside, what makes this range of perceived experiences in other people valuable to us?

This is a topic as big as the history of civilization. Here I will just make a suggestion about how it relates to the will: The premature satiation hypothesis predicts that vicarious experience will be a good source of occasions for emotional reward, but will become less valuable to the extent that you can bring it under your control, because your control will inevitably undermine your appetite. The greatest rewards from other people come through gambles. Gambles that are rigged – interactions that are predictable, people you can boss around, relationships you're poised to leave if they turn disappointing – push your emotional experiences in the direction of daydreams.

To some extent, people can occasion your emotions without currently interacting with you – by means of the stories or memories they've created that can "live on" even after their deaths; but as you become increasingly familiar with these stories or memories, they become stale. Ongoing interaction obviously resists habituation better. A person who makes a particular reaction from another person the occasion for an emotion always runs the risk that the other will evoke an unwanted urge like anger or disgust or fear, or will suggest nothing at all. Of course, it's possible to cheat at this game, to hear only what you want in what the other says, or to fail to give importance to the other's responses – not to gamble on her, the error of narcissism. But this is tantamount to exchanging a mutual game of cards for a game of solitaire, and perhaps even to cheating at solitaire; such an impulse is punished by a loss of suspense, and hence of all but the shortest-range reward.

What makes a game of empathy mutual is your depending on the other person's plays to occasion your emotions. From a physical standpoint, everyone actually plays by herself, but most people learn to barter adequately surprising plays for equally surprising plays by others. To be a good player, you need to know what emotions the others want and roughly what choices of yours occasion them – and then preserve the occasioning process by not making these choices too often or too predictably. Mixing them with a risk of occasions for contrary emotions will also preserve them. Of course, everyone tries to increase her short-range reward by manipulating you to give the right occasioning cues and by predicting these cues before they occur. People have to rely on you to keep this task adequately challenging, just as you have to rely on them in exchange.

Given adequate challenge, the emotional payoff comes when the other person gives you a rewarding occasion. Predicting other people becomes a highly rewarded activity for its emotion-occasioning value, quite aside from how it may help you influence them.

11.2.1 Empathy as Modeling

However, this is only part of the story. So far, there's no reason to think that gambling on other people's behavior is any better than gambling on a horse race or on your ability to solve a puzzle. The fact that this puzzle responds strategically to your choices might make it more challenging, but it wouldn't qualitatively change the experience of succeeding or failing. But because this kind of puzzle is built like the person solving it – that is, because it's another person – it may foster what is likely to be a much richer strategy of occasioning emotions.

First of all, this similarity supplies a different way of solving the puzzle. Since other people's choices depend more on their interaction with you than on anything you know about them in advance, you soon learn that the best way to predict them is to use your own experience to model theirs. You say, "If I were her, and were angry at me but amused by me and hoped for a job with me, what would I do if I (the real me) were to say X?" You entertain the other's likely emotions and notice where they pull you. In effect you create a model of the other person using your own emotional equipment. It's a familiar experience to hold conversations with such a model – "If I say X, I can just hear her say Y. . . ." If the model isn't arbitrary – if it's disciplined by observation – it's apt to behave much more like the actual other person than a nonempathic model would, for instance one made like the model of an economy from statistical data. Even infants can be shown to predict a person's behavior by a "theory of mind," that is, by empathic modeling, which in some situations makes them much better predictors of an adult human's behavior than are adult apes using trial and error.[7] Thus the best way to predict people is to put yourself in their shoes.

However, this empathic modeling process yields more than just prediction. Putting yourself in the other person's shoes means adopting the criteria that you think she's using to occasion emotion. For the time being, you entertain what you think would be her emotions. But of course, they are hers only in the sense that you're having them according to a theory about her. *You* are the person through whose brain they're percolating. If you have enough discipline to keep your model honest, you can use it to occasion emotions just as you use your own prospects.

Since emotions don't require a turnkey, just available appetite and adequately rare occasions to preserve this appetite, you can sometimes experience the emotions you're modeling in the other person as substantially as the ones you have *as yourself*. To model the other people is to *have* her expected feelings; and nothing makes these vicarious feelings differ in kind from real ones. However, the impact of this phenomenon will be limited by the uniqueness of your relationship with the other person, just as the impact of "texts" à la constructivism is limited by their factuality; your vicarious experiences from strangers picked for the purpose will be little more than daydreams.

In this way, models of other people can provide occasions for emotion continually over time, not just intermittent wins and losses in a game of prediction. Of course, allowing your own models of other people to occasion your emotions partially hedges your gamble on what other people are really experiencing, which at the low extreme of risk means just daydreaming; but a well-drawn model gives you the same incentives as its subject while you're impersonating her, and thus generates occasions for emotion somewhat the way she would if she were present. Authors of fiction report that even their characters can take on this property, that they "demand" or "refuse" to say certain things as a story develops. The premature satiation hypothesis thus holds that patterns of vicarious emotion can be relatively autonomous, regardless of whom they're modeled after, but these patterns will become stereotyped and predictable unless you refresh them with ongoing observations.

To the extent that we've gambled on another person's discernible feelings, these feelings become a commodity that we'll work for. If we don't cheapen it too much – by discerning feelings without an adequate basis, or changing empathic objects too quickly when they occasion aversive experiences, or picking objects who won't respond, like film stars – we may have a regular source of unique and surprising occasions for emotion. Information for refreshing our models of other people becomes the limited good that constrains this otherwise too-available resource. This is how other people come to compete for our interest on the same footing as the goods of commerce.

Models of other people are probably the form in which a child first organizes her experience. The psychoanalysts have written a great deal about how children construct selves through the "introjection" of others, that is, through identifying themselves with the people who've impressed them. Kleinian psychoanalysts, who may have listened the most of anyone to children's self-descriptions, suggest that "internal objects" are the basic tools of a continual foraging for emotional reward that they call "phantasy."[8] Certainly young children's theories of themselves are made up of a wide variety of human models.[9]

Just as allegory was a precursor of science, vicarious experience may be the starting place of individuals' conception of the world. The other people whom she incorporates through modeling may or may not be separated sharply from the entity she perceives as having her own emotions, that is, her self. Except in the case of a hunger, which is dependent on an event like eating or injury that physically must either happen to her or not, it may be somewhat arbitrary whether she calls the experience hers, as opposed to someone else's experienced empathically. That is, empathy with a friend's hunger is different from being hungry yourself, but empathy with her grief or joy need not be.

This difference may be of theoretical value in explaining some experiences, especially the negative empathy that I'll discuss presently. It also raises the possibility that both emotions and patterns of occasion for them can be fairly contagious. A pattern that you copy may "be" you for a while, or for ever after. The self that an adult recognizes as her own may be only the most constant group within a population of emotion-pacing models, rather than descriptions chosen for according to their accuracy in characterizing her attributes.[10]

11.2.2 Negative Empathy

An economist, Julian Simon, had begun before his recent death to examine vicarious reward as a possible economic good,

> viewing the unit of consciousness as composed of continuously extended rings of "interest" or "sympathy" or "empathy" around the core of the self-person, by close analogy to the notion of continuous successive temporal persons.[11]

His theory counts all empathic relationships as positive, so that each person rewards herself proportionately to the other's reward. Relationships of this sort could be called "sympathetic." But people also reward themselves according to others' misfortunes – not through indifference, but by an actual aesthetic appreciation of their pain. The extreme of this relationship is the sadism of the torturer, as I noted earlier, but there are many ordinary relationships that have a negative sign. Some kinds of rivalry still make sweet revenge socially acceptable, like our pleasure at seeing the driver who cut us off stopped by the police, or at seeing a person with vicious opinions embarrassed. Such experiences should also be counted as empathic, since they involve modeling – and thus to some extent *having* – the other person's feelings.

Instances of negative empathy raise two questions: What could make an emotion that we avoid ourselves attractive as a vicarious experience? And why is this attraction unusually strong in cases where the victim has expressed an impulse that we share but want to avoid, that is, when she makes a good scapegoat? My answers are somewhat intuitive, as opposed to being strongly suggested by the properties of hyperbolic curves; but I think it's important for any theory of empathy to offer at least a possible explanation for the negative case. I suspect that I'm dealing with the human, civilized variant of a very basic process, the one that tells an animal who's friend and who's foe; unfortunately, accounts of this process in animals are too stimulus-oriented to be helpful.

I can answer the first question only with the reminder that in hyperbolic discounting theory all emotions must be rewarding, and a change of duration of preference should not be as momentous as a reversal of value. Aversive emotions are preferred in the pain or itch range; negative empathy, even when deliberately cultivated, is rarely perceived as your greatest long-range good – more frequently, as a temptation in the addiction range.

Vicarious or even imagined pain can probably become attractive in somewhat the way that a positive component can be distilled from negative emotions. Just as a scary movie or roller coaster can evoke thrill from fear by removing the actual danger, so negative empathy may evoke some kind of gratification from pain, remorse, envy, or chagrin, by removing some element of cost from them – I won't speculate as to what. A similar transformation can be seen when your own awful experience arises as a hypothetical. There is often a fascination to imagining what it would be like to be tortured, for instance, and children are sometimes drawn to rehearse agonizing choices like "what if your boat were sinking, and you could save only your mother or your father?" These aren't pleasurable pastimes, but often aren't avoided, either.

As for the selection of objects, when people seek vicarious aversive experiences, they don't usually do so indiscriminately. In particular, if a part of our emotional experience has become a nuisance, an image that attaches pain to it is somehow satisfying: I even remember someone's rueful joke that he wanted to put his extracted tooth in a dish of sugar so that he could "watch it ache." Vicarious anguish feels like riddance. If someone's triumph would create in us an overwhelming temptation to envy or regret, or to copy harmful traits – her suffering will be reassuring.

How empathic modeling may make negative objects – villians, enemies, scapegoats – useful and even necessary is another big topic. What concerns us immediately is how it might reflect the limits of what the will can do. Briefly, a resort to negative empathy may seem worth its cost where your will can't control seductive emotional patterns.

The free availability of emotional reward isn't an unmixed blessing. Not only does indulgence ad lib deteriorate through premature satiation, but reward patterns that are temporarily preferred in the moderately long run, once learned, will be hard to get rid of for the sake of your longest-run preference. Just as a drug addict will know even after years of sobriety that intense pleasure is only a short trip away, so if you've overcome an addictive emotional pattern – dependency, promiscuity, timidity, exploitiveness, and so on – you'll always be able to reach for it under pressure. Having learned better long-range patterns doesn't mean having forgotten how to activate the old ones that gratify an urge quickly; and unlike the drug addict, you can't keep the unwanted activity distant by avoiding drug neighborhoods.

In addition, directly controlling addictive emotional patterns would probably mean avoiding emotion before it gets aroused – inhibition or isolation of your affect – rather than using willpower. Emotional patterns are both immediately rewarding and poorly marked by cues that could serve as criteria for rules, which should make them poor subjects for intertemporal bargaining. Furthermore, when an emotion can be totally controlled by will it becomes reduced to triviality, the very development that you seek empathic experiences in order to avoid. To preserve your emotionality and still restrict seductive emotional patterns that have become a nuisance, you have to find some strategy that involves neither willpower nor inhibition of emotion.

Here's where the thrill of vicarious punishment may offer a solution of sorts. You select as objects of your negative empathy people who give in to a particular temptation and stand some chance of being punished.

You go over this drama in fantasy, often with the guidance of your culture; if possible, you arrange to see it enacted in real life – the poseur humiliated, the driver who cuts ahead ticketed, the boy who cries wolf getting poetic justice, even the high-living jewel thief coming to a bad end. The temptation we experience doesn't have to be suppressed – it's gratified; and the mechanism by which we brand the role as alien not only makes the punishment empathically attractive, it creates an obstacle to adopting the role ourselves. My guess is that we can root against a scenario more easily than we can suppress it; or at least, rooting against it does less damage to our emotionality.[12]

To restate this admittedly sketchy hypothesis: Your readiness to experience other people's emotions creates an incentive to control their influence on you. If you can't resist a particular person's seductiveness with your will, you can at least interpret her as an enemy interest, the voice of the Devil. In the realm of empathy you can't kill cheap thrills; you have to spoil them by seducing the interests that are based on them into taking a poison pill. Scapegoating – the creation of pain for the person you fear you are, the younger sibling showing the behavior you've barely outgrown or the criminal who does what you're tempted to do – has seemed irrational in utility theory when reward was thought of as limited by the scarcity of external turnkeys. In the world of emotional reward, however, it may be one of the few available devices for limiting those seductive patterns that are too rewarding to reject outright.

To summarize the now rather long line of inference from the simple fact of hyperbolic discounting: This discounting will lead farsighted organisms into limited warfare relationships with their own future selves. To the extent that they perceive prisoners' dilemmas in these relationships, they will cooperate with these selves in a pattern that has the properties of will. However, hyperbolic discounting will also motivate individuals to satiate their available appetite prematurely, and the need for discrete benchmarks in intertemporal cooperation renders will unable to control this urge. Pacing of appetite for emotional reward requires gambling on surprising outcomes. Other people are especially valuable as objects of such gambles, because the models we make of them can pace our emotions directly. However, such models can grow wildly, and seductive but inferior ones can't be well controlled by direct effort. Negative empathy seems to be a way to distance the roles we want as part of ourselves from tempting alternatives, in an area where the will is ineffective.

11.3 THE INDIRECTION PUZZLE

I've described how the will can't stop the premature satiation of suspense. I'll now argue that will can actually make premature satiation worse. Your will needs conspicuous, discrete criteria of success or failure to maintain the incentive to cooperate with your future selves at each choice-point. If the criteria are subtle – "eat what you'll be glad of in retrospect," "follow your true heart," or the self-referential "do as much as you have to in order to maintain intertemporal trust" – then there will be too much room for impulses to dominate individual choices without getting caught. Remember our hypothesis of what the will needs in order to recruit motivation: You must expect to obey it in the future *if and only if* you obey it currently. Subtle criteria make this contingency escapable and thus take away its power. This is the very reasoning that leads the will often to serve compulsion range interests because of their better definability, as I argued in Chapter 9.

But systematically following well-defined criteria is exactly what makes your behavior predictable, by other people as well as yourself. It's a great way to achieve a goal as efficiently as possible, so that you can go on and do something else. It's a terrible way to enjoy an activity for its own sake because it kills appetite. You inevitably learn to anticipate every step of the activity, so that it eventually becomes second nature, making it so uninteresting that people used to think that ingrained habits were run by the spinal cord. You can't use will to prevent this anticipation, because clear criteria for rules directing attention aren't available, and even if they were, attention probably moves too quickly to be made contingent on testing for them.

So a too-powerful will tends to undermine its own motivational basis, creating a growing incentive to find evasions. The awkwardness of getting reward in a well-off society is that the *creation* of appetite often requires undoing the work of *satisfying* appetite. The availability of physiological appetites like those for food and sex regenerates as a function of time, but that of appetites for safety or wealth or comfort doesn't. If you're comfortable, you have it made, and staying comfortable may not take much effort. Once your emotional appetite for comfort has been satiated, it won't be a source of much further reward unless something restores your need for it. You have to face a challenge, some kind of doubt or delay.

However, you can't simply *try* to get satisfaction slowly or inefficiently; always to be reining in your own impatience would take more effort than it repaid. Besides, the circumstance that made seeking a particular satisfaction more than a daydream-like activity to begin with must have been some way of seeing it as necessary, as something more than a mere game; deliberately going slow contradicts that belief.

Where we haven't committed ourselves to maximizing the goods that satisfy appetites, we can recognize available appetite as a resource: People not uncommonly work up an appetite for dinner, boast of an appetite for sex, complain of a jaded appetite for entertainment, and so on. By contrast, there's clearly an appetite available for hoarding – for collecting things or getting rich – but to whet the appetite by gambling and intermittently losing your hoard isn't seen as maximizing your utility. We call gamblers foolish because we see value as inhering in their goods, not in how well they exploit their available appetite. Yet there is often a grudging acknowledgment that they have some kind of rationality: "Perhaps nowadays gambling appeals because the rest of life is enervatingly predictable."[13]

To deal with this contradiction, you usually have to discover some fact that requires you to put your satisfaction at risk. To climb mountains or jump out of airplanes as a test of manhood, to stay with an abusive lover as a test of loyalty, to join a religion that demands self-abasement, to play the stock market or the horses as a way to get rich, even to bet your dignity on staying in the forefront of fashion leads to repeated losses or at least the credible threat of losses. You get your appetite back while struggling not to. However, where appetites have to be restored by repudiating hard-won accomplishments, such recognition would often strike us as irrational.

In utility literature there is scant appreciation of the value of risk as a way to create appetite. The canniest is at the societal level, in Albert Hirschman's "principle of the hiding hand," which addresses appetite in terms of the heightened creativity that setbacks motivate:

> Creativity always comes as a surprise to us; therefore we can never count on it and we dare not believe in it until it has happened. In other words, we would not consciously engage upon tasks whose success clearly requires that creativity be forthcoming. Hence, the only way in which we can bring our creative resources fully into play is by misjudging the nature of the task, by presenting it to ourselves as more routine, simple, undemanding of genuine creativity than it will turn out to be. . . . We are

apparently on the trail here of some sort of invisible or hidden hand that beneficially hides difficulties from us.[14]

According to this hypothesis, the old psychoanalytic cliché that gamblers unconsciously want to lose turns out to be partially correct: They're moved by a need to restore their available appetites by losing, but must serve this need without contradicting their wholehearted attempts to win. This is just the intrapsychic version of a familiar phenomenon: If one sports team wins too regularly it diminishes the excitement of the game, and eventually attendance and income. It's in the winning team's interest as well as its competitors' to have a governing body impose some kind of handicap, like last pick in next season's player draft. What the team can't do, without both impairing its morale and removing the spark from the game, is try less hard to win.

Gambling has kept a startling number of devotees in thrall over the centuries, including many rich people whose felt need to get more money has always puzzled observers. And pure gambling – just games with numbers – seems to be a degraded form of letting your emotions depend on surprises. Such gambling takes the strategy of using risk to maintain available appetite to its logical conclusion by stripping risks down to their basic math. It's a degraded form because, as I noted earlier, even outcomes that are literally unpredictable habituate somewhat if there is a narrow range of possibilities. On the other hand, people who can tolerate more doubt and ambiguity wind up gambling on the complex texture of social outcomes, although they may still be more or less reckless. As Jon Elster has pointed out, Stendhal described the taste for interpersonal adventure as gambling in *The Red and the Black:* "What can a young woman hazard? All that she has most precious: her honor, her lifelong reputation." Halfway between the pure gamblers and the social ones in their taste for complexity are the daredevils and mountain climbers who are lured into taking physical risks, sometimes even after losing close family members and body parts to their quests.[15]

11.3.1 Indirection

Any self-control tactic may reduce surprise as it reduces the dangers you face. However, three of the four possible tactics (extrapsychic commitments, attention control and emotion control [see Section 5.1]) may also have the opposite effect. Physical extrapsychic devices and restrictions on attention prevent reward for limited periods of time, and thus are apt to function as challenges as much as controls. Staying away from food, or alcohol, or avoiding information about them for a time will leave you with a good potential appetite for them. While isolation of affect reduces your receptiveness to emotional reward, the cultivation of contrary emotions (the converse form of emotion control) and openness to social influence (the commonest extrapsychic control) may both refresh available appetite. Since personal rules, the fourth tactic, are based on systemization, they're going to be the self-control tactic that least accommodates your complementary needs for satisfaction and deprivation.

The more you make satisfaction depend on a condition outside of your control – the more you believe in the objective value of wealth, safety, comfort, and so on – the more you define your need to refresh your appetite for this condition as impulsive. That is, belief in the desirability of these conditions themselves commits you to guard them from any tendency you have to put them at risk. This is all the more true for the value of concrete objects associated with them: money, trophies, promises, those amassable things that could be generally called wealth. Furthermore, as I suggested at the beginning of this chapter, the more you've made the relevant beliefs themselves depend on criteria that are outside of your control, the more you differentiate these quests from mere games, from make-believe.

Thus, whereas the will usually comes to superintend the getting and maintaining of the objects of appetite, the creating or maintaining of the potential for appetites has to come from some evasion of this will. This evasion can happen crudely through the pitfalls to the will that I described earlier. Rationalizations, blind spots, circumscribed lapse districts (see Section 9.1.2), and so on defeat your resolutions, but the resulting loss of reward may be mitigated or sometimes even reversed by its stimulation of your appetite. This primitive strategy may sometimes be successful enough to make you nurse some otherwise controllable addictions,[16] but the overall costs are high. An approach that does less violence to the will involves believing in some seemingly rational or arguably necessary activity that makes the direct routes to a reward less of a sure thing. That is, you need to find *indirect* routes to success: dummy activities that are only partially maintained by their ostensible purpose, but mostly stay desirable to the extent that they maintain available appetite by creating good gambles or by directing your efforts toward tasks whose mastery won't give you arbitrary control over their reward.

Activities that are spoiled by counting them, or counting on them, have to be undertaken through indirection if they are to stay valuable. For instance, romance undertaken for sex or even "to be loved" is thought of as crass, as are some of the most lucrative professions if undertaken for money or performance art if done for effect. Too great an awareness of the motivational contingencies for sex, affection, money, or applause spoils the effort, and not only because it undeceives the other people involved. Beliefs about the intrinsic worth of these activities are valued beyond whatever truth they may have, because they promote the needed indirection. Similarly, the specific tasks that various schools of psychotherapy believe in turn out to be unnecessary when the effectiveness of seemingly contradictory teachings is compared; perhaps the empathic engagement that has been shown to make the difference is awkward unless attention is directed away from it.

There are other incentives for indirection besides maintaining available appetite, such as avoiding occasions for self-consciousness, competitiveness, panic, or performance anxiety. Any goal that excites contrary urges, even trying too hard to get to sleep, may need to be approached via a detour; and even small distractions can function as such urges, so that for instance, you may set an arbitrary goal for when to stop an activity rather than intermittently asking yourself whether you're tired of it yet. However, these examples don't arise because of efficiency at reward-getting per se, and thus aren't part of our topic.

A wide variety of activities rely on indirection at one stage or another. Some disparate examples:

- We study supposedly as a means to having knowledge, and studying would drift into idle reverie without that focus; but elderly people with little prospective need for the knowledge, or sometimes the ability to form new memories, often ignore these limitations so as to continue to have a purpose for studying.
- We think of the point of competitive sports as winning and thus that an athlete who can beat another should be paid more than the other. In a recent National Public Radio commentary, Frank DeFord punctured this indirection when he pointed out that the point of sports is entertainment, that female tennis players entertain as well as men, and that they thus should be paid equally even though they can usually be beaten by men of similar standing.[17]
- Dramatic, artistic, and even scientific creative processes often rely

191

upon meditation rituals to summon the relevant muses. I am personally conscious of going for walks or washing dishes in order to *not* work too directly on a problem. The direct approach of "find what works best" spoils the effort in its early phases.

- Likewise in the realm of the spiritual: From priesthood to fortune-telling, contact with the intuitive seems to need some kind of divination. This is all the more true for approaches that cultivate a sense of empathy with a god. Several religions forbid the attempt to make their deity more tangible by drawing pictures of him, and Orthodox Judaism forbids even naming him. The experience of God's presence is supposed to come through some kind of invitation that he may or may not accept, not through invocation.

- People who like to nurse grudges need pretexts. They would undermine their anger by acknowledging a need to stay thwarted, and paranoids are terribly threatened by the suggestion that they arrange to feel persecuted.

- Maybe the most elementary indirection is the tactic of limiting self-reward by believing reward to be intrinsically dependent on external facts, which I described in Section 11.1. While the value of an activity actually comes from how it supports an ongoing appetitive process, our guess about this value attaches to the *things* that the activity seeks. For instance, we have to be continually reminded that "time is money," because we insist that money is more real.

We use indirection most often for pacing with positive appetites, because these appetites are the most prone to habituation. We weave it in complex ways into other strategies, not the least because concealment makes it more durable. Let's look at an apparent example in greater detail:

The fastest and surest route to sexual satiation is obviously masturbation. However, this habituates in adolescence and becomes a minor activity in most people, not because it's punished but because it can't compete with alternatives that better maintain sexual appetite. Aside from the value of romantic relationships in pacing emotions, people learn to use them in pacing sex, not because these maximize satiation but because they optimize longing.

Traditional sex-role assignments arranged challenges in the cooperative task of pacing sex, quite aside from what these assignments may have done to encourage fidelity. In the past, Western tradition strongly suggested that women shouldn't cultivate a taste for sex, not just because of women's greater vulnerability to venereal disease and pregnancy, but because "fast" women were distasteful. This perception conveniently spared men the need to maintain obstacles of their own. Men could cultivate an unambivalent goal-directedness in this area as long as they maintained taboos against masturbation and the "easy kind" of women. Women, by contrast, had to learn optimal pacing strategies while ostensibly concerning themselves with higher tasks – coyness in preference to willingness, but for the sake of virtue; clothing (which permits teasing) in preference to nakedness, but for the sake of modesty. Furthermore, the most effective pacing – at least the most durable – required conviction about the value of the higher tasks in their own right. To be caught being modest as a ploy marked you as fast. The extent of the need to approach sex indirectly is shown by the fact that the other traditional naming taboo – besides that for the deity – has been for the female genital.

The Western historical attitude toward sexuality has ostensibly held that sexual pleasure is proportional to indulgence but that it happens to be difficult, dangerous, or perhaps even evil because of external givens. The idea that these beliefs have been shaped by the requirements of maintaining sexual appetite has had to be regarded as merely cynical, because to believe otherwise would be to contradict them and thus spoil them as indirections. The extent to which these attitudes remain, of course, is arguable; but if the more open competitiveness of modern culture is breaking down the old rationales for optimizing sexual longing by blocking direct access, we should expect there to be a growing market for new ones. Middle-class heterosexuals are said to be vastly overestimating their risk of contracting acquired immune deficiency syndrome (AIDS); perhaps this is one sign of such a market.[18]

The strategy of indirection goes a step beyond the harnessing of emotions to external facts that I discussed in the section on construction of fact; it finds beliefs that specifically divert effort away from the efficient satisfaction of the relevant appetites. Indirect tasks are a form of self-deception and are thus vulnerable to exposure, but they're maintained by some relatively long-range rewards that are spoiled by shortcuts. The necessary blind spots may seem preposterous to people who don't share that particular indirection strategy; a vulnerability to wit is frequently a sign that an activity is indirect. Most of the activities just described are examples: piety, the rituals that creative people use for inspiration, sexual prudery, pretension, and cultivated grudges. Indeed, it could be argued that piercing indirections is the basic mechanism of wit.

Wit is often felt to go too far, in which case it is called cynicism. After all, it relies on the discernment of base motives under ostensibly lofty ones.[19] A wit (or cynic) thinks of herself as a devotee of simple truth, and her targets as hypocrites, but the latter may just be trying to use indirection to improve emotional appetites – to the benefit of themselves and others, perhaps including the cynic. However, these targets would be hard put to claim such a justification, since most indirections can't function when acknowledged as such. In the absence of some commonly held rationale for them – piety, morality, good form, and so on – strategies of indirection lose ground, and it's hard to make sense of what's been lost. There are only complaints like those of etiquette columnist Miss Manners:

> With the entire population going crazy trying to think of new ways to shock jaded fellow citizens, there is no one left in the crucial job of being shocked. . . . Miss Manners proposes that some of us volunteer.[20]

Probably the greatest – but most debatable – indirections are those that become compulsions when taken too much as goals in their own right. Of course, how much is too much depends on an individual's strategy: Someone who plays bridge for fun may look on someone who plays to win as playing compulsively; but if she directly tries to maximize the fun, she may spoil it by a laxity that makes the game trivial because of premature satiation. A clearer overuse of indirection is the literal-mindedness and consequent boorishness of nerds – the kind that leads them to answer inquiries about their health in full detail and give true opinions of others' wearing apparel. They fail to appreciate the limited purpose of small talk in pacing the exchange of emotional occasions.[21]

Two fables reveal our culture's longstanding intuition about indirection. The goose that laid the golden eggs was cut up by a greedy owner to get to a supposedly greater store inside – but the carcass contained no gold at all. This seems to be a direct warning against trying to short-circuit routes to reward. Similarly, the recipe for stone soup was given by a wise rabbi to selfish villagers, who wouldn't contribute their vegetables to the common pot; however, they didn't mind contributing if it was just to enhance the feeding power of a magical stone in the pot.

194

Here the urge evaded is social greed, not personal impatience, but the indirection is just as clear. Within this metaphor, the error of the nerd would be to study the stone itself to unmask the nature of its magic.

Western society shares – or used to share – many articles of faith that function as indirections. One of these is avoidance of the crassness of calculation that makes the economics of utility look selfish. For that matter, it's a social sin to be caught "having a motive," even though all schools of psychology that have looked at motivation regularly conclude that all behavior is motivated. Maybe discomfort with the direct discussion of motives was a factor in putting both Freudian analysis and behaviorism out of fashion, and in creating the popularity of a cognitive psychology that goes out of its way to avoid discussing motives. As psychology in general becomes more explicit, people express fears of a cheapening, a reduction in subtlety, of our perceptions of each other.

People have always had a sense that some emotional endeavors are fragile and undermined by direct observation. Perhaps the exact specification of what we mean to each other, if it were possible, would undermine necessary indirections; we probably couldn't construct interpersonal relationships using explicit instructions. To some extent, we can recognize the dummy activity as an indirection – but if the satisfaction has to come from pursuing the goal against great odds, knowledge that "it's only a game" will make us too prone to give up during the rough spots. Hence a paradox: To get the most emotional reward from an activity in its own right, you often have to believe in the instrumental value of the activity. There are many examples of the form "You have to have faith, but it doesn't matter in what." Indirection seems to be the only robust solution that people have found to this paradox.

However, although belief in the instrumental need for particular goods may make striving for the goods seem less arbitrary, this belief necessarily blinds people to the need for a corresponding appetite. In writing about a person's folly in staying nearly satiated, "driving a cart with a permanently tired horse," Konrad Lorenz marveled that "the most stupid human being on earth should see through that error, yet people don't."[22] The explanation is probably that seeing through the error would expose the indirection that focuses our attention on the goods, rather than on the aesthetics of getting them.

We've always had trouble conceiving of a pressure to behave that is at the same time a resource. A bottle of wine that "demands to be drunk" or money that "burns a hole in your pocket" are intuitive enough, but appetites per se for drinking or spending aren't usually seen as goods. Plato saw something of this problem in the emotion of love. In his *Symposium* Socrates says that Love is the child of Plenty (Poros) and Poverty (Penia) and has some of the qualities of each: Love doesn't *possess* Plenty (beauty, wisdom, etc.), for then he would be satisfied and wouldn't be Love; but, unlike Poverty, he appreciates these things. "That which is always flowing in is always flowing out, and so he is never in want and never in wealth" but represents a "mean" between the two.[23] Many writers since then have said that love is a blessing but desire a curse; they haven't been able to specify what makes the difference.

The finding that discounting is hyperbolic lets us understand one of the most puzzling characteristics of well-off societies: that we can't optimize appetite directly, but have to foster it indirectly by "believing in" the importance of what are actually arbitrary tasks, the real value of which is only that they obstruct speedy satiation. However, analyses of social construction and of the projection of meaning, including the present hypothesis, are apt to be unwelcome because of their threat to this very strategy. Indeed, a major factor in the decay of civilizations that have been peaceful for long periods may be the replacement of indirect processes by efficient ones; as they become efficient, they become unaccountably less rewarding. In historian Arnold Toynbee's phrase, the piper loses his cunning.[24]

Even in intellectual endeavors, our culture can't seem to find a stable balance between creating and overcoming challenges. There is a pendulum of favor that swings between "getting to the bottom of things" in one direction and mystical holisms, rejections of crass reductionism in the other. When it swings in the former direction it fosters science, organization, a love of clear, explicit thought, simple form, and comprehensive theory – in short, classicism. When it swings the other way, it fosters subtlety, an ambivalence toward science, and a love of the intense and unfathomable emotions evoked when the world is mysterious – that is, romanticism. The ultimate breakdown of the will seems to occur when efficiency has pushed the pendulum further in the direction of systemization – and attenuation of available appetite – than people can stand. The will is no good at pushing the other way. It can only accede to being bypassed by indirections that have more vigor until the pendulum has again swung well into unsystematic territory.

11.4 SUMMARY

Impatience for premature satiation undoes the advantages that a farseeing intelligence and an efficient will might otherwise confer, especially in people whose physical needs have largely been met. Intelligence means imagination – a potentially rich fantasy life – but overvaluation of nearer rewards tends to keep appetite nipped in the bud. An efficient will means dependable success in waiting for long-range goals, but overvaluation of nearer rewards tends to make such success hollow, again by overly motivating anticipation. Willpower focuses your motivation on reaching milestones toward satisfaction; it thus not only fails to preserve appetite, but may forbid activities that renew appetite, because they involve abandoning hard-won milestones. Gambling, the prototypical means of refreshing appetite, is widely held to be irrational.

Three processes may counteract the willfulness of intelligent organisms, who adopt them insofar as these processes improve their pacing of emotional rewards: (1) Cues that aren't adequately rare or surprising drop away as occasions for emotional reward. The survivors are often but not always facts that stand up to tests of objectivity. For the purpose of pacing emotion, as opposed to accomplishing instrumental tasks, facts are often "constructed" according to how unique and/or surprising they are; the crucial factor is not accuracy per se, but avoiding the arbitrariness of make-believe. (2) Other people provide rich occasions for emotion, not only because they may be optimally unpredictable in the same sense that good puzzles are, but even more because empathically modeling their emotions is an effective way to pace your own. Malice and cruelty are also forms of empathy, perhaps attempts at controlling seductive empathic processes when your will can't do so. (3) Since your will spoils your appetite by policing your progress toward concrete milestones, you often have an incentive to adopt indirect routes to your goals, dummy activities that reward by their very *inefficiency* in satisfying appetites. Because identifying an activity as indirect spoils it for that purpose, this property is often unconscious in the Freudian sense and recognizable mostly when it becomes the butt of wit.

CHAPTER 12

CONCLUSIONS

People's patterns of making self-defeating choices have seemed paradoxical from Plato's time down to the present. A patchwork of lore has accumulated to explain each particular paradox, but every local solution has been inconsistent with the solution that some other piece in the puzzle has seemed to require. As in the harder sciences, increased precision of measurement has revealed the possibility of a more comprehensive solution, which I present under the name picoeconomics (micromicroeconomics).

Choice experiments that were sensitive enough to test the difference between exponential and hyperbolic discount curves provided the necessary advance. Hyperbolic discounting confronts conventional utility theory with the likelihood that the conventional theory was not describing elementary principles of choice, but a higher-order cultural invention that doesn't necessarily operate in all people or in all situations. By demonstrating the basic instability of choice, this finding has promoted the problem of estimating value from a trivial matter of psychometrics into the crucial element of motivational conflict. Preferences that are temporary aren't aberrations anymore, but the starting place for a strategic understanding of functions that used to be thought of as organs: the ego, the will, even the self.

However much it has inconvenienced utility theory, the temporary preference phenomenon finally lets it explain self-defeating behavior. Furthermore, although hyperbolic valuation seems complex when compared with the exponential kind, it fits so many aspects of motivational conflict that it promises to simplify that subject substantially.

Processes that pay off quickly tend to be temporarily preferred to richer but slower-paying processes, a phenomenon that can't be changed by insight per se. However, when people come to look at their current choices as predictors of what they will choose in the future, a logic much like that in the familiar bargaining game, repeated prisoner's dilemma, should recruit additional incentive to choose the richer processes. This mechanism predicts all the major properties that have been ascribed to both the power and freedom of the will.

Further examination of this mechanism reveals how the will is apt to create its own distortion of objective valuation. Four predictions fit commonly observed motivational patterns: A choice may become more valuable as a precedent than as an event in itself, making people legalistic; signs that predict lapses tend to become self-confirming, leading to failures of will so intractable that they seem like symptoms of disease; there will be motivation not to recognize lapses, which creates an underworld much like the Freudian unconscious; and distinct boundaries will recruit motivation better than subtle boundaries, which impairs the ability of will-based strategies to exploit emotional rewards.

Other aspects of temporary preference may have a fundamental influence on what the will can do:

Hyperbolic discounting suggests a distinction between reward and pleasure that allows us to account for the often-observed seductiveness of pain and "negative" emotions. Conversely, the likelihood that this discounting pattern hastens our consumption of a reward where slower consumption would be richer explains why we seek external occasions for rewards that are otherwise at our disposal. The existence of both strong lures to entertain aversive mental processes and intrinsic constraints on freely available, pleasurable ones makes it possible to do without the hoary theory of classical conditioning. Instead: Emotions and hungers (together: appetites) recur to the extent that there is reward for them to do so. This means that the conditioned stimuli for appetites are not automatic triggers, but signs that emitting these appetites will be more rewarding than not emitting them. These cues don't *release* appetites, they *occasion* them.

The urge to satisfy appetite prematurely teaches efficiency of reward-getting but brings about the decline of pleasures once they've become familiar. This problem provides a primary motive for the separation of belief from fantasy. Instrumental needs aside, beliefs determined by relatively rare events that are outside of your control are better occasions for feeling than your own arbitrary constructions, and hence come to be experienced as more meaningful. However, uniquely well-established social constructions may function about as well as objective facts in this regard. Similar logic explains the value of empathic interaction with other people, apart from any motives for practical cooperation: To gamble, in effect, on the experiences of others keeps your occasions for emotion surprising and thus counteracts learned habituation.

Finally, there is an inevitable clash between two kinds of reward-getting strategies: Belief in the importance of external tasks – amassing wealth, controlling people, discovering knowledge itself – leads to behaviors that rush to completion; but a tacit realization of the importance of appetite motivates a search for obstacles to solutions or for gambles that will intermittently undo them. Consciousness of the second task spoils the very belief in the first task that makes the first task strict enough to be an optimal pacer of reward. Thus the second task tends to be learned indirectly, and culturally transmitted via beliefs that seem superstitious or otherwise irrational to conventional utility analysis.

Although picoeconomics can be a tool to find potentials for greater self-control, it reveals situations where increasing efficiency at self-control is not in a person's longest-range interest. Ultimately, the will is a limited solution to the impulsiveness created by the hyperbolic discounting of prospective rewards. Will can't control the impatience for emotional reward that creates the need for surprise, and its overuse against addiction-range preferences creates compulsions. Compulsions in turn erode surprise, so that compulsive people are apt to get just as little long-range pleasure as impulsive ones.

All of these phenomena are predicted by the hyperbolic shape of the discount curve, although perhaps not uniquely. The basic temporary preference phenomenon has been well demonstrated, but other thinkers may draw different implications from it. My hypotheses may only illustrate the strategic patterns that hyperbolic discounting could produce. They can't be verified directly by controlled experiment because they deal with recursive phenomena.

Developing a definitive theory will be a matter of trying out successive models to test their parsimony, ideally with material from all the different schools that have observed the relevant choice-making; Chapter 8 was an attempt at this for the phenomenon of will. However, pattern fitting will always depend to some extent on what strikes individual observers as parsimonious. Patterns different from the ones I've proposed may turn out to fit experience better; but I would argue that some such intertemporal bargaining model will be necessary to accommodate the robust empirical finding of hyperbolic discounting.

NOTES

Preface

1. Respectively, Ainslie (1992, 1999a, 1999b, 2000, and unpublished manuscript).

Chapter 1. Introduction

1. For instance, Baumeister & Heatherton (1996), Becker & Murphy (1988), Polivy (1998), Rachlin (1995a).
2. Plato's *Protagoras* (sections 356–357) in Jowett's translation (1892/1937). His theories and Aristotle's are thoroughly discussed in Charlton (1988, pp. 13–59).
3. Averill (1988).
4. Galen (1963, p. 47); This man-vs.-animal figure has also had a long life.
5. Romans 7: 15–23.
6. Mourant (1967).
7. Kyokai (1996, pp. 228–242). Even primitive religions deal with temptation:
    The creator wished his children to be immortal.
    He told them to wait by the river.
    "Wait for the third canoe," he said.
    "For in the first canoe or in the second canoe
    Will be death."
    After a time the first canoe passed.
    In it a basket of rotten meat.
    "This must surely be death," they said
    And let the canoe pass by and vanish.
    Time passed.
    Until one day the second canoe appeared.
    In it a young man.
    Strange and alien, but who waved and greeted them like a brother.
    They waded out and drew the canoe in to the river bank.
    Embraced the stranger, asked him who he was.
    He was death . . .
    (Amazonian Indian lore adapted by Hampton, 1976, pp. 51–52)

8. Quoted by Hirschman (1977, p. 22).
9. Vanderveldt & Odenwald (1952); Ricoeur (1971).
10. Kobasa & Maddi (1983); Perls et al. (1958).
11. Freud's two principles (1911, p. 223); superego (1923).
12. Indeed, it's been suggested that the war itself was an exercise in will, undertaken by Germany in the knowledge that it was likely to lose, lest honor be lost. Economist Avner Offer has analyzed how codes of honor committed all the participants to decisions that were far removed from what their preferences would have been if honor weren't at stake (1995). A related factor may have been that all but one of the 12 articles in the behavioral science literature before 1940 that contained "strength of will" in their titles or abstracts were written by Germans (search of the PsycLIT database, 1887–1998). Weakness of will, or akrasia, did not appear at all in this database before being reintroduced by philosopher of mind Amelie Rorty (1980). Willpower is likewise a new usage. Because of extra meanings, "will" itself can't be searched by computer, but the use of "volition" peaks in 1900–1909 at 1400 per 100,000 articles, then falls to 750 in the 1910s, 460 in the 1920s, 290 in the 1930s, 140 in the 1940s, and has stayed below 100 ever since (total N = 1432 out of more than 1 million articles scanned; ibid.).

    Another belief attributes the change to "Freud, in destroying the Victorian concept of willpower" (Rollo May, 1967). However, Freud didn't destroy the concept; he only pointed out some severe limitations.
13. Comparative response to schedules of reward: Madden et al. (1998). Animal models of addiction are reviewed in Altman et al. (1996). Behaviorally, pigeons detect and respond to tiny changes in frequencies of electric shock even when these are not signaled by cues (Herrnstein, 1969). Human obtuseness to reward is especially conspicuous in children from ages 6 to 12, perhaps because this is when they first begin to override their feelings with preconceptions of the world (Sonuga-Barke et al., 1989).
14. Samuelson (1976); Becker (1976).
15. Sorensen (1992).
16. Crews (1995 p. 12).
17. See the many sources reviewed in Ellenberger (1970).
18. Vaughan & Herrnstein (1987).
19. However, this analogy can't be used to explain the motivation for behaviors directly. It has a link missing: Selection of a behavior is not the same thing as selection of an organism. The process that selects behaviors have been selected in turn to be part of the organism's hereditary makeup, presumably because that particular kind of behavior selection maximizes the organism's surviving offspring. Given natural selection of organisms, a behavior selection process that sometimes retains self-defeating behaviors must still be accounted for. See Chapter 3, note 22. I examine the distinction between the selection of organisms and the selection of behaviors at more length in *Picoeconomics* (1992, pp. 179–184).
20. Gardner (1997).
21. In this book I'll refer most often to his work on emotion (1999b).

22. For example, just 10 years ago a prominant behaviorist, Howard Rachlin, proposed that pain shouldn't be regarded as a subjective experience, but just as a behavior to get external rewards. These rewards might be anything from avoiding injury to getting sympathy, but they could never be something that occurred entirely within the person's mind (1985).

Chapter 2. The Dichotomy at the Root of Decision Science

1. Skinner (1953, pp. 244, 152).
2. Among philosophers see Bratman (1987, 1999); Davidson (1980, pp. 21–42); Parfit (1984). Among psychologists see Baumeister & Heatherton (1996); Kuhl, 1994; Perris et al. (1988); Polivy (1998); Williams et al. (1988); the writers in Magaro (1991); and summaries in Karoly (1993) and Mischel et al. (1996).
3. Parfit (1984, p. 152).
4. Baumeister & Heatherton (1996).
5. Polivy (1998, p. 182); errors in generalization: Beck (1976); Ellis & Grieger (1977).
6. Elner & Hughes (1978); Houston et al. (1980). Common laboratory animals like rats and pigeons are so good at responding to small changes in the contingencies by which their behavior earns food (e.g., Herrnstein & Loveland, 1975) that foraging theorists have come to speak of them as directly maximizing caloric intake (e.g., Johnson & Collier, 1987). Their choices are equally accurate when trying to avoid electric shock (Herrnstein, 1969).
7. I usually use "she" for any person of unspecified gender, perhaps short for "s/he," but for Economic Man, this offends the ear.
8. Economists: Samuelson (1937); Becker (1976). Simon (1995) begins to use behavioral language, and Atkinson & Birch (1970) are rooted entirely in psychology.
9. Richard Thaler (1991) catalogs a number of such seemingly irrational tendencies.
10. Glantz & Pearce (1989); an original description of one empathtically compelling people, the !Kung, is found in Thomas (1989).
11. Wray & Dickerson (1981).
12. Thus mathematician Oskar Morgenstern (1979) observed, "I know of no axiomatic system worth its name that specifically incorporates a specific pleasure or utility of gambling together with a general theory of utility."
13. A strict definition of the primrose path was given by Herrnstein & Prelec (1992).
14. This is often reported, e.g., by Kirby et al. (1999) and by Vuchinich & Simpson (1998).
15. Becker & Murphy (1988); Becker et al. (1994).
16. Ryle (1949/1984).
17. A majority of both patients with addictive problems and people drawn randomly from the general population say that an explicit process of decision

making "makes action possible/likely" and/or makes them "feel a sense of commitment after deciding"; many specifically mention "willpower" (McCartney, 1997).

18. This is the only way I'll use "conditioning," although some writers say "operant conditioning" to refer to learning goal-directed behavior.

19. "Enough is left unexplained to justify the hypothesis of a compulsion to repeat – something that seems more primitive, more elementary, more instinctual than the pleasure principle which it over-rides" (1920, p. 23).

20. Two-factor theory was first clearly articulated by Mowrer (1947); see also Rescorla & Solomon (1967) and recent applications like O'Brien et al. (1986) and Loewenstein (1996).

21. Miller (1969).

22. Biofeedback: Basmajian et al. (1989). This does not mean, as biofeedback researchers once hoped, that current technology can bring all conditionable responses under the control of differential reward (Dworkin & Miller, 1986); some innate reward may dominate a choice to the point where no incentive offered by an experimenter can compete with it. Donahoe et al. (1993) made an explicit computer model of just such a competition. Behaviorists have avoided theorizing that internal rewards exist, since they can't be studied; but this is a discipline to avoid sloppy thought, not a belief about nature (see Baum & Heath, 1992). Punished withdrawal symptoms: Wolpe et al. (1980).

23. O'Brien et al. (1986).

24. Ainslie & Engel (1974).

25. Donahoe et al. (1993, p. 21). I made a similar argument in the case of "conditioned" aversion (1987, p. 129).

26. Rescorla (1988).

27. Donahoe et al. (1993, 1997). Hilgard and Marquis (1940) suggested that the difference between conditioned and motivated responses might just be the details of how these were taught. As late as the 1950s, psychologists believed that there was only one underlying principle of learning, although they saw that principle as closer to conditioning than to goal-seeking; this slant, too, has been revived (Mackintosh, 1983, pp. 77–112). Both patterns consist of some kind of cue followed by some kind of behavior followed by some kind of reinforcement. The difference is that in conditioning the experimenter can't arbitrarily pick the behavior that a particular reinforcer will select for or, conversely, select the reinforcer for a particular behavior. A subject seems to have to make a specific, perhaps inborn, response in anticipation of a specific reinforcer.

If you can use motivation to detach a response from the reinforcer that seemed to govern it, so that the cue leads to a different response, you're said to have shown that the response is goal-directed; failing that, theorists have assumed it to be conditioned. However, it's a long way from failure to motivate a change to the conclusion that the change is unmotivatable, or that the existing behavior is unmotivated. If I have a strong personal preference that you can't pay me to give up, does that mean it's conditioned? Does being able to see my motives make any difference? The examples just listed suggest that the dichotomy is shaky, anyway, but it was always based only on the success or failure of our motivating procedures.

28. Atnip (1977); Dickinson (1980); Hearst (1975, pp. 181–223); Herrnstein (1969); discussion in Ainslie (1992, pp.39–48). Even the learning of information is held to depend on its being either emotionally meaningful or surprising (Dickinson, 1980, pp. 123–167), properties that will be shown to be sufficient to make an event rewarding (see Section 10.1).

29. There's even reason to believe that these responses – salivation, arousal, etc. – are sometimes rewarding in their own right, but this discussion will need to wait for some groundwork.

30. I say "probably" because this glaring distinction was not articulated at the time, surprisingly enough. Nevertheless, some sense of it may have influenced people's intuitions about what explanations made sense.

    The equivalence of rewards and conditioning stimuli is still unacceptable to many psychologists. Nevertheless, the controversy about whether there are two principles of response selection has largely died out – not because research proved either position to the satisfaction of its opponents, but because it seemed possible to argue most research results either way, and psychologists lost interest in the endless debate.

31. Decision theorist George Loewenstein (1996) has proposed a new version of two-factor theory as a mechanism for temporary preferences, which relies on the notion that people (and, presumably, animals) can't remember the motivational impact of "visceral" experiences like appetite, pain, and emotions. If you can't remember how dessert carts affect you, the argument goes, your sudden appetite will always catch you by surprise; but there is much quantitative animal data as well as clinical lore that the motivational import of these visceral experiences is remembered very well, sometimes to the point of retraumatization. See my discussion (Ainslie, 1999b). Herrnstein (1969) describes animals' precise ability to evaluate painful choices; Herrnstein and Loveland (1975) report their accuracy in weighing food options. Mendelson and Chorover (1965) describe how animals can even learn to plan on a future appetite that isn't present yet: Hunger can be turned off and on by brain stimulation; if rats that are full are put in a maze and have their hunger turned on only when they get to the food box, they still learn while satiated to run through the maze to get the combination of hunger and food.

    Furthermore, if the appetite catches you by surprise, there's no reason why you should try to commit yourself in advance not to give in. Even if you "expect to be surprised," a somewhat puzzling concept, conventional utility theory gives no reason that you should change your preference in advance from what you think it will be when that moment comes.

32. Premack (1959); see economists George Stigler and Gary Becker (1977).

33. Olds & Milner (1954).

34. Heath (1992).
35. Gardner (1997, 1999). However, some transmitter(s) besides dopamine also seem to be involved (Rocha et al., 1998).
36. Sites that generate both appetite and satisfaction: Deutsch & Howarth (1963).
37. Horvitz et al. (1997).
38. A few cells in the nucleus accumbens respond to pain: Mirenowicz & Schultz (1996); threat releases dopamine there: Tidey & Miczek (1994).
39. Hollerman et al. (1998); Schultz et al. (1997).
40. Ho et al. (1998).
41. Baumeister & Heatherton (1996).
42. *Nichomachean Ethics*, 1147a31–35.
43. Freud (1911, p. 223).
44. In Hirschman (1977, p. 23).
45. Rethy (1969).
46. This question was analyzed in detail by McFarland & Sibley (1975). I discussed it (1992, pp. 28–32) with regard to a single reward principle, in contradistinction to the idea that some kinds of goals were not commensurable (e.g., Schwartz, 1986). Shizgall and Conover summarized their work thus far in 1996.

Chapter 3. The Warp in How We Evaluate the Future

1. Becker & Murphy (1988).
2. "Some sets of commodities are simply incomparable or incommensurable" (Schwartz, 1986); see also Allison (1981), Taylor (1982).
3. An outcome that loses 20% of its value for every unit of time it is delayed is worth $(1.00 - .20)^1$, or .80 of its value, at 1 unit of delay, $(1.00 - .20)^2$, or .64 of its value, at 2 units of delay, $(1.00 - .20)^{10}$, or .107 at 10 units, .0000000002 at 100 units, and so on.
4. For most people, the availability of a good excuse is even more important; but we'll have to figure out why anybody would need to give an excuse to *herself* before talking about that.
5. Experimenters who have found that a good seems to be discounted more steeply in the period just before it's due have hypothesized that the discount rate may be proportional to the amount. In that case, as the discounted value of the good fell, its curve would become less steep (Green & Myerson, 1993). However, such a curve could never cross the curve from a smaller good, since it would approach the other curve more slowly the closer it got; and curves from separate rewards of different sizes tend to be *steeper* the smaller the reward, not shallower (Ainslie & Haendel, 1983; Green et al., 1994). Only a curve of a different shape will account for the findings, as we'll soon see.
6. Hume quoted in Hirschman (1977, p. 25); Senault (1649, p. C1).
7. Ainslie & Herrnstein (1981); Ainslie (1974).
8. The simplest hyperbola is:

$$\text{Value} = \text{Objective value} / \text{Delay}$$

However, this formula could probably never describe a natural process, since it would make value infinite at zero delay. A hyperbolic formula that makes "objective" value equal to discounted value at zero delay is:

$$\text{Value} = \text{Objective value} / (1 + \text{Delay})$$

A value would fall to $1.00 / (1 + 1)$, or $.50$, of what it would be if immediate at 1 unit of delay, $1.00 / (1 + 2)$, or $.33$, at 2 units, and $1.00 / (1 + 10)$, or $.09$, at 10 units of delay, but would still be worth $1.00/ (1 + 100)$, or $.01$, at 100 units, compared to the $.000030$ predicted by the exponential formula at 10%. This formula still allows for no differences in discount "rate," or impatience, among different people, a rigidity that will need correcting.

9. And among exponential discounters, those who discount at a lower rate will accumulate money faster than those who discount at a higher rate. In that case, however, the high disounter wouldn't mind this prospect, since she devalues the future, just as Becker and Murphy's rational addict doesn't regret her addiction.

10. Noise: Solnick et al. (1980); Navarick (1982). Video games: Millar & Navarick, 1984. Food: Ragotzy et al. (1988).

11. Green et al. (1994); Kirby & Herrnstein (1995); Ostaszewski (1996); Kirby (1997); Madden et al. (1997); Richards et al.; Vuchinich & Simpson (1998).

12. That is, older subjects have a smaller $Constant_2$ in the general discount equation (note 8; Ainslie & Haendel, 1983; Green et al., 1994; Kirby & Herrnstein, 1995), as do introverts (Ostaszewski, 1996), nonaddicts (Kirby et al., 1999), and nonsmokers (Bickel et al., 1999).

13. Herrnstein et al. (1993). These findings are consistent with an earlier description of the factors that make human subjects respond differently than animals in some experimental designs (Mawhinney, (1982).

14. Herrnstein (1961; 1997, pp. 11–99). The word "matching" comes from his original experimental design, in which pigeons pecked to get food on two independent keys that paid off at different rates. He found that relative rates of pecking matched the amounts, frequencies, and immediacies of reward. The experiment that showed this specifically for delays was Chung and Herrnstein (1967). Shortly afterward I pointed out that inverse proportionality to delay implied a hyperbolic discount curve, and began the experiments that showed reversal of preference as a function of D, using the discrete trial design that had been largely abandoned by behaviorists (Ainslie, 1970, 1974; Ainslie & Herrnstein, 1981). Other experimenters found the same phenomenon in various ways, all first with animals: Rachlin & Green (1972); Navarick & Fantino (1976); Green et al. (1981); Boehme et al. (1986).

The generalized matching law or a close variant has been verified exhaustively (deVilliers & Herrnstein, 1976; Stevenson, 1986). Arguments about whether early experiments confounded delay of reward with rate were resolved by Shull et al. (1981), who varied delay independently within timeouts from the usual two-rate design, and by Mazur (1987), who perfected an "adjusting procedure" to find indifference points in discrete-trial amount-vs.-delay experiments.

Theorists have proposed several discounting models to explain the temporary preference phenomenon without abandoning exponential discounting, such as:

- a step function in which immediate events are valued exceptionally and events at all delays are discounted exponentially (Simon, 1995);
- an exponential discount rate whose exponent itself varies as a function of delay (Green & Myerson, 1993);
- the summation of separate exponential discount rates for association and valuation (Case, 1997); and
- random variation in discount rate (a possibility first raised by Strotz, 1956, and recently expanded by Skog, 1999).

However, the data behind each of these are scanty compared to those behind hyperbolic discounting; nor do any of them squarely contradict hyperbolic discounting. The main virtue of these proposals has been to escape the awkward question raised by the hyperbolic model: If the basic psychological discount function is not exponential, how do people come to function in financial marketplaces as if it were?

15. Generalized from Mazur (1987). I compare the possible formulas in Ainslie (1992, pp. 63–76). Constant$_1$ keeps the value from going to infinity when a reward is immediate; Constant$_2$ describes how steeply a subject discounts the future.

16. Psychologist John Gibbon (1977) has pointed out that the matching law seems to be only one example of the principle by which many different physical qualities are sensed, known since the nineteenth century as the "Weber–Fechner law." According to this principle, a change in a physical stimulus like heat or light is perceived not equally to its absolute amount, but as a ratio of the change in the prior amount (Boring, 1950, pp. 280ff.) For the perception of value specifically, recognition that it is based on a ratio dates back to mathematics pioneer Daniel Bernouilli: "Any increase in wealth, no matter how insignificant, will always result in an increase in utility which is inversely proportionate to the quantity of goods already possessed" (1738/1954, p. 25). Accordingly, Gibbon's suggestion is that the ratios described by the matching law simply represent the Weber–Fechner law as applied to the perception of delay.

17. $Y = 1/X$, where Y is the magnitude in question and X is the distance to the building or goal.

18. Brunsson (1985), chapters 1 and 2; Brennan & Tullock (1982), p. 226. I'll return to the analogy between self-command and corporate leadership near the end of Section 6.1.

19. The classical work is by Máx Weber (1925/1964).

20. Navona and Gopher (1979).

21. Of course, reward ultimately depends on an inborn capacity for it to occur. A large proportion of Chinese people have a prolonged intermediate phase of alcohol metabolism that makes the alcohol sickening, and thus are not susceptible to alcoholism (Agarwal & Goedde, 1989). Strains of rats can in

fact be bred to have either high or low tendencies to press a bar to get alcohol, cocaine, or other substances, a process that can now be studied at
the level of individual neurons (Gardner, 1997). Many people can eat ad lib
without gaining weight. Thresholds for various kinds of emotionality are
also hereditary and vary greatly among individuals (Goldsmith et al., 1997).

22. Such a population resembles but is not identical to a population of species
in nature that have evolved by natural selection. It is similar in that these
processes compete for survival on the basis of a scarce resource – reward –
and succeed insofar as they can defend a niche from alternative processes
that are potentially better rewarded. It is different in that the selective principle – the reward mechanism – was itself a product of literal natural selection. In a cold climate warmth is rewarding because this effect helped
species to survive, but cold did not itself evolve so as to further natural selection. The need for warmth selects organisms with optimal reward mechanisms according to an exponential discount curve over generations (Lotka,
1957, p. 123); but within an organism, the rewarding effect of warmth
selects behaviors according to a hyperbolic discount curve over time.

23. Olds (1992). Because of neurophysiological findings, it has been suggested
that "hot" and "cool" (= passionate and reasonable) choice-making systems
may be based on information processed in the amygdala and hippocampus,
respectively, with the implication that the resulting motives are also in separate systems (Metcalfe & Jacobs, 1998; Metcalfe & Mischel, 1990).

24. Recall the related discussion in Section 2.2.3. Conversely, however concentrated the reward process is within one location, it must still have separate
components, ultimately neurons, that compete for control of whatever output pathway it has. Localization will always be relative.

25. E.g., Klein (1989).

26. Split brain: Sperry (1984); twins: Lassers & Nordan (1978); Szekely (1980).
Some comments by twins in Szekely (1980): "I feel, between my sister and
me, there's one part that's both of us. We're totally separate beings, yet it
is there, it does exist, this oneness. . . . There is something that is both of
us put together" (p. 79). "We never fight. It's very weird. Sometimes it's
like he's just an extension of myself" (p. 82). "The bond is a special thread
between twins, a psychological thread. It's an electrical window in the
mind of identical twins . . . a similar response to stimuli . . . or it may seem
to result in a heightened sense of telepathy or extrasensory perception"
(p. 158).

27. Cognitive psychologist Julius Kuhl and his colleagues have suggested what
is in effect a population model of the person, in which one part sometimes
controls others like a dictator but does better exercising "democratic leadership" (Kuhl, 1994). In this model a function called "autonomy" ("the
holistic integrated functioning through which action is centrally regulated")
"stabilizes and boosts autonomy and action, for example, by facilitating the
identification and efficient expression of goals . . . and shielding such goals
from competing impulses" (Ryan et al., 1997). However, they don't say
why this stabilization, or shielding, should be needed, and imply that one

faction's attempt to control others is a cause of rather than a response to conflict between them.

28. Cropper et al. (1991); Harvey (1994); Among other consequences, this uniformity over scale makes preference reversal a candidate for being analyzed as a fractal in chaos theory (see Gleick, 1987).

29. Laibson (1997); Harris & Laibson (1999). Their "quasi-hyperbolic function captures the qualitative property that discount rates decline (weakly) with horizon length" (1999, p. 2), and is adapted from the formula that Phelps and Pollack originally developed to describe the value of property transferred between generations (1968).

30. Foraging theory has always assumed that natural selection has shaped animals' choices to maximize aggregate net energy gain (Krebs, 1978; Maynard Smith, 1978); its proponents haven't examined the discounting process until recently. When they've done so, they've found that animals will regularly choose poorer, imminently available prey over better, delayed alternatives to the detriment of overall foraging efficiency (Kagel et al., 1986; Lea, 1979; Snyderman, 1983).

31. Offer (in preparation) *The Challenge of Affluence: Prosperity and Well-Being in the United States and Britain since 1945,* p. 11. Before the twentieth century, even under conditions of peace and prosperity, a given birth had 1 chance in 30 of killing the mother; and women had an average of five children, enough to yield a modest population growth rate when infectious disease killed half of all children before the age of five (e.g., Demos, 1971).

   Economist Robert Frank describes the usefulness of emotions as self-control devices (1988, pp. 81–84); but his examples don't appeal to a person *because* they are self-control devices, and could just as well be serving the survival of the species at her expense.

32. Erasmus (1509/1983).

33. See note 16 about the Weber–Fechner law.

34. See Simon (1983).

35. First in 1986; see also Ainslie (1992).

Chapter 4. The Warp Can Create Involuntary Behaviors

1. The Episcopal *Book of Common Prayer.*

2. See note 20, Chapter 3.

3. Elster (1999a); Rosenthal & Lesieur (1992).

4. Tolerance – the need for increasingly intense stimuli to get a given high – and withdrawal symptoms are part of many people's concept of addiction, but in the latest clinical writings they are neither necessary nor sufficient for addiction (American Psychiatric Association, 1994; discussed in Elster, 1999a and 1999b).

5. If we look only at the addiction-range interests in comparison with long-range ones, we see a contrast much like the classical one of passion vs. reason. Cognitive psychologist Seymour Epstein echoes Plato's dualistic model with a "rational system" that tries to control an "experiential system."

He explains mental conflict with a number of parallel mechanisms based on cognitive skils, but includes one that seems to reach out to bridge the difference between cognitive and hedonistic approaches:

> The experiential system has a short-term focus, is intimately associ-ated with affect, and the outcome of experiential processing is ex-perienced as self-evidently valid. In contrast, the rational system's interests are long-term, its processing is relatively affect free, and the validity of its outcomes has to be established by logic and evidence. Because long-term interests are often different from short-term in-terests, because what is considered reasonable often differs from what is pleasurable, and because beliefs derived from experience often differ from beliefs derived from logic and evidence, it is inevitable for conflict to occur between the two systems. (1998, p. 17)

He needs only a rationale for temporary preference to unify the two systems.

6. Nemiah (1977). I'll discuss the logic of compulsiveness further in Chapter 9.
7. As we'll see, there's a specific self-control skill that, when overdone, pro-duces the symptoms that clinicians call "compulsive." However, this word is often used for any strongly motivated behavior, as in "compulsive drink-ing." I'm suggesting that "impulsive" or "addictive" be used for choices that are usually regretted within days and that "compulsive" be reserved for behaviors that look like efforts at self-control. See Section 9.1.5.
8. For lack of another all-inclusive word, I'll nevertheless be using "appetite" for urges as well.
9. Seizures: Faught et al. (1986); Jeavons & Harding (1975); hallucinations: Anderson & Alpert (1974).
10. Pigeons: Appel (1963); Azrin (1961); Zimmerman & Ferster (1964); mon-keys: Spealman (1979).
11. Asymmetry: Thorndike (1935, p. 80); robustness of negative emotion: Solomon & Wynne (1954); Eysenck (1967).
12. Beecher (1959, pp. 157–190).
13. Audio analgesia: Melzack et al. (1963); Licklider (1959); hypnosis: Hilgard & Hilgard (1994, pp. 86–165).
14. Panic disorder: Clum (1989); obsessive-compulsive disorder: Marks (1997); many symptoms are discussed in Van Hasselt and Hersen (1996). The urges of obsessive-compulsive *disorder* differ from the highly controlled rules of obsessive-compulsive *personality*, for which the term "compulsion" is best reserved.
15. Behavior therapy or cognitive-behavior therapy is a set of techniques dis-covered by trial and error by various therapists and is based only loosely on the scientific methodology developed by behaviorism.
16. See Dweyer & Renner (1971).
17. Mirenowicz and Schultz (1996).
18. Granda & Hammack (1961).
19. Robinson & Berridge (1993).

20. Core emotions: Panksepp (1982); stereotyped emotions: Ekman & Friesen (1986); Izard (1971); subtle emotions: Elster (1999)b; Stearns (1986, 1994).
21. Elster (1999b, p. 205).
22. In ordinary speech, "appetite" is used for each of three related but distinct concepts: (1) a predilection for particular kinds of reward; (2) a state of being aroused to get a kind of reward; and (3) the deprivation or other physiological state that makes this arousal possible. I will consistently use "taste" to refer to the predilection. The arousal will be "appetite," but it's impractical in many cases to differentiate this from the underlying deprivation, the state that earlier biologists called "drive." Where two distinct phases are discernible, I will call them "available appetite" and "aroused appetite," as when the starving may have a lot of appetite available (be in a high drive state) but have no appetite aroused. Where this distinction is impossible or unimportant, I'll use "appetite" to mean any readiness to be rewarded. See Section 10.1.1.
23. *A Treatise of Human Nature*, II, 3, 3, quoted in Gosling (1990, p. 93).
24. For further discussion, see Ainslie (1992, pp. 101–114, 244–249).
25. Starvation: Carlson (1916, pp. 164–168); orthodox Jews: Schachter et al. (1977); addicts' craving: Meyer (1981); not having withdrawal symptoms: Wolpe et al. (1980); Elster (1999b, p. 227, note 2). See also Section 11.1, regarding emotional reward and Ainslie (1992, pp. 244–249).
26. An individual would naturally avoid aversive emotions as much as she could, but where emotions are pleasurable, exponential discounting implies that they would become preoccupying unless they were rationed by releasing stimuli that could be obtained only from outside.
27. Elster (1999b, pp. 150–153, 106).

Chapter 5. The Elementary Interaction of Interests

1. Ainslie (1974); see Section 3.1.
2. Strotz (1956) acknowledged that the problem implied a nonexponential discount curve but didn't suggest a hyperbola; Elster (1979).
3. Azrin et al. (1982); Fuller & Roth (1979).
4. Becker (1960).
5. Gilligan (1977).
6. Right thinking: Crane (1905, p. 115); stimulus control: Kanfer (1975, pp. 309–355); Goldiamond (1965); Metcalfe & Mischel (1999); value of ignorance: Carillo (1999).
7. Freud (1926/1956); Aristotle's *Nichomachean Ethics* 1147b9–15; lapses in smokers: Sjoberg & Johnson (1978).
8. Labeling by emotional salience: Zajonc (1980); calling up memories by category: Shiffrin & Schneider (1977); self-serving ethics: Rabin (1995).
9. The momentum of an appetite – a positive feedback effect that leads to potentiation rather than satiation – is what has made conditioning theories of

temporary preference so attractive. These include the latest incarnation of the passion/reason model, Metcalfe and Mischel's "hot/cool system analysis" (1999). I discuss this phenomenon at length in Ainslie (1999b).

10. Alexithymia: Nemiah (1977). This is the opposite of cultivating your vulnerability to influence, one of the extrapsychic committing devices. The fact that a person may see either one as serving her long-range interest doubtless comes from the fact that vulnerability to influence is a two-edged sword. Children: Mischel & Mischel (1983).

11. Bacon quoted in Hirschman (1977, P.22); David Hume quoted in Hirschman (1977, pp. 24–25). Economist Robert Frank gives several examples of emotions that seem to serve as self-control devices (1988, pp. 81–84).

12. Psychologist Julius Kuhl (1996) proposes a similar list of "self-regulatory . . . mechanisms and strategies," but without extrapsychic examples: "attention control," "emotion and activation control," and what sound like aspects of will – "motivation control," "goal maintenance," and "impulse control."

Each of Jon Elster's "devices for precommitment" is also an example or a subset of one of these tactics. He divides extrapsychic devices into "eliminating options," "imposing costs," "setting up rewards," "creating delays," and "changing preferences [i.e., early avoidance]." Attention control is "inducing ignorance," and preparation of emotion is "inducing passion." As I'm about to argue, "investing in bargaining power [i.e., maintaining your credibility]" is part of the mechanism of will, but Elster separates it from my core mechanism for will, bundling of choices, which he calls "bunching" and lists as an "alternative to precommitment" (2000, pp. 6, 84–86). Similarly, I believe that all of his reasons for precommitment ("overcome passion," "overcome self-interest," "overcome hyperbolic discounting," "overcome strategic time inconsistency," and "neutralize or prevent preference change") are ultimately motivated by one reason: the problem of hyperbolic discounting; however, he believes that passion, at least, is not an example of that problem (see Ainslie, 1999b; Elster, 1999b).

13. Aristotle, *Nichomachean Ethics,* 1147a24–28; Galen (1963, p. 44); new force, throw strength on weaker side, unite actions, strengthened by repetition: Sully (1884, pp. 631, 663, 669); vulnerable to nonrepetition: Bain (1859/ 1886, p. 440); held steadily in view: James (1890, p. 534).

14. Heyman (1996); Heyman & Tanz (1995).

15. Rachlin (1995a); Siegel & Rachlin (1996).

16. Baumeister & Heatherton (1996); philosophers: Bratman (quoted) (1999, pp. 50–56); McClennen (1990, pp. 157–161); others discussed in Bratman (1994, pp. 69–73).

17. Rachlin (1995a, 1995b).

18. Mazur (1986) reported that pigeons choosing between a single food reward and a series of more delayed rewards decide as if they simply added each amount divided by its delay, thus confirming less precise findings by McDiarmid and Rilling (1965). Likewise, psychologists Dani Brunner and

John Gibbon have shown that rats' choices between sequences of equal numbers of rewards that differ in temporal arrangement are best predicted by a "parallel discounting model," in which value is the simple sum of each reward discounted hyperbolically (1995; also Brunner, 1999). There's more information on how pigeons choose between series that require further responses to get their available rewards. This has uniformly confirmed Mazur's (1984) equation that described the value of such series at a given moment as the sum of the hyperbolically discounted rewards that it made available (reviewed and analyzed in Mazur, 1997). Data from some other experiments suggest that there is a more general but complex form of the matching equation that lets it predict choice of extended reward series even better (Grace, 1994; Mazur, 1997), but it doesn't change the implications for our analysis.

Human experiments that have found departures from the additivity of aversive experiences cut both ways: Frederickson and Kahneman (1993) found that earlier events in a bygone series are overshadowed by later ones, but Gilbert and his coworkers (e.g., Gilbert et al., 1999) found that subjects expect impending distress to last longer than it actually does.

19. Bratman (1999, pp. 35–57).
20. Making choices in the context of similar future choices can increase self-control; Kirby & Guastello (2000); bundling choices into series makes rats switch their preference from smaller, earlier to larger, later sucrose rewards: Ainslie & Monterosso (2000). In the latter experiment, rats given the choice between .4 second access to sugar water immediately and .6 second access at a 3.0 second delay regularly chose the immediate reward; they regularly chose a series of three .6 second rewards over a series of .4 second alternatives 3.0 seconds earlier, even though the first .4 second reward was immediate.
21. The bundling and other phenomena that follow from hyperbolic discounting are also consistent with the hyperboloid curves that some economists have adopted for their tractability (see Chapter 3, note 29). Roland Benabou and Jean Tirole have derived most of the properties of personal rules from such curves (2000).
22. At midnight the value of staying up will be

$$V_{up} = \Sigma_{i=0.5\rightarrow1.5} \, 60 \, / \, (1 + i) = 64$$

and the differential value of feeling rested at work will be

$$V_{bed} = \Sigma_{i=7.5\rightarrow16.5} \, 60 \, / \, (1 + i) = 49$$

Given only this choice, you'll probably stay up and suffer the next day.
23. The values of your alternatives are:

$$V_{up} = (\Sigma_{i=.5\rightarrow1.5} \, 60 \, / \, (1 + i)) + (\Sigma_{i=24.5\rightarrow25.5} \, 60 \, / \, (1 + i))$$
$$+ \, (\Sigma_{i=48.5\rightarrow49.5} \, 60 \, / \, (1 + i)) + \ldots$$
$$(\Sigma_{i=216.5\rightarrow217.5} \, 60 \, / \, (1 + i)) = 78$$

for staying up on the next 10 nights vs.

$$V_{\text{bed}} = (\Sigma_{i=7.5 \to 16.5}\ 60\ /\ (1 + i)) +$$
$$(\Sigma_{i=31.5 \to 40.5}\ 60\ /\ (1 + i)) + \ldots$$
$$(\Sigma_{i=223.5 \to 232.5}\ 60\ /\ (1 + i)) = 105$$

for going to bed.

24. Kant (1793/1960, pp. 15–49); Kohlberg (1963).
25. James (1890, p. 565).
26. He also illustrated the difficulty of making sense of this competition without a rationale for temporary preference. When he tried to specify the details, he got hopelessly tangled:

> One opinion is universal, the other concerns particulars, things about which perception has the deciding say. When one [opinion] arises from them the soul must, in the one case, affirm the conclusion, in cases to do with doing, act at once. . . . When, therefore, on the one hand there is the universal [opinion] forbidding to taste, and on the other, [the opinion] that everything sweet is pleasant, and this is pleasant (and it is this opinion which operates), and desire happens to be present, the one says to avoid this but desire drives; for it has the power to move each of the parts [of the body]. So it turns out that the man who acts akratically does so under the influence in a way of reason and of opinion, opinion, however, which is not opposed in itself to the right principle – it is the desire, not the opinion, which is opposed to that – but opposed incidentally. (*Nichomachean Ethics*, 1147a24–b17)

However, he is clearly discussing how seeing a particular example of desire as an example of the right universal category leads to controlling it, and how the failure to see it this way can be driven by the desire itself, thus undermining control of it. He was the first philosopher to describe this phenomenon; according to philosopher Justin Gosling, Socrates and Plato didn't mention it (1990, pp. 25–37).

27. Self-enforcing contracts are described by Macaulay (1963), and by Klein and Leffler (1981), and analyzed in terms of game theory by Stahler (1998). Howard Rachlin (1995b) incorrectly ascribes the active ingredient in the picoeconomic theory of will to "the law of exercise," an old behaviorist term for force of habit.

Chapter 6. Sophisticated Bargaining among Internal Interests

1. Amundson (1990).
2. Schelling (1960, pp. 53–80) gives a clear description of limited warfare. The prisoner's dilemma was first described by Albert Tucker in an unpublished paper (Straffin, 1980). Its strategies are explored in Axelrod (1984 and 1990).
3. Thus philosopher Michael Bratman (1999, pp. 45–50) maintains that acting to influence your future selves is a form of magical thinking as does Jon Elster (1989b, pp. 201–202).

4. Fehr & Gachter (1999).
5. I've performed this demonstration several times, using both hypthetical money with lecture audiences and real money with volunteer subjects. People generally report the reasoning I've just outlined.
6. Note that a large group – of players in this game or of successive motivational states within a person – will not dilute the effect of a single choice in the way that, say, the stock market does. Unless a stockholder is unusually conspicuous, she can buy or sell stock without having a noticeable effect on the market. But the voting in the situation I've been describing has to pass through the narrows of the present moment as one voter after another makes her choice. Successive choice-makers are each conspicuous for a time – famous for the 15 minutes (say) after they have chosen, while the next few choice-makers are choosing especially in the light of their example. This temporary leverage may often be enough to change the course of the stream of choices ever afterward.
7. Does it make a difference whether the players know when the game will end? Obviously a player who knows she's moving last has no intrinsic incentive to cooperate. If she cooperates, it's a sign that she sees her move in this game as also counting in a larger game, such as how it will affect her relationship with people in the audience whom she'll see again, or whether she goes on seeing herself as a community-minded person, or even whether she has sinned against a universal principle. By the same token, the next-to-last player shouldn't cooperate if she's following the instruction to maximize her income within the game, and neither should any of the last 10 players, who will have no chance to make enough dimes to make up for the dollar they lose by cooperating. This logic could be extended to the players right before them, since the last 10 can be expected to defect, and so on. But if this is a large audience and the known ending won't occur for 100 moves, the first player might do best by cooperating, on the assumption that the next few players at least will see cooperation as also in their interest, knowing that at some point a later player is sure to defect and switch all subsequent players to defection.

   Within an individual the bargaining logic is the same. She knows she'll die some day, and thus would have no reason to stick to her diet the day before this was likely to happen or the day before that. Where young, healthy people face impending death there's said to be just such an escape from rules, as when towns in the path of the bubonic plague had orgies or soldiers from a battlefront go wild on leave. But for most people healthy enough to have strong appetites, death seems both distant and of uncertain timing, so that their choice to cooperate or defect in a particular game sets a precedent for the indefinite future.
8. Well illustrated in Schelling (1960, pp. 53–80), and Elster (1989a, pp. 140–141).
9. Long-term recovery rates among treated, unselected alcoholics run about 50%, whereas "long-term maintenance of medically significant weight loss is rare" (Campfield et al., 1998).

10. "No government has ever been rational with conventional weapons. You expect them to be rational with nuclear weapons?" (Lee Blessing's play, *A Walk in the Woods*, 1988).
11. Wilson & Herrnstein (1985 pp. 389–403).
12. Brunsson (1985), chapters 1 and 2.
13. Brennan & Tullock (1982, p. 226).
14. Shefrin and Thaler (1988). "Outdoor psychologist" Jean Lave has described the intricate bookkeeping compartments that households create, seemingly in order to reduce the commensurability of money earmarked for different purposes (1988, pp. 131–141).
15. Discussed in Ainslie (1991).

Chapter 7. The Subjective Experience of Intertemporal Bargaining

1. This point was first made in Ogden and Richards's (1930) classic book, especially pp. 124–125.
2. "According to mediaeval ideas . . . the enactment of new law is not possible at all; and all legislation and legal reform is conceived of as the restoration of the good old law which has been violated" (Kern, 1948, p. 151; see also Robert Palmer, for whose guidance I'm indebted – 1993, pp. 254–257). Piaget (1932/1965).
3. Examples are given in Elster (1999b, pp. 127–129).
4. Danger from impaired impulse control is perhaps most apt to be experienced as guilt, although in depression or obsessional disorder guilt can occur with much less occasion, just as fear does in phobic patients or grief in people suffering from pathological mourning.
5. For instance, Jevons (1871/1911) said that "all future events . . . should act upon us with the same force as if they were present. . . ." Even more recently, while acknowledging the prevalence of discounting, Pigou (1920, pp. 24–25) called it abnormal:

> Generally speaking, everybody prefers present pleasures or satisfactions of given magnitude to future pleasures or satisfactions of equal magnitude, even when the latter are perfectly certain to occur. But this preference for present pleasures does not – the idea is self-contradictory – imply that a present pleasure of given magnitude is any greater than a future pleasure of the same magnitude. It implies only that our telescopic faculty is defective.

Many psychological writers have also disregarded delay. For instance, the literature of "need for achievement" (Raynor, 1969) did not recognize an effect of delay per se on the value of a goal until recently (Gjesme, 1983).

Modern authors who regard discounting as irrational are discussed by economists Olson and Bailey (1981). Most people nowadays manage to acknowledge as rational a discount rate of about 3% per year in constant dollars for risk-free investments; but to recognize discount rates as coming ul-

timately from compromises in intertemporal bargaining would be to high-
light the subjective nature of valuation.

6. The heirs of the medieval debate between "realism" and "nominalism" seem
to be the logical positivists and the social constructionists, e.g., Harland
(1987) and Mahoney (1991); see Ainslie (1993).

7. Rhue & Lynn (1989); Smyser & Baron (1993).

8. Ferguson (1989).

9. E.g., Marlatt & Gordon (1980). I'll say more about this subject presently
(Section 9.2.2).

Chapter 8. Getting Evidence about a Nonlinear Motivational System

1. Rapoport (1990); Smith (1992).

2. I can't locate where this apt figure was written.

3. Ryle (1949/1984); Becker & Murphy (1988); Baumeister & Heatherton
(1996); Kuhl (1994); McClennen (1990); Bratman (1999); Rachlin (1995a).

4. Pigeons that are run for many weeks in amount vs. delay experiments can
learn to modestly improve their rates of choosing larger-later rewards without special contingencies like forced bundling, but the mechanism for this is
unclear (Ainslie, 1982; Logue & Mazur, 1981; Todorov et al., 1983). Perhaps
not surprisingly, the birds don't seem to have learned recursive choice-making, which would mean using their current choices as cues predicting future
ones. Although pigeons can learn to base their current choice on a past
choice (such as "go right if you made a long response last time, left if you
made a short one: Shimp, 1983; see also Morgan & Nicholas, 1979), their ap-
titude for self-observation seems to stop there. In principle there's no reason
why a bird couldn't learn to use its own behavior as a cue predicting future
rewards, and thus bundle series of choices together; but an exhaustive study
of those pigeons that get better at waiting for larger-later rewards found that
they developed no tendency to use such self-observations (Ainslie, 1982).

    No self-referential behaviors: (Ainslie, 1982). Green et al. have also
demonstrated that pigeons don't learn to cooperate with a simulated partner
playing tit-for-tat in a repeated prisoner's dilemma (1995).

5. E.g., "The choice you make now is the best indication of how you will choose
every time. If you choose the [smaller amount] today then you will probably choose the [smaller amount] every time. . . ." (Kirby and Guastello,
2000).

6. Mutual cooperation is in each player's interest even for a single pair of
plays, but the absence of continuing interaction makes it irrational for a
player to expect this outcome.

7. It might also be that cumulative cooperations in the pair's previous history – both total and relative to defection – would predict how each subject would respond when told that the other had defected; but the results
so far haven't shown this.

8. It could be argued that an artifact of bargaining in pairs or small groups
makes the analogy to intertemporal bargaining unclear. In a pair or, de-

creasingly, in a trio or quartet, etc., it's rational for a player to punish another player's defection by defecting herself as a way to restore cooperation. This is just the strategy of tit-for-tat, which Axelrod (1984) found to be highly successful. However, in the roomful of successive bargainers that more closely models the usual intertemporal situation (see opening of Chapter 6), a player who wants to restore cooperation should not defect in response to a previous player's defection, since subsequent players are more apt to interpret it as joining a stampede toward general defection, or at best as self-serving that's only disguised as punishing the other's defection. This should be true even if the same roomful of bargainers will play repeatedly in the same order. Thus pairwise bargaining involves partially different incentives from most intertemporal bargaining. An exception where the incentives are the same would be those cases of intertemporal bargaining where successive selves are identified with two teams (or, decreasingly, three, etc.). Where a self at night has failed to go to bed at a reasonable hour, the self the next morning might meaningfully retaliate in failing to get up on time; that is, future nighttime selves might see her as having warned them as much as having simply indulged herself, and might take it as a reason to cooperate by going to bed earlier rather than continuing a stampede toward general defection.

Such subgrouping of successive motivational states doesn't seem to be generally true of intertemporal bargaining, however. Bargaining among very small numbers of subjects is usually exceptional, in that defections in response to a partner's new defection in the experimental situation may often be warnings in the spirit of tit-for-tat; and these lack a general analog in the will. On the other hand, cooperations following a partner's new cooperation would always be seen as offers of renewed cooperation, a fact that does model the intertemporal situation correctly. Thus it might seem that the asymmetry in the experiment comes from the asymmetry of the analogy, except for one thing: Tit-for-tat warnings should tend to repair cooperation, while the observed asymmetry is that defections do *more* damage than cooperations do good. Thus the artifact may be concealing an even greater asymmetry than was observed.

9. Elster (1999b, p. 20), in a thorough discussion of the limitations of experimentation (pp. 13–20).
10. Sorensen (1992).
11. Kavka (1983).
12. See McClennen (1990, pp. 230–231) on decision costs; see McClennen (1990) and Bratman (1987, pp. 106–108) on coordination.
13. Garson (1995). Various kinds of compatibilism are well disposed of by Dennett (1984). For indeterminacy: argument from subatomic indeterminacy, e.g., Landé (1961), criticized by Garson (1995); for indeterminacy at a higher level: Rockwell (1994).
14. Randomness: Broad (1962); James (1884/1967); dangers of "being a pawn": Ryan et al. (1997, pp. 721–722). Dennett (1984) points out that chaotic systems, of which the mind is presumeably one, "are the source of the 'practi-

cal' . . . independence of things that shuffles the world and makes it a place of continual opportunity" (p. 152). Of those who require true randomness he asks, "does it make any difference whether the computer uses a genuinely random sequence or a pseudo-random sequence?" (p. 151), and points out that the difference is impossible in principle to detect. However, he doesn't say why our internal chaos should feel different from nature's chaos, so that it results in choices that feel willed rather than happened upon.

15. Reason chooses passion, e.g., Baumeister & Heatherton (1996); d'Holbach quoted in Hirschman (1977, p. 27).
16. Cf. cognitive psychologists: Ryan et al. (1997, p. 708): "Autonomy does not represent a freedom from determinants but rather an attunement and alignment of the organism toward some determinants rather than others."
17. Hollis (1983, p. 250).
18. Reviewed in Ayers (1997).
19. Garson (1995, p. 372).
20. Sappington (1990).
21. Kane (1989, p. 231).
22. Pap (1961, p. 213).
23. Nozick (1993, p. 41–64), citing his original presentation of the problem in 1969. Numerous analyses of this problem have been made, among them Campbell & Sowden (1985); Quattrone & Tversky (1986); and Elster (1989b, pp. 186–214).
24. Weber (1904/1958, p. 115).
25. This is what Quattrone and Tversky (1986) said.
26. A working model of ths "diagnostic utility" has been developed by Bodner & Prelec (1995).
27. James (1890, v.2, p. 458); Darwin (1872/1979, p. 366).
28. Psychologists Irving Kirsch and Steven Jay Lynn review experiments that have demonstrated an unconscious self-prediction component to a number of goal-directed behaviors: "Response expectancies . . . elicit automatic responses in the form of self-fulfilling prophecies" (1999, p. 504).
29. For example, Hurley (1991).

Chapter 9. The Downside of Willpower

1. Aristotle: Kenny (1963, ch. 8); Kant (1793/1960, pp. 15–49); Piaget (1932/1965); Kohlberg (1963).
2. Kierkegaard: May (1958); existentialists: Ellenberger (1983); Kobasa & Maddi (1983); novelists: Evans (1975).
3. For instance, Davison (1888, pp. 156–183); Ricoeur (1971, p. 11).
4. Psychoanalysis: Hatcher (1973). The other therapies are summarized in Corsini (1984).
5. James (1890, p. 209); Loevinger (1976, pp. 15–26); Kohlberg (1973). Rachlin (1995a, 1995b) rejects my bargaining mechanism because he thinks that successive motivational states are a disguise for "part-organisms" and

thus are mentalistic in behaviorist terms. I reply in Ainslie & Gault (1997). Mele (1995, p. 60); Hollis (1983, p. 260).

6. Certainly animals predict rewards and can even learn tasks contingent on their own previous behaviors; they can learn tasks like, "respond depending on how many times you responded last time" (Shimp, 1983). It seems likely that recursive phenomena like the James–Lange–Darwin effect (see Section 8.3.3) are not uniquely human, but that an animal will use signs of its own panic, for instance, in deciding whether to fight or flee in a given situation. Likewise, knowing that it fled last time may be a determinant of fleeing this time. However, it takes a lot more thought to decide to flee or not partly by considering how it will affect your decision next time. It's the idea of the test case, rather than self-prediction itself, that's probably beyond animals' analytic propensities. I once spent a fair amount of time testing whether pigeons that learned to delay pecking for a small, immediate food reward by seeing the problem in effect as an intertemporal prisoners' dilemma; the evidence was that they did not (Ainslie, in preparation).

7. Hyperbolic discount curves provide a good formula for original sin, although it may be that the Judeo-Christian Bible used "sin" as a term for lapses after people had discovered personal rules as a self-control device – "I had not known sin, but by the law" (Romans 7:7). I suspect that a fair amount of theology deals with the anomaly of temporary preference and the inadequacy of willpower as a solution.

8. Insofar as decision making in corporations is recursive, they also become rigid (Brunsson, 1985; Olson, 1982). One factor in both corporations and individuals may be a tendency to overestimate the prospective duration and hence importance of a sense of having lapsed (Gilbert et al., 1999).

9. Bennett (1918, p. 80).

10. Elster discusses how the disease concept of addiction has worked this way (1999b, pp. 129–133).

11. I originally used the term "vice district" itself (1992, pp. 193–197), then suggested in a longer discussion of the phenomenon that "lapse district" would be more specific (1999a, pp. 71–73, 79–83).

12. "Strength" model: Baumeister & Heatherton (1996); opponent process: Polivy (1998).

13. As Erdelyi (1990) has pointed out, the unconscious but goal-directed effort to forget that the psychoanalysts call "repression" does not differ in nature from the conscious kind ("suppression"). I would suggest that its unconsciousness is shaped by the incentive to avoid losing the stakes of personal rules.

14. Aristotle: Bogen & Moravcsik (1982); for a recent example, see Sjoberg & Johnson (1978).

15. Hilgard (1977). I'll talk more about this big topic later.

16. Herrnstein et al. (1993).

17. Alexithymia: Nemiah (1977); the cost of rules for maximizing annual income: Malekzadeh & Nahavandi (1987); the constraints on emotional reward in empathic relationships: Ainslie (1995).

18. Heather (1998) has also criticized this usage.
19. It's not that either observation is mistaken; both mean that body mass (Offer, 1998; Wickelgren, 1998) and the incidence of extreme dieting (Walsh & Devlin, 1998) are increasing.
20. Sustein (1995, pp. 991–996); he discusses Bentham on pp. 1006–1007.
21. Casalino (1999).
22. Burnett (1969).
23. Thomas (1989).
24. Averaging behavior across groups: e.g., Miller (1994); examples of the volatility of the less rule-oriented societies: Jaffe et al. (1981); Huizinga (1924).
25. More complex changes in family attitudes are cataloged in Stone (1977); the prospect of individualized video plots is often described, for instance in *Time,* June 8, 1998.
26. Smith (1974).
27. As early as the 1800s in New York City, dwellers of adjoining row houses might never talk to each other over a period of decades (e.g., Day, 1948, p. 316).
28. Kohlberg (1963). Critique that an empathic or "relational" basis for morality is just as good: Gilligan (1982); critique that it's better: Gergen (1994).
29. This association is mostly a matter of clinical lore, but it occasionally appears in print – e.g., Kainer & Gourevitch (1983); Morgan (1977).
30. A rough but viable distinction is summarized in *The Economist* (June 21, 1997, pp. 87–89).
31. Leibenstein (1976).
32. Macdonald & Piggott (1993).
33. Thomas (1989).

Chapter 10. An Efficient Will Undermines Appetite

1. This idea, first elaborated by Adam Smith (1759/1976), has been put in utilitarian terms by economist Julian Simon – but see the commentaries following his article (1995).
2. Elster (1981); Wegner (1994). This idea isn't new:

   Happiness in this world, when it comes, comes incidentally. Make it the object of pursuit, and it leads us on a wild goose chase, and is never attained. Follow some other object, and very possibly we may find that we have caught happiness without dreaming of it. (Nathaniel Hawthorne)

3. The same could be said of the commercial marketplace itself, as informed by utility theory, a bookkeeping scheme that seems to have been refined in modern society alongside the will; both internal and commercial marketplaces are ways of maximizing your expectations for highly definable goods. In a variant of Gresham's law, definable goods drive subtle goods out of a systemized marketplace.

4. Elster makes a highly believable variant of this argument in experiential terms (1999b, pp. 149–165) but uses elements that, I believe, ultimately require a motivational explanation. I discuss these later.

5. The conventional view is that actors and other people who learn to summon emotions do so "by association," that is, by finding conditioned stimuli that have been paired with the "natural" stimuli for emotions. After all, an actor is taught that when she wants to seem sad, she should rehearse a sad memory of her own. In this view, goal-directed emotions are pale imitations of spontaneous ones – "parasitic" on them, in Elster's words (1999b, p. 152). But if conditioning were the mechanism of this process, her emotions ought to gradually extinguish in the absence of repeated unconditioned stimuli – just as Pavlov's dogs stopped salivating when food stopped following his bell. In fact, the emotion comes more and more directly.

    Emotions have the admittedly restricted learnability of smooth muscle and glandular responses: The urinary sphincter is a smooth muscle. Its control is learned later than anal control and never becomes as fine-tuned as skeletal muscle control; it can't beat a rhythm, for instance. But its movement is clearly voluntary and thus is not conditioned. To take a more extreme example, bulimics learn to induce vomiting by sticking a finger or spoon down their throats, and then by anticipating doing so, seemingly by conditioning their gag reflex. But they soon can vomit merely by intending to, without even imagining a gag stimulus; if the mechanism were conditioning, they should have to actually use a finger every now and then to prevent extinction.

    This isn't to say that emotions are just temporal patterns of reward. They have innate properties that make different modalities especially suitable for particular circumstances, just as eating and sex do. Even though you can learn to nurse a feeling until you summon it arbitrarily, nature has still given you predispositions to get angry when thwarted, fearful at great heights or in strange surroundings, or joyful to the point of laughter at sudden good fortune. My point is that natural stimuli are just prepared opportunities for the relevant emotion, grooves that keep an inexperienced organism from being a blank slate; but they are neither necessary nor sufficient precipitants of these emotions and can be overridden in goal-directed fashion.

6. Actually there has been a long-standing debate among actors as to the need to subjectively experience the emotions they portray; see Archer (1888); Strasberg (1988); Downs (1995). However, it's clear that the heartfelt route to scenes is eminently learnable. Many authors have described how to follow this route, but by significantly roundabout routes, altogether unlike instructions for how to build a kite or ride a bicycle. Archer interviewed a number of actors on the subject; Method teacher Lee Strasberg argued for it; Downs, against it.

7. Psychologists Brehm and Brummett (1998) even put emotion in this role.

8. Douglas (1966, p. 37); Empson (1930).

9. Lorenz (1970, p. 354).

10. Empson (1930).
11. Aesthetic researchers: Berlyne (1974); Scitovsky (1976); "The world is ambiguous" (Herzberg, 1965, p. 62); "As long as man is an ambiguous creature" (Becker, 1973, p. 92).
12. Even concrete rewards like food seem to have much of their effect at the moment that the organism is certain of getting them, not when they're actually delivered – that is, when their prospect is still a surprise (Mazur, 1997). This goes along with the finding of brain-reward sites that also respond only to surprising information (Schultz et al., 1997).
13. Rhue & Lynn (1987).
14. Frank (1988, pp. 9–12, 114–133); see Ainslie (1999a) for more on dissociation.
15. Dewsbury (1981); Fisher (1962); Wilson et al. (1963); Walker & King (1962).
16. Tomkins (1978, p. 212).
17. Lorenz (1970, pp. 355–356, 357).
18. Sartre (1948); mixed emotions: Elster (1999b, p. 41); Frijda (1986, p. 207); panic: Clum, 1989; Bouman & Emmelkamp, 1996; panic and suicide: Weissman et al. (1989); see Section 4.1.4.

Chapter 11. The Need to Maintain Appetite Eclipses the Will

1. E.g., Gergen (1985); see also Harland (1987).
2. These criteria for goodness of occasion cover much the same ground as the "components of situational meaning" that determine emotional responses in psychologist Nico Frijda's analysis: "objectivity" corresponds to being outside of your control, "relevance," "difficulty," "urgency," "seriousness," and "clarity" correspond to rarity, "reality level" to truth, and "change" and "strangeness" to surprisingness. "Valence" and "demand character" represent the value of the emotion if well occasioned (1986, pp. 204–208).
3. Perhaps negative emotions evolved to habituate less because it's more adaptive for an organism when negative or mixed emotions stay seductive as long as the occasions for them persist.
4. There has been a lively debate between authors who believe that altruism is a primary motive (e.g., Batson & Shaw, 1991) and those who think it reduces to selfish pleasure (Piliavin et al., 1982; Sen, 1977).
5. Humor from others' pain: Berger (1987); also Hobbes in LaFave et al. (1974).
6. Sadism: Benjamin (1988); buying criminals: Origo (1959); Khonds: Frazer's *The Golden Bough*, quoted in Davies (1981, pp. 78–82).
7. Povinelli et al. (1999).
8. Hinshelwood (1989, pp. 68–83, 179–208).
9. Schilder & Wechsler (1935).
10. This kind of accounting underlies the subtle and poorly defined area of "ego boundaries," which somehow play a central role in emotional health (e.g., Masterson, 1990).
11. 1995, p. 381.

12. There's a theater exercise that models the unavailability of will: One player improvises a story and then passes it to someone else, who isn't allowed to deny or negate any of the story she receives. The new player must find some element in the story thus far that motivates its characters to go in the direction she wants, and she can coerce later players only through the implications of the part she tells. An analogous process may be a way to govern emotional temptations without avoiding emotion itself.

13. George F. Will in *The Washington Post,* quoted in *The International Herald Tribune,* June 27, 1999.

14. Hirshman (1967, p. 13). Thanks to Denrell Jerker for pointing this out.

15. Stendhal, *Le Rouge et le Noir,* II.XII, quoted in Elster (1999a, p. 214). Mountain climber Willi Unsoeld described his continuing enthrallment with climbing despite (?because of) the death of his daughter with him on one climb and the loss of all his toes on another (Leamer, 1999).

16. More discussion is found in Ainslie (1999, pp. 80–83).

17. April 14, 1999.

18. Of course, it sounds odd to speak of a "market" for obstacles to reward, but such a thing is at least recognized in jokes – e.g., Garrison Keillor's commercials for "The Fearmonger's Shop" on *A Prairie Home Companion.*

19. Sometimes the target of wit is actually base. For instance, merchants, lawyers, and caregivers do best financially if they distract customers from the bargaining aspects of their relationship by cultivating professionalism; but some people's professionalism is sincere. The fact that the sincere kind may succeed the most in no way negates its authenticity. An economist, Robert Frank (1988), has described how society develops wisdom about what stances are hard to fake, so that someone selling her wares won't succeed until she happens upon genuine sincerity.

20. Martin (1991).

21. Patients with "empathy disorders" show no understanding of the empathic purposes under concrete tasks (e.g., Putnam, 1990).

22. Lorenz (1970, p. 355).

23. Plato (1892, p. 329) (*Symposium,* pp. 203–204).

24. Toynbee (1946). Economist Mancur Olsen (1982) described how the growth of legally protected special interests increasingly saps the adaptability of nations; thus destructive wars, like forest fires, may have the effect of renewing growth.

REFERENCES

Agarwal, D. P. and Goedde, H. W. (1989) Human aldehyde dehydrogenases: Their role in alcoholism. *Alcohol* 6, 517–523.

Ainslie, G. (1970) Experiment described by Howard Rachlin in his *Introduction to Modern Behaviorism*. San Francisco: Freeman, pp. 186–188.

Ainslie, G. (1974) Impulse control in pigeons. *Journal of the Experimental Analysis of Behavior* 21, 485–489.

Ainslie, G. (1975) Specious reward: A behavioral theory of impulsiveness and impulse control. *Psychological Bulletin* 82, 463–496.

Ainslie, G. (1982) Internal self-control in pigeons. Unpublished manuscript.

Ainslie, G. (1986) Beyond microeconomics: Conflict among interest in a multiple self as a determinant of value. In J. Elster (ed.), *The Multiple Self.* Cambridge: Cambridge University Press, pp. 133–175.

Ainslie, G. (1987) Aversion with only one factor. In M. Commons, J. Mazur, A. Nevin, and H. Rachlin (eds.), *Quantitative Analysis of Behavior: The Effect of Delay and of Intervening Events on Reinforcement Value,* Hillsdale, NJ: Erlbaum, pp. 127–139.

Ainslie, G. (1991) Derivation of "rational" economic behavior from hyperbolic discount curves. *American Economic Review* 81, 334–340.

Ainslie, G. (1992) *Picoeconomics: The Strategic Interaction of Successive Motivational States within the Person.* Cambridge: Cambridge University Press.

Ainslie, G. (1993) A picoeconomic rationale for social constructionism. *Behavior and Philosophy* 21, 63–75.

Ainslie, G. (1995) A utility-maximizing mechanism for vicarious reward: Comments on Julian Simon's "Interpersonal allocation continuous with intertemporal allocation." *Rationality and Society* 7, 393–403.

Ainslie, G. (1999a) The dangers of willpower: A picoeconomic understanding of addiction and dissociation. In J. Elster and O-J. Skog (eds.), *Getting Hooked: Rationality and Addiction.* Cambridge: Cambridge University Press, pp. 65–92.

Ainslie, G. (1999b) The intuitive explanation of passionate mistakes, and why it's not adequate. In J. Elster (ed.), *Addiction: Entries and Exits.* New York: Sage, pp. 209–238.

227

Ainslie, G. (2000) A research-based theory of addictive motivation. *Law and Philosophy* 19, 77–115.

Ainslie, G. and Engel, B. T. (1974) Alteration of classically conditioned heart rate by operant reinforcement in monkeys. *Journal of Comparative and Physiological Psychology* 87, 373–383.

Ainslie, G. and Gault, B. (1997) Intention isn't indivisible. *Behavioral and Brain Sciences* 20, 365–366.

Ainslie, G. and Haendel, V. (1983) The motives of the will. In E. Gottheil, K. Druley, T. Skodola, and H. Waxman (eds.), *Etiology Aspects of Alcohol and Drug Abuse.* Springfield, IL: Charles C. Thomas, pp. 119–140.

Ainslie, G. and Herrnstein, R. (1981) Preference reversal and delayed reinforcement. *Animal Learning and Behavior* 9, 476–482.

Ainslie, G. and Monterosso, J. (2000) Bundling choices into series makes rats switch preference from smaller-earlier to larger-later sucrose rewards. Unpublished manuscript.

Ainslie, G., Monterosso, J., Mullen, P.T., and Gault, B. (in preparation) Recovery from apparent defections in very long prisoner's dilemma games.

Allison, J. (1981) Economics and operant conditioning. In P. Harzen and M. D. Zeiler (eds.), *Predictability, Correlation, and Contiguity.* New York: Wiley, pp. 321–353.

Altman, J., Everitt, B. J., Glautier, S., Markou, A., Nutt, J., Oretti, R., Phillips, G. D., and Robbins, T. W. (1996) The biological, social and clinical bases of drug addiction: Commentary and debate. *Psychopharmacology* 125, 285–345.

American Psychiatric Association (1994) *Diagnostic and Statistical Manual of Mental Disorders* (4th ed.). Washington, DC: APA Press.

Amundson, R. (1990) Doctor Dennett and Doctor Pangloss: Perfection and selection in biology and psychology. *Behavioral and Brain Sciences* 13, 577–581.

Anderson, L. and Alpert, M. (1974) Operant analysis of hallucination frequency in a hospitalized schizophrenic. *Journal of Behavior Therapy and Experimental Psychiatry* 5, 13–18.

Appel, J. B. (1963) Aversive aspects of a schedule of positive reinforcement. *Journal of the Experimental Analysis of Behavior* 6, 423–428.

Archer, W. (1888) *Masks or Faces: A Study in the Psychology of Acting.* London: Lunmans.

Aristotle (1984) *The Complete Works of Aristotle.* J. Barnes (ed.). Princeton, NJ: Princeton University Press.

Atkinson, J. W. and Birch, D. (1970) *The Dynamics of Action.* New York: Wiley.

Atnip, G. (1977) Stimulus and response-reinforcer contingencies in autoshaping, operant, classical and omission training procedures in rats. *Journal of the Experimental Analysis of Behavior* 28, 59–69.

Averill, J. R. (1988) Disorders of emotion. *Journal of Social and Clinical Psychology* 6, 247–268.

Axelrod, R. M. (1984) *The Evolution of Cooperation.* New York: Basic Books.

Axelrod, R. M. (1990) The emergence of cooperation among egoists. In P. K. Moser (ed.), *Rationality in Action: Contemporary Approaches.* New York: Cambridge University Press, pp. 294–314.

References

Ayers, S. (1997) The application of chaos theory to psychology. *Theory and Psychology* 7, 373–398.

Azrin, N. H. (1961) Time-out from positive reinforcement. *Science* 133, 382–383.

Azrin, N. H., Nunn, R., and Frantz-Renshaw, S. (1982) Habit reversal vs. negative practice of self-destructive oral habit (biting, chewing, or licking of lips, cheeks, tongue, or palate). *Journal of Behavior Therapy in Experimental Psychiatry* 13, 49–54.

Bain, A. (1859/1886) *The Emotions and the Will.* New York: Appleton.

Basmajian, J. V. *Biofeedback: Principles and Practice for Clinicians* (3d ed.) Baltimore: Williams & Wilkins.

Batson, C. D. and Shaw, L. L. (1991) Evidence for altruism: Toward a pluralism or prosocial motives. *Psychological Inquiry* 2, 159–168.

Baum, W. M. and Heath, J. L. (1992) Behavioral explanations and intentional explanations in psychology. *American Psychologist* 47, 1312–1317.

Baumeister, R. F. (1984) Choking under pressure: Self-conscious ness and paradoxical effects of incentives on skillful performance. *Journal of Personality and Social Psychology* 46, 610–620.

Baumeister, R. F. and Heatherton, T. (1996) Self-regulation failure: An overview. *Psychological Inquiry* 7, 1–15.

Beck, A. T. (1976) *Cognitive Therapy and the Emotional Disorders.* New York: International Universities Press.

Becker, E. (1973) *The Denial of Death.* New York: Free Press.

Becker, G. S. (1976) *The Economic Approach to Human Behavior.* Chicago: Chicago University Press.

Becker, G. S., Grossman, M. and Murphy, K. M. (1994) An empirical analysis of cigarette addiction. *American Economic Review* 84, 396–418.

Becker, G. S. and Murphy, K. (1988) A theory of rational addiction. *Journal of Political Economy* 96, 75–700.

Becker, H. S. (1960) Notes on the concept of commitment. *American Journal of Sociology* 66, 32–40.

Beecher, H. (1959) *Measurement of Subjective Responses.* New York: Oxford University Press.

Benabou, R. and Tirole, J. (2000) Personal rules. Paper delivered at the ECARES-CEPR Conference on Psychology and Economics, Brussels, June 9–11.

Benjamin, J. (1988) *The Bonds of Love.* New York: Pantheon.

Bennett, A. (1918) *Self and Self-Management.* New York: George H. Doran.

Berger, A. A. (1987) Humor: An introduction. Special issue: Humor, the psyche, and society. *American Behavioral Scientist* 30, 6–15.

Berlyne, D. E. (1974) *Studies in the New Experimental Aesthetics.* Washington, DC: Hemisphere.

Bernoulli, D. (1738/1954) Exposition of a new theory on the measurement of risk. *Econometrica* 22, 23–26.

Bickel, W. K., Odum, A. L., and Madden, G. J. (1999) Impulsivity and cigarette smoking: Delay discounting in current, never, and ex-smokers. *Psychopharmacology* 146, 447–454.

Blessing, L. (1988) *A Walk in the Woods.* New York: New American Library.

Bodner, R. and Prelec, D. (1995) The diagnostic value of actions in a self-signaling model. Paper delivered at the Norwegian Research Council Working Group on Addiction, Oslo, Norway, May 26, 1995.

Boehme, R., Blakely, E., and Poling, A. (1986) Runway length as a determinant of self-control in rats. *The Psychological Record* 36, 285–288.

Bogen, J. and Moravcsik, J. (1982) Aristotle's forbidden sweets. *History and Philosophy* 20, 111–127.

Boring, E. G. (1950) *A History of Experimental Psychology,* New York: Appleton-Century-Crofts.

Bouman, T. K. and Emmelkamp, P. (1996) Panic disorder and agoraphobia. In V. B. Van Hasselt and M. Hersen (eds.), *Sourcebook of Psychological Treatment Manuals for Adult Disorders.* New York: Plenum, pp. 23–63.

Bratman, M. E. (1987) *Intention, Plans, and Practical Reason.* Cambridge, MA: Harvard University Press.

Bratman, M. E. (1999) *Faces of Intention: Selected Essays on Intention and Agency.* Cambridge: Cambridge University Press.

Brehm, J. W. and Brummett, B. H. (1998) The emotional control of behavior. In M. Kofta, G. Weary, and G. Sedek (eds.), *Personal Control in Action: Cognitive and Motivational Mechanisms* New York and London: Plenum.

Brennan, G. and Tullock, G. (1982) An economic theory of military tactics: Methodological individualism at war. *Journal of Economic Behavior and Organization* 3, 225–242.

Broad, C. D. (1962) Determinism, indeterminism and libertarianism. In S. Morgenbesser and J. Walsh (eds.), *Free Will.* Englewood Cliffs, NJ: Prentice-Hall, pp. 115–132.

Brunner, D. (1999) Preference for sequences of rewards: Further tests of a parallel discounting model. *Behavioral Processes* 45, 87–99.

Brunner, D. and Gibbon, J. (1995) Value of food aggregates: Parallel versus serial discounting. *Animal Behavior* 50, 1627–1634.

Brunsson, N. (1982) *The Irrational Organization.* Stockholm: Stockholm School of Economics.

Burnett, J. (1969) *A History of the Cost of Living.* Baltimore: Penguin Books.

Campbell, R. and Sowden, L. (eds.). (1985) *Paradoxes of Rationality and Cooperation.* Vancouver: University of British Columbia.

Campfield, L. A., Smith, F. J., and Burn, P. (1998) Strategies and potential molecular targets for obesity treatment. *Science* 280, 1383–1387.

Carlson, A. J. (1916) The relation of hunger to appetite. *The Control of Hunger in Health and Disease.* Chicago: University of Chicago Press.

Carrillo, J. D. (1999) Self-control, moderate consumption, and craving. Unpublished manuscript. Universite Libre de Bruxelles.

Casalino, L. P. (1999) The unintended consequences of measuring quality on the quality of medical care. *New England Journal of Medicine* 341, 1147–1150.

Case, D. (1997) Why the delay-of-reinforcement gradient is hyperbolic. Paper presented at the 20th Annual Conference of the Society for the Quantitative Analysis of Behavior, Chicago, May 22.

Charlton, W. (1988) *Weakness of the Will.* Oxford: Blackwell.

References

Chung, S. and Herrnstein, R. J. (1967) Choice and delay of reinforcement. *Journal of the Experimental Analysis of Behavior* 10, 67–74.

Clum, G. A. (1989) Psychological interventions vs. drugs in the treatment of panic. *Behavior Therapy* 20, 429–457.

Corsini, R. J. (1984) *Current Psychotherapies*. Itasca, IL: Peacock.

Crane, A. M. (1905) *Right and Wrong Thinking and Their Results*. Boston: Lathrop.

Crews, F. (1995) *The Memory Wars: Freud's Legacy in Dispute*. New York: New York Review of Books.

Cropper, M. L., Aydede, S. K., and Portney, P. R. (1991) Discounting human lives. *American Journal of Agricultural Economics* 73, 1410–1415.

Darwin, C. (1872/1979) *The Expressions of Emotions in Man and Animals*. London: Julan Friedman Publishers.

Davidson, D. (1980) *Essays on Actions and Events*. London: Oxford University Press.

Davies, N. (1981) *Human Sacrifice in History and Today*. New York: Morrow.

Davison, W. (1888) *The Christian Conscience*. London: Woolmer.

Day, C. (1948) *The Best of Clarence Day*. New York: Knopf.

Demos, J. (1971) *A Little Commonwealth: Family Life in the Plymouth Colony*. New York: Oxford University Press.

Dennett, D. C. (1984) *Elbow Room: The Varieties of Free Will Worth Wanting*. Cambridge, MA: MIT Press.

Deutsch, J. A. and Howarth, C. I. (1963) Some tests of a theory of intracranial self-stimulation. *Psychological Review* 70, 444–460.

DeVilliers, P. (1977) Choice in concurrent schedules and a quantitative formulation of the law of effect. In W. Honig and J. Staddon (eds.), *Handbook of Operant Behavior*. Englewood Cliffs, NJ: Prentice-Hall, pp. 233–287.

DeVilliers, P. and Herrnstein, R. (1976) Toward a law of response strength. *Psychological Bulletin* 83, 1131–1153.

Dewsbury, D. A. (1981) Effects of novelty on copulatory behavior: The Coolidge effect and related phenomena. *Psychological Bulletin* 89, 464–482.

Dickinson, A. (1980) *Contemporary Animal Learning Theory*. New York: Cambridge University Press.

Donahoe, J. W., Burgos, J. E., and Palmer, D. C. (1993) A selectionist approach to reinforcement. *Journal of the Experimental Analysis of Behavior* 60, 17–40.

Donahoe, J. W., Palmer, D. C., and Burgos, J. E. (1997) The S–R issue: Its status in behavior analysis and in Donahoe and Palmer's *Learning and Complex Behavior*. *Journal of the Experimental Analysis of Behavior* 67, 193–211 (commentaries until 273).

Douglas, M. (1966) *Purity and Danger: An Analysis of Concepts of Pollution and Taboo*. London: Routledge and Kegan Paul.

Downs, D. (1995) *The Actor's Eye: Seeing and Being Seen*. New York: Applause Theatre Books.

Dweyer, P. and Renner, E. (1971) Self-punitive behavior: Masochism or confusion? *Psychological Review* 78, 333–337.

Dworkin, B. R. and Miller, N. E. (1986) Failure to replicate visceral learning in the acute curarized rat preparation. *Behavioral Neuroscience* 100, 299–314.

References

Ekman, P. and Friesen, W. V. (1986) A new pan-cultural facial expression of emotion. *Motivation and Emotion* 10, 159–168.

Ellenberger, H. F. (1970) *The Discovery of the Unconscious.* New York: Basic Books.

Ellenberger, H. F. (1983) A clinical introduction to psychiatric phenomenology and existential analysis. In R. May, E. Angel, and H. Ellenberger (eds.), *Existence: A New Division in Psychiatry and Psychology.* New York: Basic Books, pp. 92–124.

Ellis, A. and Grieger, R. (1977) *R.E.T.: Handbook of Rational-Emotive Therapy.* New York: Springer.

Elner, R. W. and Hughes, R. N. (1978) Energy maximization in the diet of the shore crab *Carinus maenas. Journal of Animal Ecology* 47, 103–116.

Elster, J. (1979) *Ulysses and the Sirens: Studies in Rationality and Irrationality.* Cambridge: Cambridge University Press.

Elster, J. (1981) States that are essentially by-products. *Social Science Information* 20, 431–473. Reprinted in Elster, J. (1983) *Sour Grapes: Studies in the Subversion of Rationality.* Cambridge: Cambridge University Press, pp. 43–108.

Elster, J. (1989a) *Nuts and Bolts for the Social Sciences.* Cambridge: Cambridge University Press.

Elster, J. (1989b) *The Cement of Society.* Cambridge: Cambridge University Press.

Elster, J. (1999a) Gambling and addiction. In J. Elster and O.-J. Skog (eds.), *Getting Hooked: Rationality and Addiction.* Cambridge: Cambridge University Press.

Elster, J. (1999b) *Strong Feelings: Emotion, Addiction, and Human Behavior.* Cambridge, MA: MIT Press.

Elster, J. (2000) *Ulysses Unbound.* Cambridge: Cambridge University Press.

Empson, W. (1930) *Seven Types of Ambiguity.* London: New Directions.

Epstein, S. (1998) Personal control from the perspective of cognitive-experiential self-theory. In M. Kofta, G. Weary, and G. Sedek (eds.), *Personal Control in Action: Cognitive and Motivational Mechanisms.* New York and London: Plenum.

Erasmus, D. (1509/1983) *The Praise of Folly.* Leonard F. Dean (ed.). Putney, VT: Hendricks House.

Erdelyi, M. H. (1990) Repression, reconstruction and defense: History and integration of the psychoanalytic and experimental frameworks. In J. L. Singer, (ed.), *Repression and Dissociation: Implications for Personality Theory, Psychopathology, and Health.* Chicago: Chicago University Press, pp. 1–31.

Evans, D. (1975) Moral weakness. *Philosophy* 50, 295–310.

Eysenck, H. J. (1967) Single trial conditioning, neurosis and the Napalkov phenomenon. *Behavior Research and Therapy* 5, 63–65.

Faught, E., Falgout, J., Nidiffer, D., and Dreifuss, F. E. (1986) Self-induced photosensitive absence seizures with ictal pleasure. *Archives of Neurology* 43, 408–410.

Fehr, E. and Gachter, S. (1999) Cooperation and punishment in public goods experiments. Paper presented at the GREMAQ/CEPR Conference on Economics and Psychology, Toulouse, France, June 19.

Ferguson, R. (1989) On crashes. *Financial Analysts Journal* 45, 42–52.

Fisher, A. (1962) Effects of stimulus variation on sexual satiation in the male rat. *Journal of Comparative and Physiological Psychology* 55, 614–620.

Frank, R. H. (1988) *Passions Within Reason.* New York: W. W. Norton.

Fredrickson, B. L. and Kahneman, D. (1993) Duration neglect in retrospective evaluations of affective episodes. *Journal of Personality and Social Psychology* 65, 45–55.

Freud, S. (1895/1956) *Project for a Scientific Psychology.* In J. Strachey and A. Freud (eds.), *The Standard Edition of the Complete Psychological Works of Sigmund Freud.* London: Hogarth, vol. 1.

Freud, S. (1911) Ibid., vol. 12. *Formulations on the Two Principles of Mental Functioning.*

Freud, S. (1916–1917) Ibid., vol. 16. *Introductory Lectures on Psycho-Analysis.*

Freud, S. (1920) Ibid., vol. 18. *Beyond the Pleasure Principle.*

Freud, S. (1923) Ibid., vol. 19. *The Ego and the Id.*

Freud, S. (1926) Ibid., vol. 20. *Inhibitions, Symptoms, and Anxiety.*

Frijda, N. H. (1986) *The Emotions.* Cambridge: Cambridge University Press.

Fuller, R. K. and Roth, H. P. (1979) Disulfiram for the treatment of alcoholism. *Annals of Internal Medicine* 90, 901–904.

Galen (1963) *Galen on the Passions and Errors of the Soul.* P. W. Harkins (trans.). Columbus, OH: Ohio: Ohio State University Press.

Gardner, E. L. (1997) Brain reward mechanisms. In J. H. Lowinson, P. Ruiz, R. B. Millman, and J. G. Langrod (eds.), *Substance Abuse: A Comprehensive Textbook* (3d ed.). Baltimore: Williams & Wilkins, pp. 51–85.

Gardner, E. L. (1999) The neurobiology and genetics of addiction: Implications of the "reward deficiency syndrome" for therapeutic strategies in chemical dependency. In J. Elster (ed.), *Addiction: Entries and Exits.* New York: Russell Sage, pp. 57–119.

Garson, J. W. (1995) Chaos and free will. *Philosophical Psychology* 8, 365–374.

Gergen, K. J. (1985) The social constructionist movement in modern psychology. *American Psychologist* 40, 266–275.

Gergen, M. (1994) Free will and psychotherapy: Complaints of the draughtsmen's daughters. *Journal of Theoretical and Philosophical Psychology* 14, 13–24.

Gibbon, J. (1977) Scalar expectancy theory and Weber's law in animal timing. *Psychological Review* 84, 279–325.

Gilbert, D. T., Pinel, E. C., Wilson, T. D., Blumberg, S. J., and Wheatley, T. P. (1999) Immune neglect: A source of durability bias in affective forecasting. Paper presented at the GREMAQ/CEPR Conference on Economics and Psychology, Toulouse, France, June 18.

Gilligan, C. (1977) In a different voice: Womens' conceptions of self and morality. *Harvard Educational Review* 47, 481–517.

Gilligan, C. (1982) *In a Different Voice: Psychological Theory and Women's Development.* Cambridge, MA: Harvard University Press.

Gjesme, T. (1983) On the concept of future time orientation: Considerations of some functions' and measurements' implications. *International Journal of Psychology* 18, 443–461.

Glantz, K. and Pearce, J. (1989) *Exiles from Eden: Psychotherapy from an Evolutionary Perspective.* New York: Norton.

Gleick, J. (1987) *Chaos: Making a New Science.* New York: Viking Penguin.

References

Goldiamond, I. (1965) Self-control procedures in personal behavior problems. *Psychological Reports* 17, 851–868.

Goldsmith, H. H., Buss, K. A., and Lemery, K. S. (1997) Toddler and childhood temperament: Expanded content, stronger genetic evidence, new evidence for the importance of environment. *Developmental Psychology* 33, 891–905.

Gosling, J. (1990) *Weakness of Will.* London: Routledge.

Grace, R. C. (1994) A contextual model of concurrent chains choice. *Journal of the Experimental Analysis of Behavior* 61, 113–129.

Granda, A. M. and Hammack, J. T. (1961) Operant behavior during sleep. *Science* 133, 1485–1486.

Green, L., Fisher, E. B., Jr., Perlow, S., and Sherman, L. (1981) Preference reversal and self-control: Choice as a function of reward amount and delay. *Behaviour Analysis Letters* 1, 43–51.

Green, L., Fry, A., and Myerson, J. (1994) Discounting of delayed rewards: A life-span comparison. *Psychonomic Science* 5, 33–36.

Green, L. and Myerson, J. (1993) Alternative frameworks for the analysis of self-control. *Behavior and Philosophy* 21, 37–47.

Green, L., Price, P. C., and Hamburger, M. E. (1995) Prisoner's dilemma and the pigeon: Control by immediate consequences. *Journal of the Experimental Analysis of Behavior* 64, 1–17.

Hampton, C. (1976) *Savages.* London: Samuel French.

Harland, R. (1987) *Superstructuralism: The Philosophy of Structuralism and Post-Structuralism.* London: Methuen.

Harris, C. and Laibson, D. (1999) Dynamic choices of hyperbolic consumers. Paper presented at the GREMAQ/CEPR Conference on Economics and Psychology, Toulouse, France, June 19.

Harvey, C. M. (1994) The reasonableness of non-constant discounting. *Journal of Public Economics* 53, 31–51.

Hatcher, R. (1973) Insight and self-observation. *Journal of the American Psychoanalytic Association* 21, 337–398.

Hearst, E. (1975) The classical-instrumental distinction: Reflexes, voluntary behavior, and categories of associative learning. In W. Estes (ed.), *Handbook of Learning and Cognitive Processes,* vol. 2. New York: Erlbaum, pp. 181–223.

Heath, R. G. (1992) Correlation of brain activity with emotion: A basis for developing treatment of violent-aggressive behavior. *Journal of the American Academy of Psychoanalysis* 20, 335–346.

Heather, N. (1998) A conceptual framework for explaining drug addiction. *Journal of Psychopharmacology* 12, 3–7.

Herrnstein, R. J. (1961) Relative and absolute strengths of response as a function of frequency of reinforcement. *Journal of the Experimental Analysis of Behavior* 4, 267–272.

Herrnstein, R. J. (1969) Method and theory in the study of avoidance. *Psychological Review* 76, 49–69.

Herrnstein, R. J. (1997) *The Matching Law: Papers in Psychology and Economics.* H. Rachlin and D. I. Laibson (eds.). New York: Sage.

Herrnstein, R. J., Loewenstein, G., Prelec, D., and Vaughan, W., Jr. (1993) Utility maximization and melioration: Internalities in individual choice. *Journal of Behavioral Decision Making* 6, 149–185.

Herrnstein, R. J. and Loveland, D.H. (1975) Maximizing and matching on concurrent ratio schedules. *Journal of the Experimental Analysis of Behavior* 24, 107–116.

Herrnstein, R. J. and Prelec, D. (1992) Melioration. In G. Loewenstein and J. Elster (eds.), *Choice Over Time*. New York: Sage, pp. 235–264.

Herzberg, F. (1965) *Work and the Nature of Man*. Cleveland: World.

Heyman, G. M. (1996) Resolving the contradictions of addiction. *Behavioral and Brain Sciences* 19, 561–610.

Heyman, G. M. and Tanz, L. (1995) How to teach a pigeon to maximize overall reinforcement rate. *Journal of the Experimental Analysis of Behavior* 64, 277–297.

Hilgard, E. R. (1977) *Divided Consciousness, Multiple Controls, and Human Thought and Action*. New York: Wiley.

Hilgard, E. R. and Hilgard, J. R. (1994) *Hypnosis in the Relief of Pain* (rev. ed.). New York: Brunner/Mazel.

Hilgard, E. R. and Marquis, D. G. (1940) *Conditioning and Learning*. New York: Appleton-Century-Crofts.

Hinshelwood, R. D. 1989) *A Dictionary of Kleinian Thought*. London: Free Association Books.

Hirschman, A. (1967) *Development Projects Observed*. Washington, DC: The Brookings Institution.

Hirschman, A. (1977) *The Passions and the Interests*. Princeton, NJ: Princeton University Press.

Ho, M.-Y., Al-Zahrani, S. S. A., Al-Ruwaitea, A. S. A., Bradshaw, C. M., and Szabadi, E. (1998) 5-Hydroxytryptamine and impulse control: Prospects for a behavioural analysis. *Journal of Psychopharmacology* 12, 68–78.

Hollerman, J. R., Tremblay, L., and Schultz, W. (1998) Influence of reward expectation on behavior-related neuronal activity in primate striatum. *Journal of Neurophysiology* 80, 947–963.

Hollis, M. (l983) Rational preferences. *The Philosophical Forum* 14, 246–262.

Horvitz, J. C., Tripp, S., and Jacobs, B. L. (1997) Burst activity of ventral tegmental dopamine neurons is elicited by sensory stimuli in the awake cat. *Brain Research* 759, 251–258.

Houston, A. I., Krebs, J. R., and Erichsen, J. T. (1980) Optimal prey choice and discrimination time in the great tit (*Parus major L.*). *Behavioral Ecology and Sociobiology* 6, 169–175.

Huizinga, J. (1924) *The Waning of the Middle Ages*. New York: St. Martin's Press.

Hurley, S. L. (1991) Newcomb's problem, prisoners' dilemma, and collective action. *Synthese* 82, 173–196.

Izard, C. E. (1971) *The Face of Emotion*. New York: Appleton-Century-Crofts.

Jaffe, Y., Shapir, N., and Yinon, Y. (1981) Aggression and its escalation. *Journal of Cross-Cultural Psychology* 12, 21–36.

James, W. (1884/1967) The dilemma of determinism. In J. McDermott (ed.), *The Writings of William James*. Chicago: University of Chicago Press, pp. 587–610.

References

James, W. (1890) *Principles of Psychology.* New York: Holt.

Jeavons, P. and Harding, G. (1975) *Photoreactive Epilepsy: A Review of the Literature and a Study of 460 Patients,* London: Heinemann.

Jevons, W. S. (1871/1911) *The Theory of Political Economy.* London: Macmillan.

Johnson, D. F. and Collier, G. H. (1987) Caloric regulation and patterns of food choice in a patchy environment: The value and cost of alternative foods. *Physiology and Behavior* 39, 351–359.

Jowett, B. (1892/1937) *The Dialogues of Plato.* New York: Random House, vol. 1. (See also Plato, 1892.)

Kagel, J. H., Battalio, R. C., and Green, L. (1983) Matching versus maximizing: Comments on Prelec's paper. *Psychological Review* 90, 380–384.

Kagel, J. H., Green, L., and Caraco, T. (1986) When foragers discount the future: Constraint or adaptation? *Animal Behavior* 34, 271, 283.

Kainer, R. G. and Gourevitch, S. J. (1983) On the distinction between narcissism and will: Two aspects of the self. *Psychoanalytic Review* 70, 535–552.

Kane, R. (1989) Two kinds of incompatibilism. *Philosophy and Phenomenological Research* 50, 220–254.

Kanfer, F. H. (1975) Self-management methods. In F. Kanfer and A. Goldstein (eds.), *Helping People Change.* Elmsford, NY: Pergamon, pp. 283–345.

Kant, I. (1793/1960) *Religion Within the Limits of Reason Alone.* T. Green and H. Hucken (trans.). New York: Harper and Row, pp. 15–49.

Karoly, P. (1993) Mechanisms of self-regulation: A systems view. In L. W. Porter and M. R. Rosenzweig (eds.), *Annual Review of Psychology,* vol. 44. Palo Alto, CA: Annual Reviews, pp. 23–52.

Kavka, G. (1983) The toxin puzzle. *Analysis* 43, 33–36.

Kenny, A. (1963) *Action, Emotion, and Will.* London: Humanities Press.

Kern, F. (1948) *Kingship and Law in the Middle Ages* (S.B. Chrimes, trans.). Westport, CT: Greenwood Press.

Kirby, K. N. (1997) Bidding on the future: Evidence against normative discounting of delayed rewards. *Journal of Experimental Psychology: General* 126, 54–70.

Kirby, K. N. and Guastello, B. (2000) Making choices in the context of similar, future choices can increase self-control. Unpublished manuscript.

Kirby, K. N. and Herrnstein, R. J. (1995) Preference reversals due to myopic discounting of delayed reward. *Psychological Science* 6, 83–89.

Kirby, K. N., Petry, N. M., and Bickel, W. K. (1999) Heroin addicts have higher discount rates for delayed rewards than non-drug-using controls. *Journal of Experimental Psychology: General* 128, 78–87.

Kirsh, I. and Lynn, S. J. (1999) Automaticity in clinical psychology. *American psychologist* 54, 504–515.

Klein, B. and Leffler, K. B. (1981) The role of market forces in assuring contractual performance. *Journal of Political Economy* 89, 615–640.

Klein, R. (1989) Introduction to the disorders of the self. In J. F. Masterson and R. Klein (eds.), *Psychotherapy of the Disorders of the Self.* New York: Brunner/ Mazel.

Kobasa, S. C. and Maddi, S. R. (1983) Existential personality theory. In R. J.

Corsini and A. J. Marsella (eds.), *Personality Theories, Research and Assessment.* Itasca, IL: Peacock.

Kofta, M., Weary, G., and Sedek, G. (1998) *Personal Control in Action: Cognitive and Motivational Mechanisms.* New York and London: Plenum.

Kohlberg, L. (1963) The development of children's orientations toward a moral order: I. Sequence in the development of moral thought. *Vita Humana* 6, 11–33.

Kohlberg, L. (1973) Continuities in childhood and adult moral development revisited. In P. B. Baltes and K. W. Schaie (eds.), *Lifespan Developmental Psychology.* New York: Academic Press, pp. 179–204.

Krebs, J. R. (1978) Optimal foraging: Decision rules for predators. In J. R. Krebs and N. B. Davies (eds.), *Behavioral Ecology.* Sunderland, MA: Sinauer.

Kuhl, J. (1994) Motivation and volition. In G. d'Ydewalle, P. Bertelson, and P. Eelen (eds.), *International Perspectives on Psychological Science,* vol. 2. Hillsdale, NJ: Erlbaum, pp. 311–340.

Kuhl, J. (1996) Who controls whom when "I control myself"? *Psychological Inquiry* 7, 61–68.

Kyokai, B. D. (1996) *The Teaching of Buddha: The Way of Practice* (893rd ed.). Tokyo: Kosaido Printing Co.

LaFave, L., Haddad, J., and Marshall, N. (1974). Humor judgments as a function of identification classes. *Sociology and Social Research* 58, 184–194.

Laibson, D. (1997) Golden eggs and hyperbolic discounting. *Quarterly Journal of Economics* 62, 443–479.

Landé, A. (1961) The case for indeterminism. In Sidney Hook (ed.), *Determinism and Freedom in the Age of Modern Science.* New York: Collier, pp. 69–75.

Lassers, E. and Nordan, R. (1978) Separation-individuation of an identical twin. *Adolescent Psychiatry* 6, 469–479.

Lave, J. (1988) *Cognition in Practice: Mind, Mathematics and Culture in Everyday Life.* Cambridge: Cambridge University Press.

Lea, S. E. G. (1979) Foraging and reinforcement schedules in the pigeon. *Animal Behavior* 27, 875–886.

Leamer, L. (1999) *Ascent: The Spiritual and Physical Quest of Legendary Mountaineer Willi Unsoeld.* Minot, ND: Quill.

Leibenstein, H. (1976) *Beyond Economic Man: A New Foundation for Microeconomics.* Cambridge, MA: Harvard University Press.

Licklider, J. C. R. (1959) On psychophysiological models. In W. A. Rosenbluth (ed.), *Sensory Communication.* Cambridge, MA: MIT Press.

Loevinger, J. (1976) *Ego Development,* San Francisco: Jossey-Bass.

Loewenstein, G. F. (1996) Out of control: Visceral influences on behavior. *Organizational Behavior and Human Decision Processes* 35, 272–292.

Loewenstein, G. F. (1999) A visceral account of addiction. In J. Elster and O.-J. Skog (eds.), *Getting Hooked: Rationality and Addiction.* Cambridge: Cambridge University Press.

Logue, A. W. and Mazur, J. E. (1981) Maintenance of self-control acquired through a fading process: Follow-up on Mazur and Logue. (1978). *Behaviour Analysis Letters* 1, 131–137.

References

Lorenz, K. (1970) The enmity between generations and its probable ethological causes. *Psychoanalytic Review* 57, 333–377.

Lotka, A. (1957) *Elements of Mathematical Biology*. New York: Dover.

Macaulay, S. (1963) Non-contractual relations in business: A preliminary study. *American Sociological Review* 28, 55–67.

Macdonald, J. and Piggott, J. (1993) *Global Quality: The New Management Culture*. San Diego, CA: Pfeiffer.

MacKintosh, N. J. (1983) *Conditioning and Associative Learning*. New York: Clarendon.

Madden, G. J., Chase, P. N., and Joyce, J. H. (1998) Making sense of sensitivity in the human operant literature. *Behavior Analyst* 21, 1–12.

Madden, G. J., Petry, N. M., Badger, G. J., and Bickel, W. K. (1997) Impulsive and self-control choices in opioid-dependent patients and non-drug-using control patients: Drug and monetary rewards. *Experimental and Clinical Psychopharmacology* 5, 256–262.

Magaro, P. A. (1991) *Cognitive Bases of Mental Disorders*. Newbury Park, CA: Sage.

Mahoney, M. J. (1991) *Human Change Processes: The Scientific Foundations of Psychotherapy*. New York: Basic Books.

Malekzadeh, A. R. and Nahavandi, A. (1987) Merger mania: Who wins? Who loses? *Journal of Business Strategy* 8, 76–79.

Marks, I. (1997) Behavior therapy for obsessive-compulsive disorder: A decade of progress. *Canadian Journal of Psychiatry* 42, 1021–1027.

Marlatt, G. A. and Gordon, J. R. (1980) Determinants of relapse: Implications for the maintenance of behavior change. In P. O. Davidson and S. M. Davidson (eds.), *Behavioral Medicine: Changing Health Lifestyles*. Elmsford, NY: Pergamon, pp. 410–452.

Martin, J. (1991) A shortage of shock sparks plea for more. *The Philadelphia Inquirer*, Feb. 3, p. 3–I.

Masterson, J. F. (1990) *Search for the Real Self: Unmasking the Personality Disorders of Our Age*. New York: Free Press.

Mawhinney, T. C. (1982) Maximizing versus matching in people versus pigeons. *Psychological Reports* 50, 267–281.

May, R. (1958) The origins and existential movement in psychology. In R. May, E. Angel, and H. F. Ellenberger (eds.), *Existence: A New Dimension in Psychiatry and Psychology*, New York: Basic Books, pp. 3–36.

May, R. (1967) The problem of will and intentionality in psychoanalysis. *Contemporary Psychoanalysis* 3, 55–70.

Maynard Smith, J. (1978) Optimization theory in evolution. *Annual Review of Ecology and Systematics* 9, 31–56.

Mazur, J. E. (1984) Tests of an equivalence rule for fixed and variable reinforcer delays. *Journal of Experimental Psychology: Animal Behavior Processes* 10, 426–436.

Mazur, J. E. (1986) Choice between single and multiple delayed reinforcers. *Journal of the Experimental Analysis of Behavior* 46, 67–77.

References

Mazur, J. E. (1987) An adjusting procedure for studying delayed reinforcement. In M. L. Commons, J. E. Mazur, J. A. Nevin, and H. Rachlin (eds.), *Quantitative Analyses of Behavior V: The Effect of Delay and of Intervening Events on Reinforcement Value.* Hillsdale, NJ: Erlbaum, pp. 55–73.

Mazur, J. E. (1997) Choice, delay, probability, and conditioned reinforcement. *Animal Learning and Behavior* 25, 131–147.

Mazur, J. E. and Logue, A. W. (1978) Choice in a self-control paradigm: Effects of a fading procedure. *Journal of the Experimental Analysis of Behavior* 30, 11–17.

McCartney, J. (1997) Between knowledge and desire: Perceptions of decision-making in the addictive behaviors. *Substance Use and Misuse,* 32, 2061–2092.

McClennen, E. F. (1990) *Rationality and Dynamic Choice.* New York: Cambridge University Press

McDiarmid, C. G. and Rilling, M. E. (1965) Reinforcement delay and reinforcement rate as determinants of schedule preference. *Psychonomic Science* 2, 195–196.

McFarland, D. J. and Sibley, R. M. (1975) The behavioral final common path. *Philosophical Transactions of the Royal Society of London* B 270, 265–293.

Mele, A. R. (1995) *Autonomous Agents: From Self-Control to Autonomy.* New York: Oxford University Press.

Melzack, R., Weisz, A. Z., and Sprague, L. T. (1963) Stratagems for controlling pain: Contributions of auditory stimulation and suggestion. *Experimental Neurology* 8, 239–247.

Mendelsohn, J. and Chorover, S. L. (1965) Lateral hypothalamic stimulation in satiated rats: T-maze learning for food. *Science* 149, 559–561.

Metcalfe, J. and Jacobs, W. (1998) Emotional memory: The effects of stress on "cool" and "hot" memory systems. In D. L. Medin (ed.), *The Psychology of Learning and Motivation,* Vol. 38: *Advances in Research and Theory.* San Diego, CA: Academic Press, pp. 187–222.

Meyer, R. (1981) Conditioning factors in alcoholism. Paper presented at the annual meeting of the American Psychiatric Association, May.

Millar, A. and Navarick, D. J. (1984) Self-control and choice in humans: Effects of video game playing as a positive reinforcer. *Learning and Motivation* 15, 203–218.

Miller, J. G. (1994) Cultural diversity in the morality of caring: Individually oriented versus duty-based interpersonal moral codes. *Cross-Cultural Research: The Journal of Comparative Social Science* 28, 3–39.

Miller, N. (1969) Learning of visceral and glandular responses. *Science* 163, 434–445.

Mirenowicz, J., and Schultz, W. (1996) Preferential activation of midbrain dopamine neurons by appetitive rather than aversive stimuli. *Nature* 379, 449–451.

Mischel, H. N. and Mischel, W. (1983) The development of children's knowledge of self-control strategies. *Child Development* 54, 603–619.

Mischel, W., Cantor, N., and Feldman, S. (1996) Principles of self-regulation: The nature of willpower and self-control. In E. T. Higgins (ed.), *Social Psychology: Handbook of Basic Principles.* New York: Guilford Press, pp. 329–360.

Morgan, M. J. and Nicholas, D. J. (1979) Discrimination between reinforced action patterns in the rat. *Learning and Motivation* 10, 1–22.

Morgan, S. R. (1977) Personality variables as predictors of empathy. *Behavioral Disorders* 2, 89–94.

Morgenstern, O. (1979) Some reflections on utility. In M. Allais and O. Hagen (eds.), *Expected Utility Hypotheses and the Allais Paradox.* Norwell, MA: Kluwer, pp. 175–183.

Mourant, J. A. (1967) Pelagius and Pelagianism. In P. Edwards (ed.), *The Encyclopedia of Philosophy,* vol. 6. New York: Macmillan, pp. 78–79.

Mowrer, O. H. (1947) On the dual nature of learning: A re-interpretation of "conditioning" and "problem solving." *Harvard Educational Review* 17, 102–148.

Navarick, D. J. (1982) Negative reinforcement and choice in humans. *Learning and Motivation* 13, 361–377.

Navarick, D. J. and Fantino, E. (1976) Self-control and general models of choice. *Journal of Experimental Psychology: Animal Behavior Processes* 2, 75–87.

Navon, D. and Gopher, D. (1979) On the economy of the human-processing system. *Psychological Review* 86, 214–255.

Nemiah, J. C. (1977) Alexithymia: Theoretical considerations. *Psychotherapy and Psychosomatics* 28, 199–206.

Nozick, R. (1969) Newcomb's problem and two principles of choice. In N. Rescher (eds.), *Essays in Honor of C. G. Hempel.* Dordrecht: Reidel, pp. 114–146.

Nozick, R. (1993) *The Nature of Rationality.* Princeton, NJ: Princeton University Press.

O'Brien, C. P., Ehrman, R. N., and Ternes, J. W. (1986) Classical conditioning in human dependence. In S. R. Goldberg and I. P. Stolerman (eds.), *Behavioral Analyses of Drug Dependence.* Orlando, FL: Academic Press, pp. 329–356.

Offer, A. (1995) Going to war in 1914: A matter of honor? *Politics and Society* 23, 213–240.

Offer, A. (1998) Epidemics of abundance: Overeating and slimming in the USA and Britain since the 1950s. *Discussion Papers in Economic and Social History* 25.

Ogden, C. and Richards, I. (1930) *The Meaning of Meanings.* New York: Harcourt Brace.

Olds, J. (1992) Mapping the mind onto the brain. In Frederick G. Worden, and J. P. Swazey (eds.), *The Neurosciences: Paths of Discovery.* Boston: Birkhaeuser, pp. 375–400.

Olds, J. and Milner, P. (1954) Positive reinforcement produced by electrical stimulation of septal area and other regions of rat brain. *Journal of Comparative and Physiological Psychology* 47, 419–427.

Olson, M. (1982) *The Rise and Decline of Nations.* New Haven, CT: Yale University Press.

Olson, M. and Bailey, M. (1981) Positive time preference. *Journal of Political Economy* 89, 1–25.

Origo, I. (1959) *The Merchant of Prato: Francesco di Marco Datini.* New York: Octagon.

Ostaszewski, P. (1996) The relation between temperament and rate of temporal discounting. *European Journal of Personality* 10, 161–172.

Palmer, R. C. (1993) *English Law in the Age of the Black Death, 1348–1381.* Chapel Hill: University of North Carolina Press.

Palmer, D. C. and Donahoe, J. W. (1992) Essentialism and selectionism in cognitive and behavior analysis. *American Psychologist* 47, 1344–1358.

Panksepp, J. (1982) Toward a general psychobiological theory of emotions. *Behavioral and Brain Sciences,* 5, 407–467.

Pap, A. (1961) Determinism, freedom, moral responsibility, and causal talk. In Sidney Hook (ed.), *Determinism and Freedom in the Age of Modern Science.* New York: Collier, pp. 200–205.

Parfit, D. (1984) *Reasons and Persons.* Oxford: Oxford University Press.

Perls, F., Hefferline, R. F., and Goodman, P. (1958) *Gestalt Therapy.* New York: Julian.

Perris, C. (1988) The foundations of cognitive psychotherapy and its standing in relation to other psychotherapies. In C. Perris, I. M. Blackburn, and H. Perris (eds.), *Cognitive Therapy: Theory and Practice.* London: Springer-Verlag.

Phelps, E. S. and Pollack, R. A. (1968) On second-best national saving and game-equilibrium growth. *Review of Economic Studies* 35, 185–199.

Piaget, J. (1932/1965) *The Moral Judgment of the Child.* New York: Free Press.

Pigou, A. C. (1920) *The Economics of Welfare.* London: Macmillan.

Piliavin, J. A., Callero, P. L., and Evans, D. E. (1982) Addiction to altruism? Opponent-process theory and habitual blood donation. *Journal of Personality and Social Psychology* 43, 1200–1213.

Plato (1892) *The Dialogues of Plato.* B. Jowett (trans.). New York: Random House, vol. 1. (See also Jowett, 1892/1937.)

Polivy, J. (1998) The effects of behavioral inhibition: Integrating internal cues, cognition, behavior, and affect. *Psychological Inquiry* 9, 181–204.

Povinelli, D. J., Bierschwale, D. T., and Cech, C. G. (1999) Comprehension of seeing as a referential act in young children, but not juvenile chimpanzees. *British Journal of Developmental Psychology* 17, 37–60.

Premack, D. (1959) Toward empirical behavior laws, I. Positive reinforcement. *Psychological Review* 66, 219–234.

Putnam, N. (1990) Revenge or tragedy: Do nerds suffer from a mild pervasive developmental disorder? In S. Feinstein (ed.), *Adolescent Psychiatry: Developmental and Clinical Studies.* Chicago: University of Chicago Press.

Quattrone, G. and Tversky, A. (1986) Self-deception and the voter's illusion. In J. Elster (ed.), *The Multiple Self.* Cambridge: Cambridge University Press, pp. 237–248.

Rabin, M. (1995) Moral preferences, moral constraints, and self-serving biases. Working Paper 95–241, Department of Economics, University of California at Berkeley.

Rachlin, H. (1985) Pain and behavior. *Behavior and Brain Sciences* 8, 43–83.

Rachlin, H. (1995a) Self-control: Beyond commitment *Behavioral and Brain Sciences* 18, 109–159.

Rachlin, H. (1995b) Behavioral economics without anomalies. *Journal of the Experimental Analysis of Behavior* 64, 396–404.

References

Rachlin, H. and Green, L. (1972) Commitment, choice, and self-control. *Journal of Experimental Analysis Behavior* 17, 15–22.

Ragotzy, S. P., Blakely, E., and Poling, A. (1988) Self-control in mentally retarded adolescents: Choice as a function of amount and delay of reinforcement. *Journal of the Experimental Analysis of Behavior* 49, 191–199.

Rapoport, A. (1990) *Experimental Studies of Interactive Decisions.* Dordrecht, the Netherlands: Kluwer Academic.

Raynor, J. O. (1969) Future orientation and motivation of immediate activity. *Psychological Review* 76, 606–610.

Rescorla, R. A. (1988) Pavlovian conditioning: It's not what you think it is. *American Psychologist* 43, 151–160.

Rescorla, R. A. and Solomon, R. L. (1967) Two-process learning theory: Relationships between Pavlovian conditioning and instrumental learning. *Psychological Review* 74, 151– 182.

Rethy, Z. (1965) Driving forces in the dynamism of willpower. *Pszichologiai Tanulmanyok* 8, 33–48.

Rhue, J. W. and Lynn, S. J. (1987) Fantasy proneness: The ability to hallucinate "as real as real." *British Journal of Experimental and Clinical Hypnosis* 4, 173–180.

Rhue, J. W. and Lynn, S. J. (1989) Fantasy proneness, hypnotizability, and absorption – A re-examination. *The International Journal of Clinical and Experimental Hypnosis* 37, 100–106.

Richards, J. B., Zhang, L., Mitchell, S. H., and deWit, H. (1999) Delay or probability discounting in a model of impulsive behavior: Effect of alcohol. *Journal of the Experimental Analysis of Behavior* 71, 121–143.

Ricoeur, P. (1971) Guilt, ethics, and religion. In J. Meta (ed.), *Moral Evil Under Challenge,* New York: Herder and Herder.

Robinson, T. E. and Berridge, K. C. (1993) The neural basis of drug craving: An incentive-sensitization theory of addiction. *Brain Research Reviews* 18, 247–291.

Rocha, B. A., Fumagalli, F., Gainetdinov, R. R., Jones, S. R., Ator, R., Giros, B., Miller, G. W., and Caron, M. G. (1998) Cocaine self-administration in dopamine-transporter knockout mice. *Nature Neuroscience* 1, 132–137.

Rockwell, W. Teed (1994) Beyond determinism and indignity: A reinterpretation of operant conditioning. *Behavior and Philosophy* 22, 53–66.

Rorty, A. O. (1980) Self-deception, akrasia and irrationality. *Social Science Information* 19, 905–922.

Rosenthal, R. J. and Lesieur, H. R. (1992) Self-reported withdrawal symptoms and pathological gambling. *American Journal of Addictions* 1, 150–154.

Russell, J. M. (1978) Saying, feeling, and self-deception. *Behaviorism* 6, 27–43.

Ryan, R. M., Kuhl, J., and Deci, E. L. (1997) Nature and autonomy: An organizational view of social and neurobiological aspects of self-regulation in behavior and development. *Development and Psychopathology* 9, 701–728.

Ryle, G. (1949/1984) *The Concept of Mind.* Chicago: University of Chicago Press.

Samuelson, P. A. (1937) A note on measurement of utility. *Review of Economic Studies* 4, 155–161.

Samuelson, P. (1976) *Economics* (10th ed.). New York: McGraw-Hill.

References

Sappington, A. A. (1990) Recent psychological approaches to the free will versus determinism issue. *Psychological Bulletin* 108, 19–29.

Sartre, J. P. (1948) *The Emotions*. B. Frechtmen (trans.). New York: Philosophical Library.

Schachter, S., Silverstein, B., and Perlick, D. (1977) Psychological and pharmacological explanations of smoking under stress. *Journal of Experimental Psychology: General* 106, 31–40.

Schelling, T. C. (1960) *The Strategy of Conflict*. Cambridge, MA: Harvard University Press.

Schilder, P. and Wechsler, D. (1935) What do children know about the interior of their bodies? *International Journal of Psychoanalysis* 16, 355–360.

Schultz, W., Dayan, P., and Montague, P. R. (1997) A neural substrate of prediction and reward. *Science* 275, 1593–1599.

Schwartz, B. (1986) *The Battle for Human Nature: Science, Morality and Modern Life*. New York: Norton.

Scitovsky, T. (1976) *The Joyless Economy: An Inquiry into Human Satisfaction and Consumer Dissatisfaction*. New York: Oxford University Press.

Sen, A. K. (1977) Rational fools: A critique of the behavioral foundations of economic theory. *Philosophy and Public Affairs* 6, 317–344.

Senault, J. F. (1649) *The Use of Passions*. Henry, Earl of Monmouth (trans.). London: Printed for J. L. and Humphrey Moseley.

Shefrin, H. M. and Thaler, R. H. (1988) The behavioral life-cycle hypothesis. *Economic Inquiry* 26, 609–643.

Shiffrin, R. M. and Schneider, W. (1977) Controlled and automatic human information processing: II. Perceptual learning, automatic attending, and a general theory. *Psychological Review* 84, 127–190.

Shimp, C. P. (1983) On metaknowledge in the pigeon: An organism's knowledge about its own behavior. *Animal Learning and Behavior* 10, 358–364.

Shizgal, P. and Conover, K. (1996) On the neural computation of utility. *Current Directions in Psychological Science* 5, 37–43.

Shull, R., Spear, D., and Bryson, A. (1981) Delay or rate of food delivery as a determiner of response rate. *Journal of the Experimental Analysis of Behavior* 35, 129–143.

Siegal, S. (1983) Classical conditioning, drug tolerance, and drug dependence. In R. Smart, F. Glaser, Y. Israel, H. Kalant, R. Popham, and W. Schmidt (eds.), *Research Advances in Alcohol and Drug Problems*, vol. 1. New York: Plenum.

Siegel, E. and Rachlin, H. (1996) Soft commitment: Self-control achieved by response persistence. *Journal of the Experimental Analysis of Behavior* 64, 117–128.

Silverstein, A., Cross, D., Brown, J., and Rachlin, H. (1998) Prior experience and patterning in a prisoner's dilemma game. *Journal of Behavioral Decision Making* 11, 123–138.

Simon, H. (1983) *Reason in Human Affairs*. Stanford, CA: Stanford University Press.

Simon, J. L. (1995) Interpersonal allocation continuous with intertemporal allocation: Binding commitments, pledges, and bequests. *Rationality and Society* 7, 367–430.

Sjoberg, L. and Johnson, T. (1978) Trying to give up smoking: A study of volitional breakdowns. *Addictive Behaviors* 3, 149–167.

Skinner, B. F. (1953) *Science and Human Behavior.* New York: Free Press.

Skog, O.-J. (1999) Rationality, irrationality, and addiction. In J. Elster and O.-J. Skog, (eds.), *Getting Hooked: Rationality and Addiction.* Cambridge: Cambridge University Press.

Smith, A. (1759/1976) *The Theory of Moral Sentiments.* Oxford: Oxford University Press.

Smith, T. S. (1974) Aestheticism and social structure: Style and social network in the dandy life. *American Sociological Review* 39, 725–743.

Smith, V. (1992) Game theory and experimental economics: Beginnings and early influences. In E. R. Weintraub (ed.), *Toward a History of Game Theory.* Durham, NC: Duke University Press.

Smyser, C. H. and Baron, D. A. (1993) Hypnotizability, absorption, and subscales of the Dissociative Experiences Scale in a nonclinical population. *Dissociation* 6, 42–46.

Snyderman, M. (1983) Optimal prey selection: Partial selection, delay of reinforcement and self-control. *Behavioral Analysis Letters* 3, 131–147.

Solnick, J., Kannenberg, C., Eckerman, D., and Waller, M. (1980) An experimental analysis of impulsivity and impulse control in humans. *Learning and Motivation* 2, 61–77.

Solomon, R. and Wynne, L. (1954) Traumatic avoidance learning: The principles of anxiety conservation and partial irreversibility. *Psychological Review* 61, 353–385.

Sonuga-Barke, E. J. S., Lea, S. E. G., and Webley, P. (1989) Children's choice: Sensitivity to changes in reinforcer density. *Journal of the Experimental Analysis of Behavior* 51, 185–197.

Sorensen, R. A. (1992) *Thought Experiments.* New York: Oxford University Press.

Spealman, R. (1979) Behavior maintained by termination of a schedule of self-administered cocaine. *Science* 204, 1231–1233.

Sperry, R. W. (1984) Consciousness, personal identity and the divided brain. *Neuropsychologia* 22, 661–673.

Stahler, F. (1998) *Economic Games and Strategic Behavior: Theory and Application.* Cheltenham, UK: Elgar.

Stearns, P. N. (1986) Historical analysis in the study of emotion. *Motivation and Emotion* 10, 185–193.

Stearns, P. N. (1994) *American Cool: Constructing a Twentieth-Century Emotional Style.* New York: New York University Press.

Stevenson, M. K. (1986) A discounting model for decisions with delayed positive or negative outcomes. *Journal of Experimental Psychology: General* 115, 131–154.

Stigler, G. and Becker, G. (1977) De gustibus non est disputandum. *American Economic Review* 67, 76–90.

Stone, L. (1977) *The Family, Sex, and Marriage: England, 1500–1800.* New York: Harper & Row.

Straffin, P. (1980) The prisoner's dilemma. *UMAP Journal* 1, 101–103.

Strasberg, L. (1987) *A Dream of Passion: The Development Method.* New York: Plume.

Strotz, R. H. (1956) Myopia and inconsistency in dynamic utility maximization. *Review of Economic Studies* 23, 166–180.

Sully, J. (1884) *Outlines of psychology.* New York: Appleton.

Sunstein, C. R. (1995) Problems with rules. *California Law Review* 83, 953–1030.

Szekely, J. (1980) *Twins on Twins.* New York: Potter. (Probably indexed under its photographers, Kathryn Abbe and Frances Gill.)

Taylor, C. (1982) The diversity of goods. In A. Sen and B. Williams (eds.), *Utilitarianism and Beyond.* Cambridge and London: Cambridge University Press, pp. 129–144.

Thaler, R. (1991) *Quasi-Rational Economics.* New York: Russell Sage.

Thomas, E. M. (1989) *The Harmless People.* New York: Vintage.

Thorndike, E. J. (1935) *The Psychology of Wants, Interests, and Attitudes.* New York City: Appleton-Century.

Tidey, J. and Miczek, K. (1994) Threat of attack increases in vivo dopamine release in frontal cortex and nucleus accumbens. *Neuroscience Abstracts* 20, 1443.

Tittle, C. R. (1980) *Sanctions and Social Deviance: The Question of Deterrence.* New York: Praeger.

Todorov, J. C., de Oliveira Castro, J., Hanna, E. S., de Sa, M. C. N., and de queiroz Barreto, M. (1983) Choice, experience, and the generalized matching law. *Journal of the Experimental Analysis of Behavior* 40, 90–111.

Tomkins, S. S. (1978) Script theory: Differential magnification of affects. *Nebraska Symposium on Motivation* 26, 201–236.

Toynbee, A. J. (1946) *A Study of History.* New York: Oxford University Press.

Vanderveldt, J. H. and Odenwald, R. P. (1952) *Psychiatry and Catholicism.* New York: McGraw-Hill.

Van Hasselt, V. B. and Hersen, M. (eds.), (1996) *Sourcebook of Psychological Treatment Manuals for Adult Disorders.* New York: Plenum.

Van Hest, A., Van der Schoot, F., Kop, P., and Van Haaren, Frans (1987) Dissociation of instrumental and Pavlovian contingencies in a discriminated instrumental procedure. *Behavioural Processes* 15, 249–258.

Vaughan, W., Jr. and Herrnstein, R. J. (1987) Stability, melioration, and natural selection. In L. Green and J. H. Kagel (eds.), *Advances in Behavioral Economics,* vol. 1. Norwood, NJ: Ablex, pp. 185–215.

Vuchinich, R. E. and Simpson, C. A. (1998) Hyperbolic temporal discounting in social drinkers and problem drinkers. *Experimental and Clinical Psychopharmacology* 6, 292–305.

Walker, W. and King, W. (1962) Effects of stimulus novelty on gnawing and eating by rats. *Journal of Comparative and Physiological Psychology* 55, 838–842.

Walsh, T. B. and Devlin, M. J. (1998) Eating disorders: Progress and problems. *Science* 280, 1387–1390.

Weber, M. (1904/1958) *The Protestant Ethic and the Spirit of Capitalism.* New York: Charles Scribner's Sons.

Weber, M. (1925/1964) *The Theory of Social and Economic Organization.* New York: Free Press.

Wegner, D. M. (1994) Ironic processes of mental control. *Psychological Review* 101, 34–52.

Weissman, M., Klerman, G., Markowitz, J. S., and Ouellette, R. (1989) Suicidal ideation and suicide attempts in panic disorder and attacks. *New England Journal of Medicine* 321, 1209–1214.

Wickelgren, I. (1998) Obesity: How big a problem? *Science* 280, 1364–1368.

Williams, J. M. G., Watts, F., MacLeod, C., and Mathews, A. (1988) *Cognitive Psychology and Emotional Disorders*. New York: Wiley.

Wilson, J., Kuehn, R., and Beach, F. (1963) Modification in the sexual behavior of male rats by changing the stimulus female. *Journal of Comparative and Physiological Psychology* 56, 636–644.

Wilson, J. Q. and Herrnstein, R. J. (1985) *Crime and Human Nature*. New York: Simon & Schuster.

Wolpe, J., Groves, G., and Fisher, S. (1980) Treatment of narcotic addiction by inhibition of craving: Contending with a cherished habit. *Comprehensive Psychiatry* 21, 308–316.

Wray, I. and Dickerson, M. G. (1981) Cessation of high frequency gambling and "withdrawal" symptoms. *British Journal of Addiction* 76, 401–405.

Yates, B. T. and Mischel, W. (1979) Young children's preferred attentional strategies for delaying gratification. *Journal of Personality and Social Psychology* 37, 286–300.

Zajonc, R. B. (1980) Feeling and thinking: Preferences need no inferences. *American Psychologist* 35, 151–175.

Zimmerman, J. and Ferster, C. B. (1964) Some notes on time-out from reinforcement. *Journal of the Experimental Analysis of Behavior* 7, 13–19.

NAME INDEX

247

248

SUBJECT INDEX

Note: Page numbers in boldface type indicate the beginning of the principal discussion of the topic.

actors, *see* emotion, controlled by
    actors
addictions, **16, 48,** 64
    atomic bargaining in, 113
    as escape from compulsions, 156
    versus itches, 53
aesthetic value
    of pain, 183
    surprise as basis, 169
akrasia, 4, 38, 79, 215n26
alcoholism, 10, 96, 111, 136, 156
alexithymia, 50, 77, 154, 213n10
altruism, 127, **179**
anorexia nervosa, 63
appetite
    as behavior, 67
    conditioned, 20
    difficulty seeing need for, 194
    as incentive to bypass will, 175,
      190
    includes emotions and hungers, **65**
    as limited resource, 166
    relation to drive, 166, 212n22
    relation to taste, 212n22
    same brain site as reward, 23
    undetermined by will, 187, **164**
    urges as example, 51
art, based on surprise, 169
attention, 23, 67

control of, **76,** 143, 150, 169, 195
finite channel, 41
in itches, 51
in pain, **54**

bargaining, 9
    atomic, 114
    interpersonal models,
      intertemporal, 121
    intertemporal, 43, 92, 112
    intertemporal, evolution, 146
    intertemporal, source of
      compulsiveness, 152, 175
    intertemporal, source of will, **90,**
      117, 129
    intertemporal, subject experience,
      106
    with known endpoint, 216n7
behaviorism, 7, 195
belief, 77
    committing effect, **107**
    as commitment, 108
    as construction, 150, 162, **175,** 199
    as indirection, **190**
Bible, 4, 146
binges, 53, 63, 149, 156
biofeedback, 20, 204n22
bright lines, **94,** 103, 115, 147, 155
Buddhism, 5

253